Connecting Faith to Life

A Discipleship Journey

Tommy Meador
Logan Catoe

Northwood Publishing
North Charleston, South Carolina

Tommy Meador and Logan Catoe/Northwood Publishing

2200 Greenridge Road

North Charleston, South Carolina/29406

www.connectingfaith2life.com

Ordering Information:
Quantity sales. Special discounts are available on quantity purchases by churches, associations, and others. For details, contact the address above or email the authors at tommy@northwoodbaptist.com or logan@northwoodbaptist.com.

Interior Design by Brittany Boyd
Cover Design by Amanda Evans

Connecting Faith to Life/ Tommy Meador and Logan Catoe. —1st ed.

ISBN 978-0-578-70008-3

Table of Contents

Introduction   7

The Basics

1. What is a Disciple? – Luke 9:23-27   11
2. A Disciples Grows – 1 Peter 2:1-12   19

The Tools

3. How to Study the Bible – 2 Timothy 3:1-17   29
4. How to Pray – Matthew 6:5-15   37

The Gospel

5. Made in God's Image for God's Glory – Genesis 1:26-31   45
6. The Reality of Spiritual Death – Ephesians 2:1-3   53
7. The Hope of New Life – Ephesians 2:4-10   61
8. Sharing the Gospel – 1 Peter 3:13-17   67

The Life

9. Live to Glorify God – Romans 12:1-2   77
10. Live to Give – 2 Corinthians 9:6-15   85

The Growth

11. Grow in Daily Confession and Repentance – Isaiah 6:1-8   93
12. Grow in the Fruit of the Spirit – Galatians 5:16-26   101
13. Grow in Obedience to God's Commands – 1 John 2:1-14   109
14. Grow in Forgiveness – Matthew 18:21-35   117
15. Grow in Your Speech – James 3:1-12   127

The Church

16. What is the Church? – Acts 2:42-47   135
17. The Ordinances of the Church – Romans 6:1-11; Mark 14:12-22   143
18. Why God Has Placed You in the Church – 1 Corinthians 12:1-31   151
19. Why God Has Placed Leaders in the Church – 1 Peter 5:1-5   159

The Story: Old Testament

20. Creation – Genesis 1-2   167
21. Fall – Genesis 3:1-24   177
22. Covenant – Genesis 12:1-9; 15:1-21   185
23. Exodus – Exodus: 12:33-51   195
24. Law- Exodus 19:1-20:21   205
25. Temple/Tabernacle - 2 Chronicles 2:1-18; 5:7-14; 7:1-3   215
26. Kingdom – 2 Samuel 2:1-17   223
27. Prophets – Isaiah 53   233
28. Exile and Restoration – 2 Kings 17:6-23; 2 Chronicles 35:17-22   255

The Story: New Testament

29. The King Comes – John 1:1-18   263
30. The King Establishes His Church – Acts 2:1-13   271
31. The King Nurtures His Church – Philippians 1:3-11 (Epistles Overview)   279
32. The King Returns – Revelation 21:1-8   289

The Mission

33. Life on Mission – Matthew 28:16-20   297

Introduction

When I was in college, my pastor made the intentional decision to disciple me. While he never once said to me, "Tommy, I'm discipling you," that's exactly what he did! We met together every week, and each week he taught me theology, how to pray, and how to live out the Christian faith. Because of his influence in my life, I made the decision early in ministry that I would do for others what had been done for me.

I'm convinced that what most churches are missing is an intentional discipleship strategy. Most churches do not have a plan to fulfill the Great Commission. Over the years, I have led churches that I've pastored to think intentionally about discipleship. I have led the churches I've pastored to develop discipleship groups. Discipleship groups are groups of four to five people of the same gender where a leader teaches the group the basics of the faith and trains the members of the group to make disciples.

I've been in ministry for over two decades now, and over two decades of ministry, I have led quite a few discipleship groups. Weekly, I have met with men to teach them to study the Bible, to pray, and to live out their faith. Weekly I have challenged men to make disciples. It's been a joy to see many men grow in their faith, and it has been a joy to see men begin to invest in the lives of others for the sake of the Gospel.

I've struggled over the years to find good curriculum that helps people understand the basics of discipleship and trains them to make disciples. This workbook is our attempt to give you a basic discipleship curriculum that will help you grow in Christ and train you to make disciples.

Logan and I have teamed up to write this curriculum, and before you begin to journey through this curriculum, here's what you need to know.

1. This curriculum is intended to be used in a group setting.

Specifically, we wrote this curriculum with discipleship groups in mind. For us, a discipleship group is a group of no more than five people of the same gender. Sure, you can benefit from this curriculum if you read through this material on your own. However, you will benefit much more if you study this in a group with a leader who has already gone through this curriculum. We believe that your best spiritual growth takes place within Christ-centered relationships.

2. This curriculum is designed to be completed in one year.

We want you to be able to go through this curriculum and then begin your own discipleship group. Because we desire to see disciples multiplied, we wanted to produce curriculum that covered the basics of discipleship as concisely as possible. We want to train you up the best we can as quickly as we can so you can become an effective disciple-maker.

3. This curriculum is designed with the head, heart, and hands in mind.

This curriculum focuses on the head. In other words, we want you to have a good knowledge of God's Word. We teach you how to study the Bible. We teach you how to share the Gospel, and we teach you the basics of biblical theology. If you are unfamiliar with biblical theology, biblical theology is an attempt to demonstrate how the Bible is one, unified book that tells the singular story of redemption. Biblical theology traces specific themes through Scripture that tell the story of Jesus.

This curriculum focuses on the heart. We want you to think like a follower of Jesus, and we want you to live like a follower of Jesus. This curriculum not only engages you in a study of biblical theology, but this study also engages you in a study of Christian character. In your group, you will discuss topics such as how to have a forgiving heart, how to make God-honoring decisions, how to be faithful in your giving, and how to live out the fruit of the Spirit. We certainly want you to have a robust knowledge of the Bible, but your knowledge of the Bible should lead you to live a life transformed by the power of God.

This curriculum focuses on the hands. As God makes you into who He wants you to be, it should affect what you do. As you grow in your knowledge of Christ and the character of Christ, it should lead you to grow in your service to Christ. God wants you to serve Him by making disciples. In this curriculum, you will learn how to share the Gospel, and you will also grow in your ability to help believers in Jesus grow in their faith. This curriculum is designed to be reproducible. In other words, we want you to be able to take this curriculum, start your own discipleship group, and help people to grow in their obedience to the Lord.

4. This curriculum is designed to get you into the Bible. Each week you will study one passage of Scripture.

We hope that the material we have written is helpful for you, but the Bible is life-transforming. The words that Logan and I have written do not have the power that the actual Bible has. In your discipleship group, you should spend a significant portion of your time talking about the Bible passage for that particular lesson. We devote an entire lesson to studying the Bible. That lesson will help you tremendously as you study the Bible each week.

We do hope that this curriculum is helpful for you as you continue to grow in your relationship with Jesus. Nothing is more important in this life than your relationship with Jesus. May God bless you richly as you grow in your love for Him. May God use you to make disciples for the glory of Jesus Christ.

1. What is a Disciple?

Know the Word

Read Luke 9:23-27 and answer the following questions.

1. What do you see? (Observation)

2. What does it mean? (Interpretation)

3. What do you do? (Application)

4. How should you pray?

If you've been around the church for a while, or even if you are brand new to the church, you have probably heard the word disciple. The word disciple is not exclusive to Christianity, but it is a word that is used prominently within the Christian faith. You probably know that the word disciple simply means a learner or a follower. For example, when I was a kid, I was a disciple of Larry Bird. I watched every game I could, read every news article about him I could find, and I tried my best to imitate him on the basketball court. Unfortunately, I do not have the genetic disposition of Larry Bird, so while I tried to imitate his basketball skills, I did so with little success.

Being a disciple of someone does not guarantee your success as a student of the one you are following. You can study finance under Warren Buffet, but that does not guarantee you'll have the same financial success he has had. You can learn golf from Tiger Woods, but that doesn't mean you will drive the ball like he does. You can study music under a world-class musician, but that does not mean you will be able to make a musical instrument sing with the same virtuosic skill that a world-class musician is able. Simply put, you are not guaranteed success by putting yourself under the tutelage of someone else.

While you might not have success as a disciple of your favorite basketball player, a world-class musician, or famed financial investor, I can guarantee that you can have success as a follower of Jesus if you submit your life to the teaching of Jesus. Jesus wants you to succeed as His follower. In fact, as a follower of Jesus, He wants you to succeed so much that He has placed His Spirit within you to teach you, transform you, and empower you to be the person that He has called you to be.

You must answer a simple question. Will you cooperate with the work that God wants to do in your life? Certainly, Jesus will not force you to be His disciple. He will not force you to learn from Him. He will not force you to conform your life to His will. You can freely choose to not put your life under the authority of Jesus but think about what you will miss! That's exactly the point Jesus is driving home in Luke 9:24-25: "24For whoever would save his life will lose it, but whoever loses his life for my sake will save it. 25For what does it profit a man if he gains the whole world and loses or forfeits himself?"

You will follow someone or something, but there's only One you can follow who will absolutely transform your life and give you eternal life: Jesus Christ. If you are on the fence as to whether you should completely submit your life to the authority and Lordship of Jesus Christ, let me make it abundantly clear: the only way to find real life is by giving your life to Jesus.

I don't know where you are in your spiritual journey. Maybe you are just starting in your faith journey as a Christian, or maybe you've been a Christian for some time, and you realize that it's past time that you began to take your faith in Christ much more seriously than you have been.

Or, maybe you're investigating Christianity and someone has invited you to study this material with them. Wherever you are in your faith journey, you need to have a clear understanding of what a disciple of Jesus does.

Consider four characteristics of a disciple:

A DISCIPLE SURRENDERS.

When you read the verses that surround Luke 9:23-27, you learn that Jesus had just asked the disciples the most important question they would ever be asked: "But who do you say that I am?" (Luke 9:20) Peter gave the correct answer: "The Christ of God" (Luke 9:20). Peter knew that Jesus was the long-awaited Messiah, but Jesus was a different kind of Messiah than Peter and the disciples expected. The Jews longed for a political leader that would deliver them from the oppression of their enemies and establish an eternal Kingdom in which Israel would rule and reign over the nations. Jesus was not that kind of king. He did not come to go to war with the nations and establish Himself as the King of the Jews who would rule from Jerusalem. Rather, He came to bring peace to all people who would place their faith in Him. Astonishingly, the way Jesus brought peace was through suffering. Jesus went to the cross and died in the place of sinful people. On the cross, Jesus suffered the wrath of God by enduring the punishment that all of humanity deserves. The victory Jesus gives His people is not through conquest but through suffering.

Jesus clearly tells His disciples this in Luke 9:21-22. Then He looks at them and tells them that if they are going to truly follow Him, they will have to embrace a life of suffering as well. They would find life by giving their lives away for the mission of Jesus and not by pursuing their own desires. Simply put, Jesus explained to His early disciples, and to us as well, that the only way to find real life is to surrender to His plan and purpose.

What about you? Have you come to a point in your life where you have surrendered to King Jesus? Have you realized the only way to find life is to say "no" to your dreams, your goals, and your ambitions and instead say a resounding "yes" to the One who gave up His own life so that you could have new life? When you surrender to Jesus, in every area of your life you are willing to say, "Not my will, but your will be done." Would that describe you? If not, you are like Jesus' original disciples – you don't really understand Jesus at all. Now, I understand that you will never surrender perfectly to Jesus, but if you are a Jesus-follower, surrender must be your heart's desire.

A DISCIPLE ABIDES.

A disciple not only surrenders to Jesus, a disciple also abides in Jesus. To abide in Jesus simply means to make your home in Him. It means that your life is centered around growing in intimacy with Him, learning to hear His voice, and enjoying communion with Him. The more you abide in Him, the more you will desire to surrender to His will for your life. Jesus said in John 15:1-4:

I am the true vine, and my Father is the vinedresser. ² Every branch in me that does not bear fruit he takes away, and every branch that does bear fruit he prunes, that it may bear more fruit. ³ Already you are clean because of the word that I have spoken to you. ⁴ Abide in me, and I in you. As the branch cannot bear fruit by itself, unless it abides in the vine, neither can you, unless you abide in me.

The fruitfulness of your walk with the Lord is dependent on you abiding in Christ. This is why half-hearted devotion never works. If your relationship with Jesus is just an addition to your life and not the totality of your life, you will never experience the full power of Christ at work in you. Jesus isn't merely a part of the disciple's life. Jesus IS the disciple's life.

How do you abide in Christ? The primary way to grow in Christ is through cultivating spiritual disciplines. We'll learn more about the spiritual disciplines in the weeks ahead, but as you cultivate spiritual disciplines in your life, you create an environment for God to work in your life. In and of themselves, spiritual disciplines do not grow you in Christ, but they do put you in position to experience growth in your relationship with Jesus. You're probably already familiar with some of the spiritual disciplines, and perhaps you already practice some of them. The most common spiritual disciplines are daily Bible study and daily prayer. You simply cannot abide in Christ without Bible study and prayer, and in the weeks ahead you will be challenged to make these disciplines a daily habit.

A DISCIPLE OBEYS.

Because a disciple desires to live a surrendered life, and because a disciple desires to grow in intimacy with Jesus, a disciple does what Jesus says. Obedience to Jesus' words is one of the defining characteristics of a disciple of Jesus. The apostle John writes in 1 John 2:3-6:

³And by this we know that we have come to know him, if we keep his commandments. ⁴ Whoever says "I know him" but does not keep his commandments is a liar, and the truth is not in him, ⁵ but whoever keeps his word, in him truly the love of God is perfected. By this we may know that we are in him: ⁶ whoever says he abides in him ought to walk in the same way in which he walked.

Jesus wants obedience in your character. The work that Christ wants to do in your life is a transforming work that changes you from the inside out. God promised through the Old Testament prophet, Ezekiel, that there would come a day that He would give people new hearts.

26 And I will give you a new heart, and a new spirit I will put within you. And I will remove the heart of stone from your flesh and give you a heart of flesh. 27 And I will put my Spirit within you and cause you to walk in my statutes and be careful to obey my rules" (Ezekiel 36:26-27).

When you allow God to change your heart, you will begin to see your heart become like the heart of Christ. A heart like the heart of Christ is a heart full of love, forgiveness, patience, kindness, grace, and many other characteristics that imitate the character of Christ. Obeying Christ is to say "yes" to putting on these inward characteristics.

Jesus wants your obedience in your lifestyle. In other words, Jesus calls you to live a life that strives to put sin to death. The apostle Paul wrote in Colossians 3:5-10:

5 Put to death therefore what is earthly in you: sexual immorality, impurity, passion, evil desire, and covetousness, which is idolatry. 6 On account of these the wrath of God is coming. 7 In these you too once walked, when you were living in them. 8 But now you must put them all away: anger, wrath, malice, slander, and obscene talk from your mouth. 9 Do not lie to one another, seeing that you have put off the old self with its practices 10 and have put on the new self, which is being renewed in knowledge after the image of its creator.

You will never grow to be like Jesus if you refuse to put away what Christ despises. How are you doing in your battle with sin? What sins are hindering you in your walk with Jesus? Are you ready to begin confessing those sins and asking God to help you put them to death?

Finally, Jesus wants your obedience in your daily decisions. Again, it's a matter of surrender. Will you decide to follow God's will or your will? Will you decide to live for His mission or your agenda? Will you decide to invest in others or invest in yourself? Will you desire to go where He leads you to go? Will you share with the people who He leads you to share with? Will you make that sacrifice for Jesus that seems so costly? Will you have that difficult conversation in order to put back together a broken relationship? If God calls you, will you leave behind the comforts of your home to plant your family in another land for the sake of the Gospel? Will you do what God tells you to do? Will you obey Him?

A DISCIPLE PRODUCES.

The evidence that you belong to Jesus is that your life produces fruit. Jesus said, "[5]I am the vine; you are the branches. Whoever abides in me and I in him, he it is that bears much fruit, for apart from me you can do nothing" (John 15:5). It is possible to be active in the church for years and attend numerous church services yet never produce any real fruit in your life.

A disciple of Christ continually grows in inward and outward fruit. Inward fruit is unseen by others, but others can see the results. Think about the fruit of the Spirit in Galatians 5:22-23. Paul writes: "[22]But the fruit of the Spirit is love, joy, peace, patience, kindness, goodness, faithfulness, [23]gentleness, self-control; against such things there is no law." You can't see what's on the inside of someone. You can't always see how God is teaching someone patience or how He is developing gentleness in the life of a believer. However, you can see the results of the fruit of the Spirit. This inward fruit is often unseen, but it is present, and it is demonstrated in how a believer lives his or her life before others.

You can't always see inward fruit, but you can see outward fruit. Truth is, you can have outward fruit without inward fruit, but you can't have inward fruit without outward fruit. In other words, you can have all the signs of spiritual life on the outside but on the inside your soul can be decaying. This was the case with the Pharisees. They had lots of outward fruit, but Jesus pointed out that on the inside they were rotting. Jesus said to the Pharisees in Matthew 23:27-28:

[27]Woe to you, scribes and Pharisees, hypocrites! For you are like whitewashed tombs, which outwardly appear beautiful, but within are full of dead people's bones and all uncleanness. [28]So you also outwardly appear righteous to others, but within you are full of hypocrisy and lawlessness.

For the Pharisees, their outward "fruit" wasn't a result of a changed heart, it was a result of their desire to be seen as righteous people in the eyes of others. However, when you are developing inward fruit with the help of the Holy Spirit, you are naturally going to produce external fruit as a result of the Spirit's work in you. Outward fruit is sharing the Gospel with other people, serving in ministry in your local church, or providing mercy and relief to those who are hurting. If you examine your own life, do you see ongoing evidence of inward and outward fruit? What is being produced in you as you walk with the Lord?

In your group, reflect on the following questions:

1. What strikes you about Luke 9:23-27? What do you think the disciples thought when they heard these words from Jesus? What challenges you in these verses? What gives you hope in these verses?

2. Think about what a disciple does. In which of these areas do you think you've seen growth in your walk with the Lord? In which of these areas do you need to see growth?

3. What do you think has prevented you from becoming the disciple Christ has called you to become?

Model the Word

1. Take time for each group member to describe what it means to be a disciple of Jesus based on this past week's lesson.

2. Think again about a close friend or family member, maybe a spouse or a child, who may be a follower of Jesus. How would you encourage that person in their faith with what you've learned from this lesson? How would you share this passage with a friend or family member? With your child? Take time for each group member to explain how they would communicate this passage to a fellow Christian they are close to.

Share the Word

1. Think about this passage from the perspective of a lost person. What do you think would be most challenging for a lost person to understand in this passage? How would you help a lost person to understand what Jesus desires in this passage?

2. The big question that a lost person might have when considering what it means to follow Jesus is "why?" How would you answer that question? Why should a lost person be willing to give up a life of pursuing their own comforts in exchange for a life in which Christ calls for suffering and self-denial?

Pray the Word

1. As a group, spend time praying for each other to have a better understanding of what it means to be a disciple of Jesus.

2. What sins are hindering you in your discipleship journey? Confess those to each other and to the Lord.

3. What are the next steps God is calling you to take in your discipleship journey? Pray for each other to have the faith to take those next steps and ask God to empower you in your journey.

Daily Bible Reading

Day 1: Luke 1-2
Day 2: Luke 3-4
Day 3: Luke 5-6
Day 4: Luke 7-8
Day 5: Luke 9-10

2. A Disciple Grows

Know the Word

Read 1 Peter 2:1-12

1. What do you see? (Observation)

2. What does it mean? (Interpretation)

3. What do you do? (Application)

4. How should you pray?

God is far more interested in who you are becoming than what you are doing. Reread that statement very carefully and think through it. I'm convinced that most Christians are far more obsessed with what they are doing for Jesus rather than who they are becoming in Jesus. Let's face it. We live in a "do" culture. We value busyness, productivity, hard-work, and checking tasks off of our to-do lists. You know the frustration you feel when you don't complete all the tasks on your to-do list. When tasks go undone, you feel like a time-waster. You feel lazy. You feel unproductive.

Unfortunately, we often approach the Christian faith in the same way we approach the rest of life. We feel really good about our faith when we check things off of our Christian "to-do" list. We feel like we've accomplished something for Jesus when we've been to church most Sundays, served in a ministry, read our Bible most days, gone on a mission trip, and put some money in the offering plate. On the other hand, we feel like we are failing in our faith when we don't do enough Christian stuff. When we fail to read our Bible every day or fail to make time for a ministry or church attendance, we feel like our faith isn't progressing. For many of us, much of our faith is based on our own accomplishments rather than trusting in what Christ has already accomplished for us through His death and resurrection.

I'm not saying we shouldn't do things for Jesus. We should absolutely be doing things for Jesus. Paul writes in Ephesians 2:10, "For we are his workmanship, created in Christ Jesus for good works, which God prepared beforehand, that we should walk in them." However, you would be far more effective in what you do for Jesus if what you do for Jesus flowed out of your becoming like Jesus. Please understand that Jesus didn't die for you just to give you some Christian stuff to do. Jesus died for you to give you a completely new life. He died and rose again to transform you.

What would it look like in your life if you stopped with the Christian check-lists, and instead you started focusing on growing in an intimate relationship with God in such a way that it transforms every area of your life? What if you grew in intimacy with God in such a way that it affected the way you think about people and talk to them? What if your relationship with God affected the way you viewed your job, your money, your time-management, your parenting, or your marriage? What if your relationship with God affected how you serve Him on a daily basis?

The heart of discipleship is not training you in how to do more Christian stuff. Rather, the heart of discipleship is helping you to experience a transformed life through continual growth in your relationship with Jesus. In 1 Peter, Peter wrote to Christians that experienced intense persecution for their faith. It would have been very easy for them to walk away from Jesus and go back to living the way they did before they became Christians. However, Peter encouraged them not only to press on in their faith, but he also encouraged them to long for pure spiritual milk like a newborn-infant longs for literal milk (1 Peter 2:2). Just like an infant needs milk to grow, believers need the nourishment of spiritual milk (God's Word) to grow in Christ. Do you thirst for spiritual milk? Do you long for spiritual growth in your life? Or, are you satisfied with where you are right now in your walk with Jesus?

The diagram below has been very helpful for me over the years. This diagram was designed by Jim Putnam, the senior pastor of Real Life Ministries in Post Falls, Idaho. He wrote a helpful book, *Real Life Discipleship: Building Churches that Make Disciples*, that gives a great overview of the different stages of spiritual growth. The diagram below shows the different stages of spiritual growth:[1]

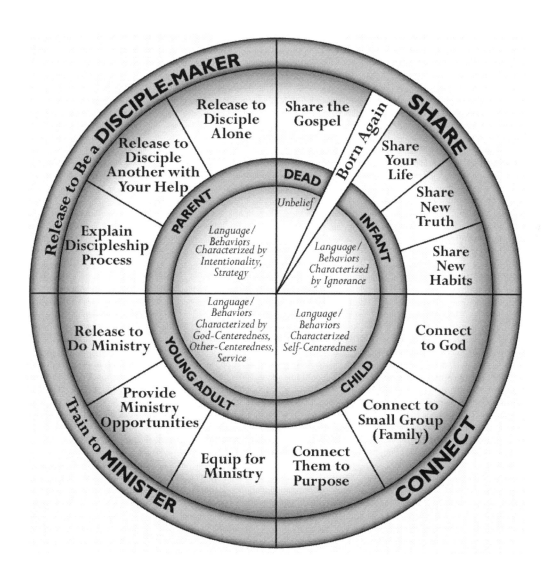

---

[1]Jim Putnam, *Real-Life Discipleship: Building Churches that Make Disciples* (Colorado Springs: NavPress, 2010), 43.

I want you to use this diagram to diagnose where you are in your spiritual journey. For instance, you might be spiritually dead. You're still questioning if God really exists, or maybe you've settled the fact that He does indeed exist, but you have yet to trust in the death and resurrection of His Son, Jesus, for your salvation. Now is the time to settle where you stand before God by believing in the death and resurrection of Jesus, repenting of your sins, and giving your life to Him.

Maybe you are a spiritual infant. If you know anything about babies, you know that a baby is dependent on her parents for everything. An infant needs to be held, fed, changed, put to bed, taken to the pediatrician, and a host of other things to ensure healthy growth. In the same way, a spiritual infant is someone who is brand-new to the faith and is dependent on the church for everything to ensure that she grows into a healthy, mature believer. An infant in Christ needs to be taught how to pray, how to find different books in the Bible, how to read the Bible, and how to obey what the Bible says. Spiritual infants are needy, and a healthy church will be willing to do all that it can to help spiritual infants in their newfound faith.

You might be a spiritual child. If you have young children, then you understand that your children are capable of learning information rapidly. As my boys make their way through school, I'm amazed at how quickly they've been able to learn to read, do complex math, and learn all kinds of scientific facts. Typically, children don't have a problem learning, but they do have a problem with obedience. (Can I get an amen?) By nature, children are selfish. They want what they want when they want it. In the same way, spiritual children are selfish. Being a spiritual child has nothing to do with how long you have been a Christian and everything to do with your maturity as a follower of Jesus. A believer can be stuck in spiritual childhood for years. For example, a believer who has gained a lot of knowledge about God but still thinks the church exists for him is a spiritual child. A believer whose primary focus is on self is a spiritual child. Let's be honest, this is where a lot of believers get stuck. Are you stuck in spiritual childhood?

You probably remember when you became a teenager or a young adult. There's a vast difference between being a young adult and being a child. A child is self-centered while a young adult is becoming more other-centered. A spiritual young adult takes more responsibility for her own spiritual development. Honestly, there are some children that may know a lot more information than young adults, but young adults are typically more responsible. A young adult still needs some help and coaching, but a young adult is growing. A spiritual young adult is one who's taking responsibility for her faith. She's studying the Bible on her own, praying more regularly, and serving in the church. She may need coaching along the way, but she's responsible.

For those of us who are parents, it's a completely different ball game, because we're not only responsible for our own lives; we're also responsible for the lives of the children that God entrusts us with! We have to feed our kids, clothe our kids, educate our kids, and teach them how to be responsible, productive citizens of society. Likewise, a spiritual parent takes responsibility not only for his own faith but also for the faith of someone else. A spiritual parent understands that the reason why God extended grace to him is because through him God desires to extend grace to someone else. A spiritual parent reproduces fully surrendered disciples of Jesus. We should all desire to be spiritual parents.

No matter what stage you find yourself in your spiritual growth, you can't make excuses for not being obedient to the command of Christ to make disciples. In other words, if you are a spiritual child, you can't say, "Well, I'm not mature enough to make disciples." No matter where you are in your journey, you are called to be obedient to Christ's command to make disciples. So, if you are a spiritual child, you better start growing up fast! As you grow, invest in the lives of others for the sake of the Gospel along the way and watch how quickly God matures you as you give your life away for the sake of the Gospel.

I have a dear missionary friend who God has used greatly over the years to plant churches and multiply disciples in a very difficult country for Christians. He created a tool that I have used repeatedly to help believers diagnose their spiritual growth. Look at the image below:

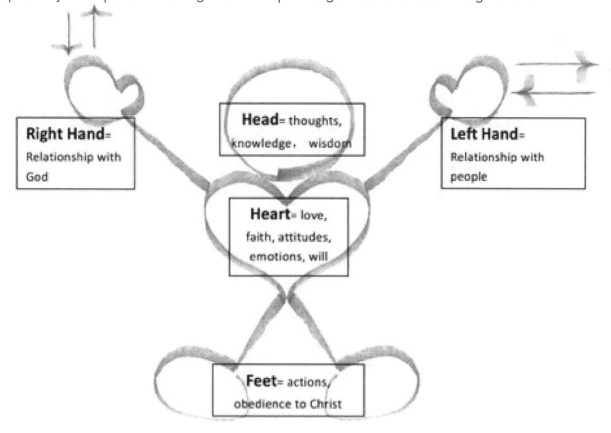

The diagram should be fairly self-explanatory. The head represents your knowledge of God and the Bible. It also represents wisdom. Wisdom is how you're able to apply your knowledge of the Bible to everyday situations.

The heart represents your will, desires, attitudes, and emotions. It represents how you are growing in the character of Christ, in the fruit of the Spirit, and your ability to discern God's will.

The right hand represents your daily relationship with God. Are you growing in intimacy with Christ? Are you regularly praying and studying the Bible? Are you closer to God right now than you were a year ago?

The left hand represents your relationships with other people. Are you loving your neighbor as yourself? Do you regularly forgive those who wrong you? Are you building Christ-centered, accountable relationships to stir others to walk with Jesus?

The feet represent your obedience to Christ. Are you living out His commands? Are you doing what the Bible says to do? Are you going where the Spirit is leading? Are you sharing your faith regularly?

The goal is to live a balanced Christian life. In other words, you want to be growing consistently in every one of these areas. The problem is, if you are like me, you are often out of balance. For example, if I was to examine myself at this moment, I probably have a bigger head than heart. I'm growing regularly in my knowledge of God's Word, but I'm not growing as regularly in the fruit of the Spirit (Galatians 5:22-23) and the character of Christ. What about you? Is your left-hand bigger than your right? Is your heart bigger than your feet? If you were to use the above image as a diagnostic tool to draw where you are in your walk with the Lord at this moment, how would you draw yourself in the space below?

If you want to grow as a disciple, you have to be honest about where you are right now. As you consider the different stages of spiritual growth, where are you? As you think about the healthy disciple diagram, would you draw yourself as healthy? Be honest about where you are in your relationship with the Lord and begin to ask God to help you to grow-up so you can become the spiritual parent that He wants you to be.

In your group, reflect on the following questions:

1. Can you think of a time in your relationship with Jesus when you longed for pure spiritual milk like a newborn baby longs for literal milk? If it's been a long time since you longed for spiritual milk, what do you think it was that caused you to lose your desire for the Word of God?

2. Think about the 1 Peter passage. As you studied the passage, how did God challenge you in your walk with Him?

3. Look at 1 Peter 2:9-12. How do these verses encourage you in your discipleship journey? Look specifically at verse 9. Why are these different descriptions of the church so significant for the discipleship process?

Model the Word

1. How would you explain the different stages of spiritual growth to someone who is just starting their faith journey? Take turns in your group explaining to each other the different stages of spiritual growth.

2. How would you explain a healthy disciple to someone who is just starting in their faith journey? Take turns in your group explaining to each other the healthy disciple diagram.

3. Look back over the different stages of spiritual growth and the healthy disciple diagram. Let each person in your group share what stage of spiritual growth they think they are in, and also share with each other how you drew yourself based off of the healthy disciple diagram. What do you think needs to change in your life right now for you to begin to grow and progress to the next stage of spiritual growth?

4. Think back over the course of your life. Who has been a spiritual parent to you? How did that person model faith for you and teach you to grow in Christ? What do you think it would take for you to be a spiritual parent?

Share the Word

1. Think about 1 Peter 2:1-12 from the perspective of an unbeliever. Specifically, look at verses 9-12 again. How could you use these verses to have a Gospel conversation with an unbeliever? What does it mean to be called out of darkness? How does one go from darkness to light?

2. For an unbeliever, the process of spiritual growth could be confusing and overwhelming. How would you explain the work that God wants to do in the life of a believer to an unbeliever?

Pray the Word

1. In your group, you've already shared what stage of spiritual growth you are in, and you've already shared how you've diagnosed yourself using the healthy disciple tool. Now, pray for each other's spiritual growth. Pray that God would give you a desire to become spiritual parents.

2. Pray for lost friends and family members by name. Pray God would give you the courage to have Gospel conversations with them.

3. Pray for your church. Pray that God would give your church a heart for discipleship and that everyone in your congregation will desire spiritual milk.

Daily Bible Reading

Day 1: Luke 11-12
Day 2: Luke 13-14
Day 3: Luke 15-16
Day 4: Luke 17-18
Day 5: Luke 19-20

3. How to Study the Bible

Know the Word
Read 2 Timothy 3:1-17

   1. What do you see? (Observation)

   2. What does it mean? (Interpretation)

   3. What do you do? (Application)

   4. How should you pray?

Have you ever been in the middle of reading the Bible and come across a verse, chapter, or even a whole book that leaves you with more questions than answers? I know I have. For the longest time in my life I had a desire to know and love God's Word, but I found more often than not I simply didn't understand what I was reading. I liked Matthew, Mark, Luke, and John because they were pretty easy to read, had a lot of stories I could remember, and they talked about Jesus. When it came to books like Isaiah and Ezekiel, full of their imagery and prophetic language, I would give them a quick read, not understand most of them, and move back to easier books to read and understand. Leviticus was full of rules and laws that may have served a purpose for Israel, but how could they possibly benefit me today? The genealogies of 1 and 2 Chronicles were dull, full of names I could hardly pronounce, and seemingly pointless for teaching me how to follow Christ. Even books in the New Testament gave me problems. Romans was complex, dense, and full of theological concepts I figured I needed a degree to understand. Let's not even mention Revelation; that seemed like more of a nightmare than a happy ending!

I convinced myself I needed a degree to understand the Bible, so that's exactly what I did! I went to seminary to gain the knowledge I thought would help me unlock all the Bible's secrets. My very first class of seminary was called Hermeneutics. At the time I had never heard that word, but I was told it was foundational for the rest of my degree. Hermeneutics is, "The discipline that studies the theory, principles, and methods used to interpret texts, especially ancient ones such as the sacred Scriptures. Traditional hermeneutics focuses primarily on the discovery of the historical meaning as intended by the author and understood by the original audience."[1] Now that sounds really fancy and complicated. You might be thinking, "I don't know anything about theories and principles for interpreting ancient texts. That's the pastors job!" Don't worry; that's not the case.

What I learned in my class is that the principles and methods for interpreting the Bible are actually pretty simple and understandable. Anyone can use and apply these principles and methods. The problem isn't that hermeneutics is complicated; the problem is that no one has taught you hermeneutics! If I asked you to make a peanut butter and jelly sandwich, but all I gave you to make it was lettuce, tomato, and bacon, you would think making a peanut butter and jelly sandwich was nearly impossible. And it would be impossible if you never got the right ingredients. You need the right tools to do the job properly. I remember being frustrated while I was taking that class. I was frustrated that I had grown up in church and had been a Christian for a long time without anyone ever teaching me how to read the Bible. I don't want you to be frustrated in your personal study of the Bible. So let's look at some basic principles for hermeneutics.

---

[1] James D. Hernado, *Dictionary of Hermeneutics: A Concise Guide to Terms, Names, Methods, and Expressions* (Springfield: Gospel House Publishing, 2005), 23.

Let's start by simplifying our definition. Hermeneutics is the science and art of how we read, study, and interpret Scripture. It's a science because it follows certain rules. It's an art because it is a skill one develops with practice. There are a lot of methods for how we should go about doing this task, and a lot of them are really good. The structure of good hermeneutics may change, but the principles are all essentially the same. The one we provide here isn't the only way to practice hermeneutics, but it's one that is both simple and helpful. There are three steps to this hermeneutic: 1. Observation 2. Interpretation 3. Application (OIA for short). Let's look at each of these steps.

1. OBSERVATION

The first step to reading the Bible well is to ask: What do I see? That may seem simplistic, but let's explore what it means. Have you ever been in a Bible study or heard a sermon and the teacher or preacher drew conclusions from the text that you would have never thought of or noticed? Why is that the case? After all, aren't you both looking at the same book? Of course you are. The problem isn't what you are seeing; the problem is what you are not seeing. Here's what I mean. A good Bible reader asks six fundamental questions about a text to help them see what is really going on: Who? What? When? Where? Why? How? My guess is you probably used these same questions growing up to solve problems or study a book. Let's look at each of these.

Who?[2] Here we ask several "who" questions. "Who is the author of the book?" The author's background will help us understand his intention for writing and relation to his audience, which leads to the next question. "To whom is the book written?" Audience is a major factor for determining the meaning of a text or passage. For example, Matthew is written to a Jewish audience, while Luke is written to a Gentile audience; both of these factors determine how we read and understand certain details within those books. Who are the characters in the book? Who is speaking? To whom is he or she speaking? Etc.

What? Here we ask several "what" questions. The most important question in this section is "What is the context?" Context is key in reading and interpreting the Bible! Context determines the circumstances that form the setting for an event, statement, or idea, and it provides the starting tools so the text to be fully understood and assessed. Scripture should not and cannot be read and properly understood apart from context. Knowing the context of a book or passage helps protect us from misinterpretation.

---

[2] Daniel Akin, "Hermeneutics," (class lecture, Southeastern Baptist Theological Seminary, Wake Forest, NC, Fall 2013); the following three sections have been adapted from Dr. Akin's lectures and notes from the course.

More "what" questions include: What is the atmosphere of the book or passage (friendly, chastening, loving)? What is the author's general topic? What is he saying about his topic? What are the key words? What do they mean? What are repeated words and phrases? What is the genre? What is the historical background? Etc.

When? When was the book written? When did this event happen in relation to other events? When was this prophecy fulfilled or has it been?

Where? Where was the book written? Where were the recipients of the book living? Where else does this topic appear in Scripture?

Why? Why was the book written? Why does he include this material and not other things? Why does the author give so much space to one topic and so little to another?

How? How many times does the author use the same word in this book, chapter, passage, or verse? How long? How much? How does he do this? How does this relate to the preceding and succeeding statement?

Observation takes time and work, but good observation allows for proper interpretation. I like to print out a passage of Scripture on a piece of paper and practice "marking up" the text. "Marking up" a text means underlining important words or phrases, circling repeated words, writing down cross references, etc. John Piper displays this technique in his series "Look at the Book" (see www.DesiringGod.org/labs). With enough practice, "marking up" the text becomes second nature. Investing in a good study Bible will greatly help you in Observation. Sometimes, historical background can be difficult to find; study Bibles provide much of that information in a concise format.

2. INTERPRETATION[3]

The second step to reading the Bible well is to ask: What does it mean? Interpretation can be done really well or it can be done quite poorly, leading to very different results. For example, Jesus says, "If your right eye causes you to sin, tear it out and throw it away. For it is better that you lose one of your members than that your whole body be thrown into hell" (Matthew 5:29). A bad interpretation of Matthew 5:29 would be to take Jesus literally and conclude that every time your eye causes you to sin God wants you to gouge it out and throw it away; if that were the case no Christians would have eyes! That can't be what He means. A better interpretation of Matthew 5:29 is to conclude that Jesus is speaking figuratively and wants His hearers to understand how serious it is to get rid of sin in their lives. Get rid of sin by any

---

[3] Ibid.

means necessary, but don't go around chopping off body parts! Remember, the more time spent in observation, the less time you will spend in interpretation and the more accurate your interpretation will be.

Here are ten general rules for interpreting the Bible:

1. Work from the assumption that the Bible is authoritative.
2. Interpret difficult passages in light of clear passages. Let Scripture interpret Scripture.
3. Interpret personal experience in light of Scripture and not Scripture in light of personal experience.
4. Remember that Scripture has only one meaning but many applications.
5. Interpret words and passages in harmony with their meaning in the time of the author; interpret them within their context! We must understand what the Scripture meant to its original audience, and what it means for us today.
6. Interpret Scripture in light of its progressive revelation.
7. Remember, you must understand the Bible grammatically (Observation) before you can understand it theologically (Interpretation).
8. A doctrine cannot be considered biblical unless it includes all that the Scripture say about it. Do not practice "selective citation" or "proof-texting."
9. Determine the genre of a book or passage. Is it narrative, prophecy, poetry, apocalyptic, etc.?
10. When two doctrines taught in the Bible appear to be contradictory, accept both as scriptural, continue to work toward resolution, and accept that we cannot "figure-out" all there is to know about God and his word.

These are not all of the rules of interpretation, nor will they guarantee correct interpretation. However, these guidelines will greatly help you in properly interpreting a text. The biggest rule of interpretation might be to practice humility. Seek help of others when you come across difficult passages. Interpretation is best done in community.

3. APPLICATION[4]

The third step to reading the Bible well is to ask: How do I apply it to my life? Bible study isn't solely for the purpose of knowing more about God. Yes, you should always be growing in your knowledge and understanding of who God is and what he has done for you, but it can't stop there, or you haven't truly studied the Bible. The Bible wasn't given to make us smarter sinners, but holy saints. We want to think rightly about God in order to live rightly before Him. Therefore, you must take what you learn from observation and interpretation and actually apply it to your life. But how do we draw applicable principles from God's Word? Often, the gravest

---

[4] Ibid.

misstep in the hermeneutical process is, oddly enough, in application. We don't want to make the Bible say something it doesn't, and we definitely don't want to practice something it isn't asking of us. Ask these questions when figuring out how to apply a Scripture:

1. Is there an example for me to follow?
2. Is there a sin to avoid/confess?
3. Is there a promise to claim?
4. Is there a prayer to repeat?
5. Is there a command to obey?
6. Is there a condition to meet?
7. Is there a verse to memorize?
8. Is there an error to avoid?
9. Is there a challenge to face?
10. Is there a principle to apply?
11. Is there a habit to change, start, or stop?
12. Is there an attitude to correct? Is there a truth to believe?

Remember, there is always one meaning of a text but many possible applications. Make sure your applications are drawn from the text you are studying at the time. The goal of studying the Bible is to live holy and pleasing lives before God. In order to do this well, we must have a good hermeneutic. Practicing Observation, Interpretation, and Application as described above will help you greatly as you seek to study, understand, and apply God's Word to your life.

In your group, reflect on the following questions:

1. How do you study the Bible right now? Is there any structure or method to your Bible study? Do you "study" the Bible at all, or do you find yourself reading and hoping for the best?

2. Have you ever read parts of Scripture you didn't understand? How did you go about trying to understand them better? Have you ever just moved on from a difficult text without trying to figure it out?

3. Look at 2 Timothy 3:1-17. What do these verses say about the Bible? How is the Bible profitable? What is the difference between those individuals mentioned in verses 1-9 and those mentioned in 10-17?

Model the Word

1. How could using Observation, Interpretation, and Application change the way you read and study the Bible? What principles did you find most helpful?

2. If someone asked you to teach them to read and understand Scripture, what would you tell them to do?

3. Look back at 2 Timothy 3:1-17 and use the process of Observation, Interpretation, and Application in your group with some of the new principles you've learned. What did you do differently from the first time?

Share the Word

1. Think about this passage from the perspective of a lost person. What do you think would be the most challenging aspect of this passage for a lost person to understand? How would you help them understand those aspects better?

2. Many non-Christians don't view the Bible as authoritative or useful for living good lives. There may be some good things from Jesus, but they may believe the Bible has too many problems to be trustworthy. What challenges have you heard from non-Christians about the Bible? How could practicing good hermeneutics help you respond to some of those challenges?

Pray the Word

1. As a group, spend time praying for a greater desire to know and love God's Word.

2. What sins are hindering you from spending more time in the Bible? Confess those to one another and to the Lord.

3. What are the next steps you need to take in reading, studying, and applying God's Word in your discipleship journey? Pray for one another to take those steps and ask God to empower you in your journey.

Daily Bible Reading

Day 1: Luke 21-22
Day 2: Luke 23-24
Day 3: Acts 1-2
Day 4: Acts 3-4
Day 5: Acts 5-6

4. How to Pray

Know the Word
Read Matthew 6:5-15

   1. What do you see? (Observation)

   2. What does it mean? (Interpretation)

   3. What do you do? (Application)

   4. How should you pray?

Martin Luther, a great Christian theologian who started the Protestant Reformation in the 16th century once said, "To be a Christian without prayer is no more possible than to be alive without breathing." Simply put, prayer should be the most natural thing a Christian can do, but let's be honest, sometimes it is the most unnatural thing a Christian can do. Christian history is replete with men like Martin Luther and John Wesley, for example, who would rise at four in the morning and spend several hours of uninterrupted prayer before they would begin their day. While we admire men and women who pray for hours on end, most of us struggle to pray for a few minutes without getting distracted. Instead of prayer being a natural outflow of our relationship with God, it is often a struggle which causes us to throw our hands in the air and say, "I just can't do this!"

Thankfully, prayer does not have to be a constant struggle. You can have a meaningful, life-changing, Christ-exalting prayer life if you will allow Jesus to teach you how to pray. In the school of prayer, I can't think of a better teacher than Jesus!

When the disciples saw how Jesus rose every morning to pray and how the Heavenly Father honored those prayers, they naturally said, "Lord, teach us to pray." Jesus responded to that request by giving them what we call The Lord's Prayer. However, it would probably be more accurately titled The Disciple's Prayer because this simple prayer was intended to help the disciples grow in their own times of prayer. Jesus gave this prayer as a model so we might know how to pray more effectively. I guarantee you, if you will take this model that Jesus gives us and learn how to model your own times of prayer in the way Jesus teaches in Matthew 6:9-13, it will radically change the way you communicate with God!

When you studied this passage on your own, you probably noted that before Jesus taught His disciples how to pray, he taught them how not to pray. The disciples had seen how the religious leaders prayed publicly to be recognized and applauded for their piety. In first century Jerusalem, the religious leaders lined the streets of Jerusalem and looked toward the temple during the daily times of prayer and loudly prayed long and verbose prayers that sounded so polished and so pious. As people passed them by, they undoubtedly thought to themselves, "I can never pray like that. God will never hear my prayers, because there's no way I can pray like the religious leaders! The Pharisees are so righteous. I'll never be like that."

While they may have sounded impressive to people, the religious leaders were not impressive to God. The religious leaders prayed empty prayers because they had no real desire to grow in intimacy with God. Jesus reminded His disciples that when they prayed, they needed to focus on actually communicating with God to build an intimate relationship with Him rather than praying to gain the attention of others. Jesus encouraged his disciples to go to a quiet, private place to pray, just as Jesus Himself did. As they poured their hearts out to God in private, they could know that God would meet with them.

Undoubtedly, you've recited the disciple's prayer in a church service, at a funeral, or at a wedding. Jesus didn't give us this prayer as a prayer to recite in a ritualistic manner. Instead, He gave us this prayer to help us approach our Heavenly Father with the full confidence that our Father is listening to us and ready to answer our prayers. The disciple's prayer is a great model for you to use as you learn to pray. Randy Pope, the author of The Journey discipleship curriculum[1], gives a helpful way to think through the disciple's prayer as a model for your own prayer life. He suggests focusing on five essential targets from the disciple's prayer: (1) God's honor, (2) God's Kingdom, (3) God's provision, (4) God's forgiveness, and (5) God's power. Let's think about each of these targets.

1. GOD'S HONOR

The Disciple's Prayer begins, "Our Father in heaven, hallowed be your name." When you pray, know who you are approaching. You are approaching your Father. You are praying to the God of all creation who has adopted you into His family through the death and resurrection of His Son. Paul wrote, "In love he predestined us for adoption to himself as sons through Jesus Christ" (Ephesians 1:5). God is your Father, and as your Father, He desires a relationship with you. He wants to hear you, to nurture you, and to care for you. Isn't it an amazing thought to think of yourself as a child of God? John wrote,

[1]See what kind of love the Father has given to us, that we should be called children of God; and so we are. The reason why the world does not know us is that it did not know him. [2]Beloved, we are God's children now, and what we will be has not yet appeared; but we know that when he appears we shall be like him, because we shall see him as he is. [3]And everyone who thus hopes in him purifies himself as he is pure (1 John 3:1-3).

While God is your Father, He is also the God of all creation. He is the sovereign King who rules and reigns over the universe. He is worthy of your worship, your reverence, and the totality of your life. When you pray, hallow His name. I know hallow is not a word you typically use in everyday conversation, but it means to honor or to regard as holy. When you pray, think about exactly who God is and approach Him with an attitude of worship and gratitude.

2. GOD'S KINGDOM

"Your Kingdom come, your will be done on earth as it is in heaven." God is not about building your kingdom. He's about building His Kingdom, and He desires for your life to be conformed to His desire to establish His Kingdom on earth. The promise of Scripture is that there is coming a day when God's Kingdom will be established fully on this earth, and no one will stand in the way of God accomplishing His will. We long for that day, and in the meantime, we pray

[1]See thejourneycurriculum.com

that His will be done on earth as it is in heaven. Right now, in God's heavenly throne room, no one stands in the way of His will being done. That's what we long for on this earth.

Prayer is a time of introspection. Is your life centered around God's Kingdom or your kingdom? Are you praying for God to use you to make His Kingdom known? Are you praying for people who are far away from Christ? Are you praying for God to use you to influence the lives of others for His Kingdom?

3. GOD'S PROVISION

"Give us this day our daily bread." More than praying for literal bread, this petition is a reminder that you are utterly dependent on God for everything. Like most people, you probably struggle with self-sufficiency. In your self-sufficiency, you often think you are able to provide for yourself without the help of anyone. After all, you're smart. Over the years you've developed skills and abilities, got a good job, and earn a good living. In your mind, you are more than able to take care of yourself. However, the reality is, you are only where you are in life because of the grace of God. Everything you have is a result of God's grace. You really do need God for everything. You are even dependent on Him to provide you with something as basic as the bread you eat.

Do your prayers express your dependency on God? Do you approach God with humility; trusting that He is the one giving you your next breath? Jesus encourages us to pray for God's provision in light of the reality that God is our Father who wants to provide us with all we need to accomplish His will in this life.

4. GOD'S FORGIVENESS

"And forgive us our debts as we have also forgiven our debtors." You've been forgiven of all your sins, but you still sin. While your present sins do not negate your eternal salvation, your present sins do affect your daily walk with the Lord. You've probably experienced it. When you sin, you don't want to pray. You don't want to read your Bible. Your ongoing sin causes distance in your daily relationship with God. Therefore, you need ongoing confession and repentance. Daily you need to come before God confessing to Him how you have sinned against Him. Notice, the assumption is that not only are you asking for forgiveness, but you are also practicing forgiveness. (See Matthew 6:14-15.) If you are unwilling to forgive others, it may be an indicator that you have not experienced the forgiveness of God yourself. If you have experienced the forgiveness of Jesus, it creates in you a heart willing to forgive those who have wronged you. When you have experienced such grace from a loving and merciful heavenly Father, how can that not make you into a person of grace?

5. GOD'S POWER

"And lead us not into temptation but deliver us from evil." Every day, you experience the temptation to turn from God and turn to sin. You also know those areas in your life in which you are prone to sin. God has the power to protect you from yourself. He has the power to change the desires of your heart. Are you asking God for His power over sin? Are you asking Him to help you to not give into those things you struggle with?

What Jesus gives us in the Disciple's Prayer is a simple model to help us to pray effectively and powerfully. I would challenge you to simply work through the five targets of the disciple's prayer on a daily basis. As you read through Scripture, you'll see these targets come up on the pages of the Bible. For example, when you read one of the Psalms that extols the greatness of God, let that psalm inform the way you hallow God's name. When you read a passage that speaks of the forgiveness of Jesus, let that passage inform the way you ask God to forgive you of your sins. I think if you focus on these five targets when you pray, and if you focus on asking the question, "how should I pray?" when you are daily reading your Bible, it will tremendously affect your prayer life.

Please don't be discouraged if your prayer life is not where you want it to be. We have all experienced the struggles of prayer! Please don't feel guilty because your prayer life is not as "good" as another believer's prayer life. Maybe you know someone who gets up every morning at 4:00 a.m. to spend an hour in prayer, and you can't imagine ever having that kind of commitment to prayer. Don't compare yourself to what somebody else is doing. Just start where you are and make it a practice to spend uninterrupted time in prayer each day. That may be ten or twenty minutes, and sometimes it may be longer. God is not watching the clock to make sure you pray the appropriate amount of time. He simply desires for you to grow in your relationship with Him.

In your group, reflect on the following questions:

1. How would you evaluate your current prayer life? If you struggle, why do you think you struggle? If you feel like your prayer life is strong, why do you think it is strong?

2. Think about the warnings Jesus gives in Matthew 6:5-8. How do you think your private prayer life should affect the way you pray in public?

3. As you look at the Disciples prayer in Matthew 6:9-13, what target do you think you struggle with the most in your prayer life? How can you improve in praying for that specific target area?

Model the Word

1. Who has been most influential in your life when it comes to prayer? Has anyone ever taught you how to pray? How would you teach a new believer to pray?

2. In your group, share with each other some practices that have helped you pray effectively. Share with each other how you approach your time of prayer each day.

3. In your group, walk through the Disciple's Prayer together and talk about how you would pray each target of the prayer. Spend some time praying together over each target.

Share the Word

1. How would you explain prayer to an unbeliever?

2. Should an unbeliever pray? Does God hear the prayers of an unbeliever? Why or why not?

3. How do you think God desires for you to pray for unbelievers?

Pray the Word

1. Pray that God would give you a renewed desire for spending time alone with Him in prayer.

2. Pray for each of your group members to grow in their desire to pray.

3. Pray for lost friends and family members by name. Pray God would give you the courage to have Gospel conversations with them.

Daily Bible Reading

Day 1: Acts 7-8
Day 2: Acts 9-10
Day 3: Acts 11-12
Day 4: Acts 13-14
Day 5: Acts 15-16

5. Made in God's Image for God's Glory

Know the Word
Read Genesis 1:26-31

1. What do you see? (Observation)

2. What does it mean? (Interpretation)

3. What do you do? (Application)

4. How should you pray?

If you're a parent, you probably look at your kids from time to time and see yourself in them. Maybe your kids share your hair color, or perhaps the shape of their face reminds you of the shape of your face. When you compare photos of yourself as a child to your children's photos, the similarities are uncanny. Not only do you see physical resemblances, but perhaps you have noticed that your kids share some of your mannerisms. Maybe your son talks with his hands just like you do. Maybe your daughter gets aggravated by the same things you get aggravated by. Maybe you don't have children yet, but when you look in the mirror you see your parents staring back at you! It's shocking!

Have you ever thought about the fact that you resemble God? On the opening page of the Bible, you are told that you are made in the image of God. Now, you don't resemble God in the sense that you physically look like God. God is not a physical being; He's a spiritual being. Jesus told the woman at the well in John 4:24, "God is spirit, and those who worship him must worship in spirit and truth." While you might not look like God in a physical sense, His fingerprints are all over your life. What does it mean to be made in the image of God? Theologian Wayne Grudem writes, "The fact that man is in the image of God means that man is like God and represents God."[1] If you're going to understand the Gospel message, you must begin with a right understanding of what it means to be made in the image of God.

YOU ARE LIKE GOD.

Humans aren't merely another animal in the animal kingdom. Instead, humans are distinct from every other creature God created. As a human, you are obviously a physical being, but you are also a spiritual being. We have no indication in Scripture that any other creature in the animal kingdom has a spirit, but you do. The Apostle Paul writes, "Now may the God of peace himself sanctify you completely and may your whole spirit and soul and body be kept blameless at the coming of our Lord Jesus Christ" (1 Thessalonians 5:23). Since you are a spiritual being, you are able to have a relationship with God and live with Him forever. However, if you reject God, you will live apart from Him for all eternity.

You are distinct because you are a spiritual being. You are also distinct because you are a moral being. As a spiritual and moral being you are like God. You know the difference between right and wrong, and you are able to choose between right and wrong. You are able to judge between what is beautiful and pleasing and what is not beautiful and pleasing.

You are like God in other ways as well. Like God, you have knowledge and intellect. You are able to think and make decisions based on your knowledge of the truth. Like God, you are relational. God is triune (three distinct persons yet one God), and for all of eternity the

---

[1] Wayne A. Grudem, *Systematic Theology: An Introduction to Biblical Doctrine* (Leicester, England; Grand Rapids, MI: Inter-Varsity Press; Zondervan Pub. House, 2004), 442.

three persons of the Trinity - the Father, the Son, and the Holy Spirit - have been in a perfect relationship with each other. Like God, humans desire to live in intimate relationships with others. You desire to know and to be known. All of these distinctions set you apart from the animal kingdom and serve as a reminder that you are made in the image of God.

Obviously, we're just scratching the surface of the ways you are like God, and to be honest, Scripture does not specifically spell out the ways in which we are like God. We're just told that we are made in His image. However, we are certainly told in Scripture what God is like. In some ways, we will never be like God. For example, we will never know everything. We will never be all powerful. We will never be infinite. These are a few characteristics of God that are completely unique to Him. In Scripture, we also see characteristics of God that we can imitate. We can imitate His love, His grace, His mercy, His kindness, His forgiveness, His patience, and so many other of His characteristics. So, any time you show selfless love, you are bearing the image of God. Any time you patiently endure with someone, you are bearing the image of God. Any time you imitate the character of God, you are bearing the image of God.

YOU REPRESENT GOD.

We are like God, and we represent God by living out the unique responsibilities He has given to all who bear His image. According to Genesis 1:26-31, God has given us the responsibility of having dominion over His world. In other words, our God who rules and reigns over creation has called us to rule with Him. What a sobering thought! We are His representatives on earth who have been given a divine responsibility to care for and subdue His creation while knowing that ultimately everything belongs to the King of kings and Lord of lords. How should knowing that this world belongs to the King of kings and Lord of lords affect the way that you care for His creation?

We not only have the responsibility of living out the image of God by caring for His creation in a way that honors Him, but we also have the responsibility of spreading the image of God by being fruitful and multiplying (Genesis 1:28). If you think back to the Garden of Eden, it was just Adam and Eve living on a massive planet that needed subduing. Obviously, Adam and Eve could not have dominion over the entire earth. Adam and Eve were limited to the Garden of Eden, and the Garden of Eden was more than enough for them to handle. But, as Adam and Eve had children, those children would begin to populate the earth and spread God's image throughout His creation.

Now, I don't want to get in your business concerning the number of children you have or the number of children you are going to have, but for those of us who are Christ followers, every child we have is an opportunity to spread God's image in this world. When you raise your children to know God, love God, and serve God, they are able to go into the world and spread God's image in a way that brings glory to God! What a tremendous responsibility!

YOU ARE VALUED BY GOD.

Only humanity is made in the image of God, and the Bible reminds us that because we are made in the image of God, we have distinct value. David writes in Psalm 8:3-8:

3When I look at your heavens, the work of your fingers, the moon and the stars, which you have set in place, 4what is man that you are mindful of him, and the son of man that you care for him? 5Yet you have made him a little lower than the heavenly beings and crowned him with glory and honor. 6You have given him dominion over the works of your hands; you have put all things under his feet, 7all sheep and oxen, and also the beasts of the field, 8 the birds of the heavens, and the fish of the sea, whatever passes along the paths of the seas.

To David, it was evident that God made humanity distinct from the rest of creation, and it caused David to rejoice. In Psalm 8:1 David writes, "O Lord, our LORD, how majestic is your name in all the earth." When you realize how much God values you, what other response should you have other than to worship the One who distinctly and wonderfully made you for His glory?

Every person on the face of the planet is made in the image of God. Therefore, every person on the face of the planet has intrinsic worth and value in the eyes of God. This means that every person is worth your dignity and respect, and every person is worth us showing them kindness, love, mercy, and grace. If every person on the face of the planet is valued in the eyes of God, then every person needs an opportunity to hear the Gospel.

When the reformer John Calvin reflected on what it means to be made in the image of God, he essentially explained that people are mirrors. In other words, God intended for us to reflect who He is in the way that we live our lives. As previously discussed, when we love sacrificially, we reflect His love. When we give generously, we reflect His generosity. When we show kindness, we reflect His kindness.

While God intended for us to mirror His character, we have a huge problem. We're broken mirrors. Because of our sin, the image of God in us has been shattered to pieces. I tried to illustrate this in a sermon one time. I was attempting to explain to my congregation what it meant to be made in the image of God. On the stage, I had a full-length mirror, and I talked about how each of us reflects the character of God in the way that we live in this world. Then, at the appropriate time, I took a hammer and smashed the mirror on stage. It sounded like a shotgun had gone off, and glass flew in a million different directions. On top of that, I cut my hand on the glass right in the middle of my sermon! I spent the rest of the message trying to preach while blood gushed from my hand. Needless to say, I didn't think through all of the consequences of smashing glass on stage. After the sermon, several men tried to help me clean up the mess I had made. It was a difficult task. Tiny pieces of glass were everywhere.

While the sermon illustration didn't go quite as I had planned, there were two realities about that broken mirror I was trying to communicate to my congregation. First, because the mirror was broken, it could no longer reflect a full image like it was designed to do. It was no longer a full-length mirror. If I held up a broken piece of the mirror, I could only see a partial image. If I held a broken piece up to my face, I might have been able to see my hair in that broken piece, but I couldn't see my feet. The tiny pieces of the mirror were not able to reflect my whole body.

Second, after the mirror was broken, it was impossible to put the mirror back together. There was not enough super glue in the world to put that mirror back together. Even if we were somehow able to gather every single sliver of glass from that broken mirror and piece it back together, we would never be able to remove the cracks from the mirror. It is impossible to put a broken mirror back together.

You are a broken mirror. Because of sin, you are unable to adequately represent God. Sure, you can love, but not perfectly as God does. You can forgive and show mercy, but not perfectly like God. In your life, and in every life, glimpses of the image of God can be seen, but you are a broken mirror. God's image cannot be clearly seen in your life.

On top of that, there's nothing you can do about it. You can't fix yourself! Thankfully, there is One who can fix you. This is the Good News that the Christian faith proclaims. Jesus, who was fully man and at the same time fully God, entered into this broken world and lived perfectly as the ultimate image of God. In everything He did, He reflected the glory of His Father. He perfectly showed us the love of the Father, the mercy of the Father, the forgiveness of the Father. Then, the One who perfectly bore the image of God on this earth went to a cross and was broken for us. Three days later, Jesus rose from the grave, so for all of us who trust Him, we can experience forgiveness and a renewed relationship with God.

For those of us who have placed our faith in Jesus, our Savior is working a miracle in us. He's putting the pieces of the mirror back together. He is the only One who is able to restore the image of God within us. As you daily give your life to Him, He is daily putting the pieces back together. Ultimately, there will come a day when you stand before the God of all creation, who made you in His image, as an unbroken mirror, fully restored, and completely in the likeness of Jesus, the One who died and rose again for you.

In your group, reflect on the following questions:

1. Knowing that every person is made in the image of God, how should this affect the way you view people?

2. Look at Genesis 9:6. How does this verse help your understanding of the image of God? Is it possible for lost people to reflect the image of God? Why or why not?

3. What new insights have you gained from this study of the image of God?

Model the Word

1. In your group, take turns explaining what it means to be made in the image of God with each other.

2. How does knowing that you are made in the image of God affect your understanding of the purpose of your life? Take turns discussing ways that you have seen growth in reflecting the image of God in your life. Also, take turns discussing where you need to grow in reflecting the image of God in your life.

3. What do you think it means for a twenty-first-century person to "have dominion" over the earth? How can Christians do a better job of "having dominion" over the earth, and how can Christians do a better job of spreading the image of God throughout the earth?

Share the Word

1. How would you explain the image of God to an unbeliever?

2. Do you think it's important for a lost person to understand what it means to be made in the image of God? How can use this doctrine in a Gospel conversation with an unbeliever?

3. How should knowing every person is made in the image of God affect the way you share the Gospel?

Pray the Word

1. Pray for a renewed desire to reflect the image of God in your own life.

2. Pray for each of your group members to grow in the character of Christ.

3. Pray with thanksgiving that Jesus died and rose again so that what is broken in you could be put back together.

Daily Bible Reading

Day 1: Acts 17-18
Day 2: Acts 19-20
Day 3: Acts 21-22
Day 4: Acts 23-24
Day 5: Acts 25-26

6. The Reality of Spiritual Death

Know the Word
Read Ephesians 2:1-3

1. What do you see? (Observation)

2. What does it mean? (Interpretation)

3. What do you do? (Application)

4. How should you pray?

Death and taxes--the only things we can't avoid in this life, right? Well, you may be able to avoid your taxes, but that probably wouldn't go well for you in the long run! Death, on the other hand, is absolutely unavoidable. The author of Ecclesiastes assures his readers that no matter whether people are good or evil, clean or unclean, loving or hateful, rich or poor, everyone will die (Ecc. 9:1-6). If you have ever been to a funeral or had someone in your family or close to you die, you know it's difficult to see a lifeless body lying in a casket.

I was a child when I saw a dead body for the first time at a funeral visitation. I was terrified! All I could think about was that lifeless body suddenly sitting up in the casket and looking at me. As adults, even though going to a funeral is still a sad experience, we know dead bodies don't come to life—when it's dead it's dead. Upon death, a person's soul goes either to be in the presence of God or apart from Him in torment. The body is left behind until the resurrection occurs when souls will be reunited with their bodies and made new. Therefore, when we see dead bodies at funerals, we know, unlike some children, there is no way those bodies are going to sit up in the casket—that would take a miracle!

Physical death isn't the only aspect of death; there is also the reality of spiritual death. What exactly does it mean to be spiritually dead? And how is that similar or dissimilar to being physically dead? A closer look at Genesis 2-3 provides some clarity.

When God created Adam, He placed him in the garden of Eden. The garden was lush, beautiful, and provided Adam everything he needed to live. However, the primary thing that made Eden so wonderful was the presence of God. It was in the garden that man could live fully and freely in God's presence, without any sin, shame, or death. Moses writes:

15The LORD God took the man and put him in the garden of Eden to work it and keep it. 16And the LORD God commanded the man, saying, "You may surely eat of every tree of the garden, 17but of the tree of the knowledge of good and evil you shall not eat, for in the day that you eat of it you shall surely die" (Genesis 2:15-17).

The command was simple enough: Eat fruit from the tree of the knowledge of good and evil and you will die. After God gave Adam the command, He saw that it was not good for Adam to be alone, so He created his wife, Eve. Notice that Eve had not yet been created when God gave Adam the original command about the fruit of the tree; therefore, what Eve knew about the command came from Adam. The serpent, then, being the craftiest of all the beasts, addresses Eve first and not Adam.

¹He said to the woman, "Did God actually say, 'You shall not eat of any tree in the garden?'" ²And the woman said to the serpent, "We may eat of the fruit of the trees in the garden, ³but God said, 'You shall not eat of the fruit of the tree that is in the midst of the garden, neither shall you touch it, lest you die." ⁴But the serpent said to the woman, "You will not surely die. ⁵For God knows that when you eat of it your eyes will be opened, and you will be like God, knowing good and evil." ⁶So when the woman saw that the tree was good for food, and that it was a delight to the eyes, and that the tree was to be desired to make one wise, she took of its fruit and ate, and she also gave some to her husband who was with her, and he ate.
⁷Then the eyes of both were opened, and they knew that they were naked. And they sewed fig leaves together and made themselves loincloths (Genesis 3:1b-7).

Several things are important to note. First, the serpent questions whether God actually said they shouldn't eat from "any tree." Eve rightly states they could eat freely of the trees in the garden, and she even rightly says they shouldn't eat of the tree in the midst of the garden or they would die, but she wrongly states they shouldn't "touch it". Her sentiment is correct, but her information is partly wrong. Either Adam didn't convey God's command correctly to Eve or she misremembered what Adam told to her.

Second, the serpent causes Eve to question God's intention, claiming God simply knows that if she eats of the fruit, she will become like Him, knowing good and evil, but surely she wouldn't die. Eve is enticed by the proposition of being like God and desires to be wise, so she takes and eats of the fruit. Oddly enough, she turns and gives Adam the fruit as well, which implies that he was present for the entire encounter but chose to remain silent rather than speak up in obedience to God.

Third, upon eating the fruit sin enters into their world, their eyes are opened to the reality of sin, and they become ashamed of their nakedness, attempting to cover themselves with fig leaves. Once sin enters, everything about their lives change.

In Genesis 3, Adam and Eve hide from God as he walks through the garden. The God they once were happy to fellowship with they now hide from because of their sin and shame. As God calls out to them, asking their whereabouts, Adam says they hid because they were naked. We see the results of sin as Adam blames Eve and Eve blames the serpent for their wrongdoing. God then gives curses to all three, which ultimately results in Adam and Eve being kicked out of Eden, which, remember, is where the presence of God is.

TWO TYPES OF DEATH

What are we to make of God's decree that on the day the humans eat of the tree of the knowledge of good and evil they would surely die (Gen. 2:17)? It doesn't seem as if Adam and Eve actually died on that day. So, what does it mean? There are two ways we see them die: physically and spiritually.

Physically? They don't physically die! God sends them out and we see them live for a long time, right? While they don't die on the spot, they certainly do begin the process of dying. God promises Adam that he will return to the dust he came from (Gen. 3:19); in other words, one of the consequences of Adam's sin was his eventual death. Adam and Eve began to physically die on that day.

The key thing we want to see for this week is that they also died spiritually on that day. Prior to sin, Adam and Eve were in an unhindered relationship with God. They dwelt in His presence with no fear of judgment, condemnation, punishment, or death. When no sin is involved, being in the presence of God is a wonderful, joyous thing! However, as we see post-fall and throughout the Old Testament, entering into the presence of God in a sinful state is more of a terrifying experience than anything, often leading to death. Because God is holy, nothing sinful can be in His presence. When sin entered into the world, the once unhindered relationship Adam and Eve had with God became broken and distorted. No longer could they walk and talk with God freely; no longer could they bask in the joy and glory of his presence. God had to kick them out of Eden and away from His presence.

Adam and Eve's broken relationship with God meant they also died spiritually. Sin separated them from God. In Genesis 3:21 we see God graciously clothe them with animal skins, which meant something had to die and blood had to be shed for their sin to be covered. However, they still had to be kicked out of his presence because sin affected every aspect of their lives. Adam and Eve experienced spiritual death, or separation from God.

SPIRITUAL DEATH TODAY

In Romans 5:12-21, Paul plainly states that because of Adam's disobedience, sin and death spread to all people. There isn't a single person who has ever lived or ever will live who isn't separated from God, because all have sinned and fall short his glory (Rom. 3:23). Just like Adam, our sin earns us death; we die because of sin. Therefore, just like Adam, we have two types of death problems: physical and spiritual. Jesus Christ fixes his church's physical death problem through his resurrection, which will ultimately be applied to the church one day (we will look at that in a later session).

Before we look at how Jesus Christ fixes our spiritual death problem (next week), here are a few characteristics of those who are spiritually dead Paul mentions in Ephesians 2.

1. EVIL FLESH AND MINDS

Paul says those who are spiritually dead indulge and readily give into the desires of the flesh and mind. Paul identifies some but not all of the works of the flesh in Galatians 5:19-21: "Now the deeds of the flesh are evident, which are: immorality, impurity, sensuality, idolatry, sorcery, enmities, strife, jealousy, outbursts of anger, disputes, dissensions, factions, envying, drunkenness, carousing, and things like these, of which I forewarned you, that those who practice such things will not inherit the kingdom of God" (ESV). Those who are in Christ still battle and fight the flesh, but fighting against sin is much different than seeking it out and willfully giving into it.

In the same vein, the sin of the mind is closely connected to the sin of the flesh. Here is a helpful way to think about the relationship between the two: thinking leads to doing. It's very rare that people suddenly find themselves struggling with serious and costly sins such as adultery, impurity, dissensions, jealousy and the like. Typically, these types of sin form over time by the accumulation of evil thoughts. This is why Paul is so adamant about controlling and monitoring the things you think about because the things you think about can and will become what you do. Not only does he warn against evil thoughts he also commands believers to think about holy things. Paul writes, "Finally, brothers, whatever is true, whatever is honorable, whatever is just, whatever is pure, whatever is lovely, whatever is commendable, if there is any excellence, if there is anything worthy of praise, think about these things" (Phil. 4:8). Those who are spiritually dead do not set their minds on things worthy of praise; rather, they set their minds on things worthy of death.

2. WALKING WITH THE WORLD

Those who are spiritually dead live in accordance with the world and not the word of God. Jesus says that a tree is known by the fruit it produces. Good trees bear good fruit; bad trees bear bad fruit (Matt. 7:17-20). An easy way to tell if someone is spiritually dead is by the fruit they produce. Those who have been made alive in Christ Jesus produce the fruit of the Spirit, while those who are dead in their trespasses and sins produce the deeds of the flesh as listed above (see Gal. 5:19-21). This isn't to say that in order to be spiritually alive one must produce every fruit of the Spirit in abundance; however, those who are alive in Christ will produce some fruit, and as they progress in their walk with Christ that fruit will increase.

3. CHILDREN OF DISOBEDIENCE

"Children of disobedience" is an interesting term. When children disobey, we punish them because they intentionally did something they knew they weren't supposed to do, which means they were given a command to obey or instructions to follow and they willingly did something contrary to that. In order to be disobedient, you have to be given a command to obey. We don't punish little babies if they do something we don't want them to do—we know they are innocent and don't intentionally do wrong things, but older children are well aware of what is right and wrong; therefore, we punish them for disobedience.

In the same way, Paul says that all people who are spiritually dead are children of disobedience. Whether Jew or Gentile, all people willingly turn against and disobey the God of the universe. The prince of the power of the air—Satan—tempts people into disobedience, just like he did in the garden of Eden. Those who are disobedient walk with the world and follow their sinful flesh and minds.

4. CHILDREN OF WRATH

The ultimate characteristic of those who are spiritually dead is also the most terrifying one. Paul concludes that because of all the other characteristics that define those who are dead in their sins and trespasses, those people are worthy of God's wrath and judgment. Wrath and judgment are for all those who are spiritually dead, which is every person who has lived. As we read the first three verses of Ephesians chapter 2, we see how dire the state of humanity is. There is nothing those who are spiritually dead deserve other than the full wrath, punishment, and judgment of God, both physical and spiritual death.

By God's grace and mercy, the story doesn't stop there. We'll look next week at the solution to this tragic situation.

In your group, reflect on the following questions:

1. Read Ephesians 2:1-3. What words or phrases stand out to you?

2. What does it mean to be "dead in trespasses and sins"?

3. What are the two types of death you discussed this week? How are those similar? How are they different?

4. What are some of the characteristics of those who are spiritually dead?

Model the Word

1. As a follower of Christ, you are not spiritually dead; however, we battle with our flesh and minds daily and we fight against many of the sins that are defined by being spiritually dead. Read Galatians 5:19-20. What areas of sin that are mentioned in that passage do you struggle with? What steps can you take to remove those sin areas?

2. Because you are a follower of Christ, the fruits of the Spirit apply to you! Look at the same passage and think about these questions. Which of the fruits of the Spirit do you see in your life? Which of those fruits do you need to grow in? What practical steps can you take this week to begin to grow in some areas you may be weak?

Share the Word

1. How would you use this passage to teach a lost person about what it means to be spiritually dead?

2. How could you use this passage to encourage a believer who may be struggling with sin issues and doubting their faith?

Pray the Word

1. As a group, spend time praying for one another concerning the sin struggles you mentioned above.

2. Which fruits of the Spirit do you need to see growth in? Pray that God would work in those areas of your life.

3. Pray for the name(s) of a person you know is spiritually dead. Share the name of that person with the group and spend time praying that God would provide an opportunity for you to share the gospel with that person and that ultimately God would save him or her.

Daily Bible Reading

Day 1: Acts 27-28
Day 2: Galatians 1-2
Day 3: Galatians 3-4
Day 4: Galatians 5-6
Day 5: 1 Thessalonians 1-2

7. The Hope of New Life

Know the Word
Read Ephesians 2:4-10

1. What do you see? (Observation)

2. What does it mean? (Interpretation)

3. What do you do? (Application)

4. How should you pray?

Have you ever received a gift you didn't deserve? I don't mean something like socks for Christmas--you probably deserved that. I'm talking about a substantial gift, something you weren't expecting, and something you couldn't repay. Maybe it was a brand new car or an all expense paid vacation. Someone may have stepped in to pay a medical bill you couldn't afford, or even provided a spare kidney or blood cells for a transfusion.

When I was in high school, a new student transferred in to our school because he had gotten into some serious legal trouble at his previous school. He was living with his grandmother who was a member of our church, and this individual started coming to our youth group. He had a lot of problems and knew he needed to turn his life around. Our youth group and many at our school embraced him and tried to make him feel at home and loved.

Problematically, he had a court date to pay for a ticket associated with his previous issues, and he didn't have enough money to pay the fine. His grandmother didn't have enough money to help him, and if he didn't pay the fine, he had to go to jail. We certainly didn't want him to go to jail, so several of my friends rallied together and, mostly with our parent's help (we didn't have any money!), raised the money to pay for his ticket.

I remember going to his grandmother's house and knocking on the door. He was surprised to see us and had no clue what we had been doing. As I explained what we had done and why we had done it, I handed him the money to pay for his fine. He was overcome with emotion and joy. At that moment, he realized he received a gift he didn't deserve and couldn't repay. He hadn't done anything to earn the money; it was freely given to him. And we didn't do it out of obligation; we loved him and wanted him to know and love Jesus. His life was different after that moment. He didn't go on to live the perfect life--he still needed a lot of growth. But, because of a gift, his life changed, and he realized he needed to live differently moving forward.

EPHESIANS 2:4-10

These verses contain some of the most transparent and robust language about the nature of salvation. Last week, we looked at the reality of spiritual death. In Ephesians 2:1-3, Paul paints a dire picture of the human condition. Humanity is characterized by evil and disobedience, destined for the wrath of God. If all we had was the first three verses, we would be hopeless, but God is amazing and merciful and provides salvation through Jesus Christ. Let's examine these verses.

DEAD IN SIN

Paul doesn't want to confuse his readers by causing them to think they somehow earned favor with God or initiated their salvation--they were dead! Dead means dead. What can a dead person do? Absolutely nothing. Someone who is alive can at least try to clean themselves up, work hard to get right with God, or do some good in an attempt to earn God's favor. But that's not how salvation works. Those apart from Christ can't improve their situation, even if they wanted to.

There are many lies and misconceptions about salvation. One lie says people can earn God's favor through good works. If they are "good" enough of a person, God will ultimately save them. Paul refutes such thinking and says there isn't one single person who is good enough to earn God's favor; none are good, no not one (Rom. 3:10-12). In verse 8 he reiterates the point just in case someone missed it the first time. Another lie says people can initiate their salvation. All they need to do is consider whether or not they want to follow Jesus. If they think about it long enough, they will realize their need for God. But this thinking doesn't correlate with Paul's words in these verses. Those who are dead have no ability or capacity to initiate anything. If God doesn't start the work, humans are doomed. A third lie says people are far too sinful to ever be forgiven by a holy God. If those who are dead are going to come to life, it will take a miracle! Well, a miracle is exactly what we see.

MADE ALIVE IN CHRIST

Verse 4 starts, "But God." This may be the best but in the whole Bible! Christians once were dead in sin, BUT GOD made us alive in Christ. Christians once followed after Satan and their own flesh, giving in to worldly desires, BUT GOD raised us with Christ to sit in the heavenly places. Christians were once children of wrath and disobedience, BUT GOD saved us so that we may spend eternity with Him, worshipping Him for who He is and what He has done. We were in a hopeless, helpless, and horrible situation that was going to result with an eternity in hell, BUT GOD, by His grace and mercy, which is lavishly bestowed upon us, chose to raise dead people to the new life that is in Jesus Christ. This is the good news of salvation!

We use words like grace and mercy a lot without knowing precisely what they mean. They describe two different aspects of God's salvation. Grace is unmerited favor. Therefore, when Paul says "by grace you have been saved," it means that God favors you, but you did nothing to earn or "merit" that favor. It's His choice. Grace is His gift to give. Mercy, on the other hand, is compassion or forgiveness shown to someone who deserves punishment. To say, "God, being rich in mercy" (Eph. 2:4a), means that God could punish us because that's what we deserve, but He chooses to forgive us instead. In God's mercy He doesn't punish us, and in His grace, He blesses us more than we could possibly imagine.

CREATED FOR GOOD WORKS

It would be easy to stop at verse 9, and, so often, that is what people do when they talk about salvation. Sadly, I've presented and have heard the gospel presented in such a way that the only things that are mentioned are sin, death, separation from God, and a solution to the problem. In this sense, salvation becomes nothing but a way to get to heaven after death. But that isn't the gospel at all! If we are going to preach a complete gospel, we can't ignore what Paul says in verse 10 of this beautiful chapter.

Those who have been made alive are "created in Christ Jesus for good works, which God prepared beforehand, that we should walk in them" (Eph. 2:10). God doesn't merely save you from something; He saves you for something. If you have new life, you are to live and walk and act in such a way that anyone could look at you and tell you are no longer dead. In Ephesians 4:17-6:20, Paul describes how those who have new life should live. Those who experience new life are changed inside and out. Your desires, goals, ambitions, emotions, and character should be aimed at pleasing and glorifying God. If your inner self is changed. Your outer self should reflect the change as well. Salvation isn't just about character change; it's also about action change. If you've been made alive in Christ, you've been called to be on his mission and make disciples. Get rid of the old and put on the new. You have been made alive in Christ! Rejoice in the gospel, and live in such a way that glorifies God and causes people to know you've been made new.

In your group, reflect on the following questions:

1. When did you come to faith? What was your life like before Christ and after you met Christ?

2. What does Ephesians 2:4-10 say about those who are in Christ? What verses, phrases, or words stand out?

3. What are grace and mercy? How does God show us grace and mercy?

Model the Word

1. How would you explain "new life" to someone? What are the characteristics of someone who was once dead but is now alive in Christ?

2. What areas of your life are still characteristic of someone who is dead? What sins are holding you back from walking fully in the newness of life?

3. Paul says Christians are created in Christ Jesus for good works. What are some of the "good works" of the Christian life? How are you doing in this area?

Share the Word

1. Think about this passage from the perspective of an unbeliever. How could you use these verses to share the gospel with someone?

2. Consider someone who is dead in sin and someone who is alive in Christ. How should their lives look in comparison to one another?

3. How can your testimony help an unbeliever understand these verses?

Pray the Word

1. Think about areas of your life that aren't representative of the new life. Pray God would work in and through you to rid you of sin and transform you more into the image of Christ.

2. As a group, reflect on what God has done for you by raising you from death to new life. Pray a prayer of thankfulness for who God is and what He has done for you.

Daily Bible Reading

Day 1: 1 Thessalonians 3-4
Day 2: 1 Thessalonians 5
Day 3: 2 Thessalonians 1-2
Day 4: 2 Thessalonians 3
Day 5: 1 Corinthians 1-2

8. Sharing the Gospel

Know the Word
1 Peter 3:13-17

1. What do you see? (Observation)

2. What does it mean? (Interpretation)

3. What do you do? (Application)

4. How should you pray?

When is the last time you shared the gospel? What are you feeling after reading that question? You might feel pretty good. Maybe you shared the gospel with someone today or this past week. The likelihood, however, is that you either haven't shared the gospel in a while or you may have never even shared it at all. You might be feeling shame or condemnation right now. I don't want you to feel that way! Remember, Paul says there is no condemnation for those who are in Christ Jesus (Rom. 8:1). So, let's start there: whether or not you've shared the gospel thousands of times or have never shared it, if you are in Jesus Christ, the Father looks at you and sees his Son standing in your place.

I'm not going to guilt trip you into forcing a gospel conversation with someone so you can check your evangelism box. I'm not interested in box-checking; I'm interested in life change. Before we can talk about how to share the gospel, we must first understand the gospel. The gospel says you are saved by the grace of God through faith in who Jesus is and what He has done for you. If you are in Christ, you are no longer dead in your sins and trespasses; you are a new creation. The old has gone, and the new is here. By the Spirit, you can worship and obey God. And that, I think, is what God is really after. He desires that you worship and obey Him. Not because He is some megalomaniac who wants to control every part of your life, but because He loves you and He knows what is best for you. Sharing the gospel is an act of both worship and obedience.

CHOSEN TO SHARE THE GOSPEL

We share the gospel primarily as an act of worship and obedience to God. As you may know, "gospel" means good news, and, for our purpose, it refers to the good news of Jesus Christ. If people don't hear the good news, they can't respond in worship and obedience. But why us? Why does God want us to share the gospel? Why doesn't He just save people? In His infinite grace and mercy, God has chosen followers of Jesus to be the ones who take the gospel to a lost and dying world. He has chosen you and me to be on His mission.

The question still remains: couldn't God do the work of sharing the gospel better than us? Well, yes and no. Now before you quit reading because I said yes and no, let me explain. We'll start with the obvious: Yes, of course God could do the work better! If Jesus wanted to, He could have shared the good news with everyone He came in contact with and could have opened their eyes and hearts to understand who He was. He would have been the best evangelist of all-time if He wanted to be. But that's not what He wanted. Time and time again, we read about Jesus veiling His identity and even commanding people not to tell anyone about who He was. Jesus told people not to talk about Him! He also wasn't very popular by the end of His time on earth. Think about it. For a guy who had authority over the weather, cast out demons, healed the sick, and brought the dead back to life, Jesus sure didn't have a huge following by the time of His death and resurrection. He was far more hated than liked, and once He was no longer performing miracles for the crowds, the crowds left. After His resurrection and before His ascension, all that remained was a small group of His disciples.

Here's where we get to the no of this question. I know it seems strange and wrong to say God can't do the work of sharing the gospel better than us. It isn't because He doesn't have the power (He's all-powerful). It isn't because He doesn't have the authority (He's sovereign). And it isn't because He doesn't have the ability (He's undoubtedly abler). It is because He chose not to be the one to share the gospel, and He chose for us to be the ones who do. We can't overlook this amazing fact. He chose His people to be the ones to share the good news to a lost and dying world. In choosing His people to do the work He has also equipped his people for the work. Let's look at how God has chosen and equipped His people.

EQUIPPED TO SHARE THE GOSPEL

John chapters 14-16 are remarkable. Jesus makes several important statements about His relationship to the Father and His relationship to the Holy Spirit. He also talks about the future impact the Holy Spirit will have on the disciples. After His famous proclamation that He is the way, truth, and life, as well as telling His disciples that He and the Father are one, Jesus says, "Truly, truly, I say to you, whoever believes in me will also do the works that I do; and greater works than these will he do, because I am going to the Father" (Jn. 14:12). Wow, what a statement from Jesus! How is it possible that anyone can do greater works than Jesus?

Before we get to the greater works, we must first figure out how followers of Jesus can even do equal works. Jesus is God, and God is all-powerful. That means someone equal to Jesus in power needs to be involved in this work. The only persons equal in power to the second person of the Trinity are the Father and the Spirit. Bingo! Here's what Jesus tells His disciples:

[7]Nevertheless, I tell you the truth: it is to your advantage that I go away, for if I do not go away, the Helper will not come to you. But if I go, I will send him to you. [8]And when he comes, he will convict the world concerning sin and righteousness and judgment: [9]concerning sin, because they do not believe in me; [10]concerning righteousness, because I go to the Father, and you will see me no longer; [11]concerning judgment, because the ruler of this world is judged" (John 16:7-11).

There is a lot we could unpack from these verses, but we know the Holy Spirit, the "helper," must be involved if we are to do works equal to Jesus. Now we must address how it is that Christians can do greater works than Jesus. Notice Jesus says it's to the disciple's "advantage" for Him to leave so that the Holy Spirit can come. Think for a moment: why would that be an advantage for the disciples? Wouldn't it always be better to have Jesus around? According to Jesus, apparently not.

Jesus is fully God (John 1; Col. 2:9). Every quality and characteristic of God is present in Jesus Christ. Jesus is also fully man (Phil. 2:1-11; Heb. 2:5-18). He was born into flesh like ours to die a death like ours. One of the characteristics of being human is that you can't be everywhere all the time. Jesus walked from one city to the next, preaching the good news and teaching about the kingdom of God. Jesus could have walked His whole life and never made it to everyone on earth.

Jesus knew that if all the nations were going to be reached with the gospel, there had to be a more effective way. That's where the Holy Spirit comes in. Rather than Jesus being the one to walk around and talk to everyone, He sent the Spirit to indwell believers so that they could be the ones to share the gospel. Jesus knew twelve disciples filled with the Holy Spirit could reach more people in a shorter amount of time. As those twelve went out and shared the gospel, more people came to faith, resulting in more people able to go out and share. The Holy Spirit provided the means for exponential growth in the church.

PREPARED TO SHARE THE GOSPEL

Ok, God has chosen you and equipped you, but are you prepared to share the gospel? Think about the text for today. Peter writes, "always be prepared to make a defense to anyone who asks you for a reason for the hope that is in you" (1 Pet. 3:15). One reason you may not share the gospel as often as you would like is that you are not prepared. The Bible is a big and often complex book, and it can be intimidating to think about communicating its message to someone else. You don't need to know everything about the Bible to share the gospel. If you know a few key components, you can share the good news of Jesus with anyone at any time.

There are many methods for sharing the gospel. You may be familiar with the Romans Road, the Bridge Method, or even the Evangecube. Today, you are going to learn the 3 Circles method. The 3 Circles is helpful, simple, and you can share it anywhere. The 3 Cirles was designed by Jimmy Scroggins, the lead pastor of Family Church in West Palm Beach, Florida. This isn't the only way to share the gospel with others. This is merely a tool that will help you feel more comfortable and confident in evangelism.

Here's what the 3 Circles looks like:

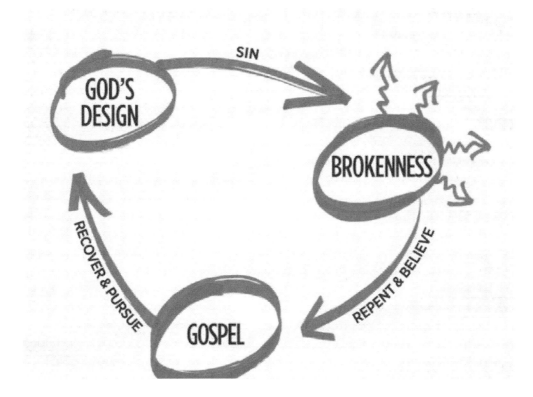

At this point, you should be familiar with what the gospel is. We've looked at the reality of spiritual death and the hope of new life in previous lessons. The purpose of this lesson is to take what you already know and teach you how to share it with someone else. Rather than going back and defining these terms, you are going to work on learning this method and practice sharing it with those in your group. Watch the videos below. Each video displays someone sharing/teaching the 3 Circles. Each presentation is slightly different. After you watch the videos, answer the questions provided below and discuss them with your group. There is also a space provided below for you to draw the 3 Circles.

- https://www.youtube.com/watch?v=tjpt1gbVnOE
- https://www.youtube.com/watch?v=NYU-a2wlbxc
- https://www.youtube.com/watch?v=R1yOeNbrQR0&t=6s

1. What are the similarities between the three gospel presentations? What are the key components to sharing the 3 Circles?

2. What are some of the differences between them?

3. Do you find one of the videos/methods more effective for communicating the gospel than the others? Why or why not?

4. Did any of the videos leave out important details? If so, what was left out?

5. Which of the videos emphasized teaching and helping others "go" and share their faith? Is this important? Why or why not?

PRACTICE

Now it's your turn. In the space provided below, practice drawing and explaining the 3 Circles. Try to complete it without looking at the example.

How did you do? Don't be discouraged if you forgot some details. Practice makes perfect. This week, practice drawing out the 3 Circles on a piece of paper or napkin. As you meet with your group week, take time to practice sharing the 3 Circles with one another. You can draw it out and explain it, or explain the example provided.

Remember, God has chosen and equipped you to share the gospel; it's your responsibility to be prepared. Those who are far from God will not and cannot be saved if they do not hear the amazing message of Jesus Christ. Think about 3 people you know who need to hear the good news of Jesus. Write their names here and begin to pray for opportunities to share with them.

1.

2.

3.

I challenge you to share the gospel with one of those people this week. That may be a scary task, and that's okay. God has not called us to save anyone—that's his responsibility and his work. He has simply called us to be faithful to share this amazing story.

In your group, reflect on the following questions:

1. When is the last time you shared the gospel with someone?

2. Personally, what are the biggest obstacles/hindrances to you sharing the gospel more?

3. What does 1 Peter 3:13-17 teach you about sharing your faith? What verses, phrases, or words stand out?

Model the Word

1. How would you go about teaching someone else to share his or her faith? Who can you teach the 3 Circles to?

2. Has anyone shared the gospel with you before? What strategy or method did they use?

3. How can/do you go about getting into gospel conversations? What are some easy or helpful ways to get into gospel conversations?

Share the Word

1. Peter says to make a defense for your faith with "gentleness and respect." How can you share with others both gently and respectfully?

2. Think about this passage from the perspective of an unbeliever. How could you use these verses to share the gospel with them?

3. What are the key elements of a gospel presentation that people must know to be saved?

Pray the Word

1. As a group, pray for the names you wrote above. Pray for God to provide opportunities to share the gospel.

2. Pray for those in your group. Ask God to provide each person boldness as they go and share the gospel.

Daily Bible Reading

Day 1: 1 Corinthians 3-4
Day 2: 1 Corinthians 5-6
Day 3: 1 Corinthians 7-8
Day 4: 1 Corinthians 9-10
Day 5: 1 Corinthians 11-12

9. Live to Glorify God

Know the Word
Read Romans 12:1-2

1. What do you see? (Observation)

2. What does it mean? (Interpretation)

3. What do you do? (Application)

4. How should you pray?

If you've been a Christian for any length of time, you've undoubtedly asked this question, "What is God's will for my life?" You're dying for the answer to that question, aren't you? You want to know whom God wants you to marry, where He wants you to go to school, where He wants you to go to work, how many children He wants you to have, what type of car to buy, what neighborhood to live in, and what mission trip to go on. You wish God worked like a Magic 8 Ball. You wish you could shake your Bible really hard and the answer to all your questions would surface to the top. Wouldn't that be nice?

If you've always wondered what God's will is for your life, I have excellent news for you. God's will is not a mystery to figure out. There is no secret formula for uncovering the will of God. God clearly spells out His will for you in the Bible. In fact, I'm going to go ahead and tell you exactly what the Bible says about God's will for your life. Are you ready? God's will for your life is that you live to live to glorify Him. It's as simple as that. God's will for your life is that in your attitudes, your conversations, your daily routine, and your decisions you bring Him honor and glory. While it sounds easy enough, you and I know it's not as easy it sounds. However, let's try to answer the question, "How do I glorify God in my decisions?"

KNOW GOD'S REVEALED WILL

Romans is a long letter the Apostle Paul wrote to the church in Rome. The church was primarily made up of non-Jewish people who had converted to faith in Jesus Christ. They came from pagan backgrounds, and they were learning what it meant to follow Jesus as Lord of their lives. Much of this letter is an explanation of what Paul believes about Jesus and the work of salvation that Jesus accomplished for humanity. As the letter comes to its conclusion, Paul explains to his readers how they should live in light of what Jesus has done for them.

Romans 12:1-2 is a landmark passage of Scripture. In this passage, Paul explains how you should live in light of what Jesus has done through His death and resurrection. What Paul writes is a high order! Since you've experienced God's gift of salvation, you owe God your life by daily giving God your life as a living sacrifice.

Think about the phrase living sacrifice. It seems like an oxymoron because living and sacrifice do not go together. If you lived in the first century, whether you were a pagan or a Jew, you were very familiar with the concept of sacrifice. All types of religious adherents made their way to the temples of their gods to offer sacrifices. Every time a worshipper made a sacrifice, the same thing happened. The sacrificial animal died. The worshipper saw it happen right before his eyes. He saw the blood pour out of the animal as it lay lifeless on the altar. In the mind of a first-century worshipper, there was no such thing as a living sacrifice because sacrifices always died. Sacrifices were dead sacrifices not living sacrifices.

Jesus changed all of that. He is the ultimate living sacrifice. On the cross, He laid down His life as a sacrifice for our sins. In His death, he suffered the punishment for our sin so that we could be forgiven and brought into a relationship with our Heavenly Father. Just as the Israelites sacrificed an animal on the altar, the Heavenly Father sacrificed His Son on the cross for you. For those who witnessed His death over 2,000 years ago, they were convinced Jesus was dead and buried in a borrowed tomb. However, Jesus did not stay dead. Three days later, He rose from the dead, completely defeating sin and death so we could have the gift of eternal life. Jesus is our living sacrifice. He laid down His life for us, only to take it up again through His resurrection.

Now Jesus is at the right hand of the Father ruling and reigning over creation and interceding on our behalf. He is still at work in our lives!

So, what does it mean for you to be a living sacrifice? To be a living sacrifice is to daily lay your life down before God and say, "I am dead to everything I desire for me and alive to everything you desire for me." Know God's revealed will! This passage tells you exactly what God's will for your life is. God's will for your life is that you glorify Him by surrendering to His desires.

How do you do it? It starts with a negative. Do not be conformed to this world (Romans 12:2). To be conformed means to be pressed into the mold of this world. It's to adopt the world's way of thinking. It's to apply what you learn from the world to your everyday life. You cannot live out the will of God when you are being pressed into the mold of this world. Let me ask you a simple question, and I want you to be honest with yourself as you answer this question: What has a more significant influence over your life; the ways of this world or the ways of God? Every day you are bombarded with the influence of this world; whether it is through media or even casual conversations at your job. How often do you let casual conversations or the media shape how you think? Think about how this world is trying to press you into a mold that is contrary to Scripture. How often are you more shaped by this world than you are Scripture?

The reality is that you might claim Christianity, but you often don't think and live like a Christian. Instead, you often think and live like an unbeliever. Because of the world's influence over you, you have become an expert in the things of this world, and you are often ignorant toward the things of God. What you need is a transformed mind. You need to think like Jesus so that you can live your life consistent with God's will. This is what Paul is getting to.

Follow the progression: God's will for you is for you to glorify Him by daily surrendering to His desires. However, you struggle because you are consistently following the influence of this world. You need transformation! You need to think like God thinks in order to act like God wants you to act. So, you need the Spirit's help to renew your mind day in and day out so you are consistently thinking the things of God so you might live the ways of God.

God has revealed His will. He has clearly told you how to live. You don't have to ask the question, "What is God's will for my life?" God's will is that you live for Him. We're so busy looking for the hidden that we ignore the obvious. We're so busy trying to figure out whom God wants us to marry, what job He wants us to take, and where He wants us to live that we forget that ultimately God's will for us is to live for His glory. Just think. If you would let God renew your mind by getting in the Bible daily to learn about the God who loves you, it would transform you. The only way your mind is going to be renewed is for you to know God's Word. As you prayerfully and intentionally read the Bible, God will make His Word come alive in you. He will transform you and renew you.

MAKE DECISIONS BY APPLYING GOD'S REVEALED WILL TO YOUR PERSONAL CIRCUMSTANCES.

So, you know God wants you to live out His will – a life that glorifies Him by surrendering to His desires instead of yours. But, how do you make decisions that are consistent with God's will? How do you avoid messing it up? Notice what Paul says in Romans 12:2. He says that when our minds are renewed, we gain the ability to test. In other words, we're able to evaluate our circumstances in light of God's revealed will and then make decisions that are consistent with what we know God wants from us.

There isn't a magic formula for figuring out God's will for your life. You read the Word, think the Word, and do the Word. Moreover, if you read the Word, think the Word, and do the Word, you will find yourself in the center of God's will every single time. Let me give you some practical steps you can take to apply God's revealed will to your present circumstances so you can make decisions that are consistent with God's will for your life.

Think biblically. Don't think like the world. When you are facing a decision, start with God's Word rather than your feelings. Does the Bible address your particular circumstances in any way? How would God want you to respond to your circumstances based on what He has said in His Word? Are you trying to determine whom to marry? Quit focusing on finding "the one" and see what God says about marriage and what kind of spouse you should be. Are you trying to determine where you should work? What does God say about work and vocation? I know the Bible doesn't touch on every subject under the sun. For example, the Bible doesn't have much to say about school or college, but it does have much to say about how God wants you to live regardless of what school you attend. The Bible doesn't say much about what kind of house you should buy, but it does have much to say about being a good steward of the resources God has given you. The Bible may not speak to every situation you face, but the Bible does inform every situation you face. Regardless of the situation, you have the responsibility to respond in a way that is consistent with what the Bible teaches.

Pray. Simple enough, right? Ask God to help you make wise decisions that are consistent with His revealed will. Ask the Spirit to help you to understand His Word.

Seek godly counsel. Proverbs 15:22 says, "Without counsel plans fail, but with many advisers they succeed." The keyword is godly. Talk to people who think biblically and pray fervently. I can't tell you how helpful it has been in my life to have trusted counselors who saturate themselves in the Bible and prayer. The best counselors are those who will merely speak God's Word into your life and help you apply God's Word to your circumstances.

Use wisdom. James says to ask for wisdom and God will give it to you (James 1:5). As you seek to apply wisdom to the choices you make, be more concerned with making a wise choice rather than the right choice. Wisdom is the ability to apply biblical knowledge to your present circumstances. You can only use godly wisdom if you know the Word. Think about a decision you're struggling to make. In light of what you know about what the Bible says, what is the wisest course of action? If you have three companies that are offering you a job, what's the most prudent choice? What job best utilizes your abilities and skills? What job puts you in a position to make the most impact for the Kingdom of God? When you are counseling your children on whom to marry, don't ask them the question, "What does your heart say?" Who cares what their heart says? Instead, help your children to consider the character of the person they are marrying and make a wise choice based on what the Bible says about marriage. The same goes for any other decision. Be wise.

Make a decision and move on. If you have thought biblically, prayed, sought godly counsel, used godly wisdom, and made a decision, there's no need to second-guess that decision. I never second guess if Staci is the woman I should have married. Why? Because I married her. I know that she is the one for me because I made a covenant with her. So, when we don't see eye to eye, and when marriage gets tough, I don't wonder, "Did I miss God in this somehow?" No. I decided to marry Staci based on godly wisdom, prayer, biblical thinking, and wise counsel. I am convinced that I was in the center of God's will when I chose to marry Staci. The same is true about my time at Northwood. I am convinced that today I am in the center of God's will in being the pastor of Northwood because several years ago, I prayed, considered the Word, sought counsel, used wisdom, and made a decision. Every day isn't easy, but I have seen evidence that I am right where God wants me in this season of my life.

MAKE EVERY DECISION WITH THE GOSPEL IN MIND.

As you seek to make decisions that are consistent with the will of God you cannot lose sight of the fact that you are on mission. When you make a decision, ask the question, "What implications does this decision have for the spread of the Gospel?" If you are trying to choose a school, is there a strong church close to that school that is going to equip you to become more effective in making Christ known? If you are buying a car, how will buying that $50,000 car strain your budget in such a way that you will not be able to give generously to Gospel-centered ministries? How will that job you are considering help you make disciples? Will that job put you around lost people with whom you can build Gospel-centered relationships? Will that job take you away from your primary responsibility of making disciples of your children? Will that job take you away from your commitment to the local church where God has placed you to serve and use your spiritual giftedness to build up the body? What about that house you are considering? Will it put you in a neighborhood that is unreached? Or, can you use your home as a gathering place for believers for Bible study and prayer? How will your home be an asset for the ministry of the Gospel? We too often make decisions based on what's in it for us rather than how our decisions affect the work of the Kingdom. Our decisions need to be wise, but they also need to be strategic. When you make a life decision, are you considering how that decision will affect the mission that God has you on this earth for?

In your group, reflect on the following questions:

1. Practically speaking, how do you live as a living sacrifice on a daily basis?

2. In what ways does your life demonstrate that you are conformed to the world? In what ways does your life demonstrate that you have been transformed by the Spirit of God?

3. How has this study helped you to think about following God's will?

Model the Word

1. In your group, share a time when you've had to make a significant life decision. How did you make that decision? Based on this study, how would you have approached that decision differently?

2. In your group, take turns discussing decisions that you currently need to make. How can you counsel each other with the Bible, prayer, and wisdom?

3. How can you do a better job of holding members of your group accountable for renewing your minds instead of conforming to the world?

Share the Word

1. How would you explain God's will to an unbeliever?

2. How does Romans 12:1-2 help you to share the Gospel?

3. How would you explain transformation to an unbeliever?

Pray the Word

1. Pray for a renewed desire to reflect the image of God in your own life.

2. Pray for each of your group members to grow in the character of Christ.

3. Pray with thanksgiving that Jesus died and rose again so that what is broken in you could be put back together.

Daily Bible Reading

Day 1: 1 Corinthians 13-14
Day 2: 1 Corinthians 15-16
Day 3: 2 Corinthians 1-2
Day 4: 2 Corinthians 3-4
Day 5: 2 Corinthians 5-6

10. Live to Give

Know the Word
Read 2 Corinthians 9:6-15

   1. What do you see? (Observation)

   2. What does it mean? (Interpretation)

   3. What do you do? (Application)

   4. How should you pray?

The best way you can spend your life is to give your life away. However, you and I know that's not the philosophy of this world. The philosophy of this world is that the best way you can spend your life is to gain for your pleasure. Therefore, we work forty to sixty hours a week to earn a paycheck so we can spend our hard-earned money on the things that we want in an attempt to make our lives better. All the while, Jesus calls us to a radical perspective of wealth and possessions. Jesus says:

19Do not lay up for yourselves treasures on earth, where moth and rust destroy and where thieves break in and steal, 20but lay up for yourselves treasures in heaven, where neither moth nor rust destroys and where thieves do not break in and steal. 21For where your treasure is, there your heart will be also (Matthew 6:19-21).

Be honest. What does the way that you spend your money say about where your heart really lies? Does the way that you spend the financial resources God has blessed you with demonstrate that you are laying up treasures in heaven or treasures on this earth? How would your life change if you saw your money as a gift from God to be used for His purpose and His Kingdom?

In 2 Corinthians 9, Paul challenged a group of wealthy believers to give generously to a love offering for a group of poor believers in Jerusalem. Paul wrote to the church at Corinth while he was on a missionary journey, and on his journey, he had already visited with churches in Macedonia. The churches of Macedonia, even though they were poor, set the example for other churches by giving sacrificially and abundantly to the love offering for the Jerusalem believers. (See 2 Corinthians 8:1-5.)

Paul challenged the church at Corinth to give as well, and he wanted them to think about the sacrificial love offering the poor believers in Macedonia made as they thought about how they should give their love offering. More significantly, Paul wanted the believers in Corinth to think about the sacrifice Christ had made for them. If they understood the sacrifice Christ had made for them, they wouldn't be able to help but to give generously. After all, Jesus had graciously given everything to them. Paul wrote in 2 Corinthians 8:9, "For you know the grace of our Lord Jesus Christ, that though he was rich, yet for your sake he became poor, so that you by his poverty might become rich."

Grasp the significance of what Paul is saying. Jesus Christ had everything, but He willingly gave up everything by coming to this fallen world, living as a homeless, itinerant preacher, and subjecting Himself to shame and suffering so that his people could have everything. Ultimately, we were the ones who were poor. Apart from Christ, we were spiritually bankrupt and on our way to an eternity apart from Him, but through His death and resurrection, Jesus made us the wealthiest people on the face of the planet. He has given us an eternal inheritance that is far more valuable than anything this world offers. Peter describes this eternal inheritance as "imperishable, undefiled, and unfading" (1 Peter 1:4). Paul says in Ephesians 1:3 that Christ has given us "every spiritual blessing in the heavenly places."

How I want to live before God in response to what He has done for me is with open hands. With open hands I want to be able to say to God, "Whatever I have is yours, take it and use it as you please." I also want to be able to say to God, "My hands are open, whatever you decide to give me, even if it means difficult circumstances that you choose to use in my life for your glory and my good, I'm willing to receive."

Unfortunately, many of us choose to live close-handed lives. With clenched fists we say to God, "What I have is mine. God, do not take my resources. My money is mine to spend how I please. My time is mine to use as I desire. Hands off." The problem with living a closed-handed life is that your hands are also closed to receive whatever God wants to give you. With a close-handed life, you close yourself to the blessings God may want to bring into your life. Living closed-handedly is no way for a Christ follower to live.

When you realize what Christ gave up for you so that you could have the riches of heaven, how can you not be motivated to live an open-handed life in which you say to God, "Lord, what I have is yours, take it and use it as you please?" If you understand what Paul means in 2 Corinthians 8:9, then it makes sense to live as Paul describes in 2 Corinthians 9: cheerfully and with a heart of thanksgiving.

How are you doing with your giving? Let's be honest. Most of us live a close-handed life. We don't mind serving in the church and volunteering our time, but when it comes to letting go of our financial resources for the purpose of God's Kingdom, we clench our fist and say to God, "You can't have my money! I've worked too hard for it!" We have a tendency to believe three lies about wealth that keep us from giving cheerfully, sacrificially, and regularly:

1. THE MORE I GAIN, THE MORE SATISFIED I WILL BE.

You probably think to yourself, "If I have more money, I can buy more stuff, and that stuff will satisfy me." You know it's a lie, but you buy into it daily. Look around your home. How much useless junk have you collected over the years? When you bought that gadget a few years back you thought to yourself, "I have to have this. It will make my life so much easier," but now that gadget is stuck in the back of a closet collecting dusts with about ten other gadgets that you thought you had to have. Those gadgets obviously did not satisfy you, but you probably already have your eyes on another gadget you can't wait to buy. You can't seem to break the cycle of buying more stuff thinking that the more you have the more satisfied you will be. Do not believe the lie of the enemy!

2. THE MORE I GAIN, THE MORE SECURE I WILL BE.

You might think, "When I have enough money, I will be able to solve my problems and finally be secure." Indeed, it is wise to save for emergencies and catastrophes. It is wise to invest your money into a retirement fund. However, it is unwise to put your faith in what you have in the bank. When you give regularly, you let go of your self-financed security and trust that God knows how to take care of you whether you have a lot or a little. Certainly, you should save and invest, but it is sinful to look to anything other than Jesus for your security.

3. THE MORE I GAIN, THE MORE IMPRESSIVE I WILL BE.

You want the dream home, two cars in the garage, kids in private school, a fully funded retirement fund, and extravagant vacations because if you have all that, people will look at you and say, "He's done well for himself." Don't you want to hear those words? However, you know that you can look like you've done well for yourself but inwardly be miserable. Why do we tend to care so much about what others think about us? Shouldn't we be more concerned with living our lives to please the One who gave up everything for us?

Think about what Paul writes in 2 Corinthians 9:11. "You will be enriched in every way to be generous in every way, which through us will produce thanksgiving to God." Paul is clear. You have been blessed by God to be a blessing to others. You might not feel blessed. You may feel as if you are lacking and cannot give generously. However, consider again what Paul says in 2 Corinthians 9:8-9, "And God is able to make all grace abound to you, so that having all sufficiency in all things at all times, you may abound in every good work. As it is written, 'He has distributed freely, he has given to the poor; his righteousness endures forever.'"

God has a way of providing for you even in your poverty. When you give even when you are struggling financially, know that you will be blessed. Do you remember the widow who gave all that she had? (Luke 2:1-4) Besides, even if you feel like you are impoverished, you likely are not. Sure, you may have your financial struggles, but compared to the rest of the world, as an American, you are rich. More than likely, your basic needs are met every week, and if you did a little rearranging of your budget, you could free up some money to give away for the sake of the Gospel. Bottom line: when you consider what Christ has given for your redemption, you really have no excuse not to give and every reason to give.

If you are not in the habit of giving, take a step of faith and start. Just like studying the Bible or daily prayer, giving is a discipline. The more you habitually give, the more natural it will become for you, and the more your generous your heart will become. So, let me encourage you to just get started. Let me also give you some practical ways to start giving if you are not in the habit of regular giving.

GIVE CHEERFULLY.

We give cheerfully because of what Christ has given for us. It's not drudgery to give, it's a delight, especially when you constantly reflect on God's generosity towards you. Let His generosity motivate you to be generous.

GIVE REGULARLY.

Paul wrote in 1 Corinthians 16:2, "On the first day of every week, each of you is to put something aside and store it up, as he may prosper, so that there will be no collecting when I come." Generous people give regularly. Many believers are in the practice of tithing. Tithing is giving ten percent of your income to a local church. In the Old Testament, a tithe was required of the Israelites. However, in the New Testament, the tithe is rarely mentioned. Jesus affirms tithing, but He doesn't command it, and we don't find tithing mentioned in the epistles. This begs a question. If the New Testament is relatively silent concerning tithing, should we tithe?

I believe we are under grace, and not under the law of the Old Testament. So, I don't give out of religious obligation. Instead, I give as a result of the gift that God has given me through Jesus Christ. Therefore, grace compels me to go beyond the Old Testament obligation of a tithe. For me, a tithe is the right place to start, but it's not where I want to stop with my giving. I want to discipline myself to give away more and more as God's Spirit leads me to give. For you, I'd encourage you just to start giving regularly, but set some goals. Don't be content with giving a certain percentage. What would it look like to start giving regularly right now and then increasing the amount you give over the next year or two?

GIVE SYSTEMATICALLY TO THE CHURCH.

If God works primarily through the church to accomplish His plan to reach the nations with the Gospel, then the church is where my money is going. The church has a responsibility to evaluate how resources are being used for God's Kingdom so that financial gifts are not used wastefully but instead wisely for the spread of the Gospel. I prayerfully give to my local church trusting that God is going to give wisdom to the leadership of my church to use the resources I give to further God's Kingdom in my local community and beyond. I should be seeing the fruit of my giving in the local church. In other words, I should see my local church giving generously to international missions, investing in the local community for the sake of the Gospel, and training up leaders who will affect Gospel change for generations to come.

GIVE SYSTEMATICALLY TO OTHER ORGANIZATIONS.

While I believe the bulk of your giving should be to your local church, it is good to give to missionaries, Christian radio, relief organizations, and other Gospel-centered ministries. For years, my wife and I have supported missionaries who are a part of organizations where those missionaries have to raise their own support. You may choose to give to a Gospel-centered relief organization or to an organization that provides for children who are in need.

GIVE SPONTANEOUSLY.

Needs will always be present in the lives of people. Budget money just to give away to bless other people. Find ways to bless a struggling neighbor or a friend or family member how who's going through a tough time financially. Your spontaneous giving opens up all kinds of opportunities to share the Gospel.

In your group, reflect on the following questions:

1. How have you been doing in your financial giving? If you are struggling to give, why do you think it has been a struggle?

2. What does it mean to give under compulsion? How is giving under compulsion different than giving cheerfully?

3. Why do you think the Gospel is a more powerful motivator for giving than guilt or religious obligation?

Model the Word

1. In your group, talk about times when you have given financially and seen God bless you as a result. How did He bless you?

2. In your group, talk about ways that you can be a financial blessing to others in need. What can you do as a group to help someone for the sake of the Gospel?

3. How can you do a better job of holding members of your group accountable in financial giving?

Share the Word

1. How would you use 2 Corinthians 8:9 to explain the Gospel to an unbeliever?

2. If an unbeliever were to ask you why you give so much of your money to a church, how would you respond?

Pray the Word

1. Pray for a renewed desire to give as God's Spirit leads you.

2. Pray for each of your group members to grow in their desire to give.

3. Pray with thanksgiving that Jesus willingly lived impoverished so you could live in spiritual wealth.

Daily Bible Reading

Day 1: 2 Corinthians 7-8
Day 2: 2 Corinthians 9-10
Day 3: 2 Corinthians 11-12
Day 4: 2 Corinthians 13
Day 5: Romans 1-2

11. Grow in Daily Confession and Repentance

Know the Word
Read Isaiah 6:1-8

1. What do you see? (Observation)

2. What does it mean? (Interpretation)

3. What do you do? (Application)

4. How should you pray?

What is the most magnificent sight you have ever seen? Maybe you have had the opportunity to visit the Grand Canyon, or maybe you traveled to another country and were impressed by snow-capped mountain ranges. I've had the chance to visit Israel a few times, and my favorite site in Israel is Masada. Masada was a fortress built by King Herod in the region of the Dead Sea. Masada was built on the plateau of a high cliff. As you stand on top of Masada and look out over the region, all you can see for miles is the Judean Dessert surrounding the Dead Sea. I would never have thought that the Judean Dessert would be an impressive sight, but it is breathtaking!

When you witness a breathtaking sight such as the Grand Canyon, Niagara Falls, the Himalaya Mountains, or another natural wonder of the world, you probably have the same response that I do. You are left in absolute awe because you are reminded that we serve an impressive God who has created an amazing world. In Romans 1:20, Paul writes: "For his invisible attributes, namely, his eternal power and divine nature, have been clearly perceived, ever since the creation of the world, in the things that have been made. So they are without excuse." In other words, when you see the beauty of God's creation, you can't help but know that there is a Divine Creator who made everything you see.

It's one thing to look at God's creation and be in awe of who He is as you marvel at His creation. It's another thing to come face to face with the King of the Universe. This is precisely what happened with the prophet Isaiah after the King of Judah, Uzziah, died. King Uzziah reigned over Judah for over fifty years. For the most part, he was a good king, but later in his reign, he made some terrible decisions. His death was a national tragedy, and young Isaiah was undoubtedly shaken by the death of his king.

Isaiah went to the temple to mourn, and he was not expecting what he saw: God sitting on a throne with angels surrounding Him crying, "Holy, Holy, Holy!" As they cried out, the foundation of the temple shook, and smoke filled the temple. It was an impressive sight. It was a scary sight! How would you react if you walked into your local church this Sunday and saw God sitting on a throne with mighty angels surrounding Him?

God didn't stop by the temple just to say, "Hello." In those moments of national tragedy, Isaiah needed the reminder that the real King was present. Sure, King Uzziah had served Israel well, and sure, his death left a leadership vacuum in Judah. However, the true King was still on the throne ruling and reigning over His people There was no need for Isaiah or the nation of Judah to worry about what would happen after the death of King Uzziah. God was on His throne. Everything would be fine.

It's an amazing story, and as you grow as a disciple of Jesus, you need what Isaiah needed on that day when he walked into the temple.

YOU NEED TO SEE THE HOLY PERFECTION OF GOD.

You've probably been around the church long enough to have heard the word holy used. In fact, you've probably heard the word quite a few times, but do you know what it means? Holy means to be "set apart." To be holy is to be different from everything else, and when God appeared to Isaiah, He reminded Isaiah that He was different than everything else. There is no one like our God. He is far above His creation, ruling as He desires.

You need to be reminded regularly that God is holy. He is perfect in every way. You need to be reminded that God is above His creation working out His plan according to His will. Simply put: He is God, and you are not. Our absolutely holy God is worthy of complete worship like the seraphim worshipped Him in the temple. Like God was teaching Isaiah, God is also worthy of your complete trust.

YOU NEED TO SEE YOUR UNHOLY IMPERFECTION.

When Isaiah saw the holy perfection of God up close and personal, his response was to fall on his face confessing his sins and the sins of his people because in that moment Isaiah not only Isaiah see the holiness of God, he saw his own unholy imperfection. Isaiah immediately confessed his sins, and his confession wasn't a mere, "Oops. I'm sorry God. I won't let that happen again." Rather, his confession was gut-wrenching. "Woe is me! For I am lost…" (Isaiah 6:5) In that moment of confession, Isaiah saw his sin for what it was: rebellion against a holy God; not merely a mistake.

In God's grace, He sent seraphim to touch the lips of Isaiah with burning coal. It seems weird, but God was burning the sin away. Isaiah was experiencing the sweet grace of relief through the pain of discipline. Be honest. It can be rather painful to go through the process of letting go of sin. However, the end result for Isaiah was that his guilt was taken away. (Isaiah 6:7) Isaiah's restoration from sin started with a confession, and your restoration from the daily sins you commit will always begin with confession as well.

You need the discipline of daily confession because you daily struggle with sin. Your sin regularly hinders your intimacy with God, your earthly relationships, and the work God wants to do through you for His Kingdom. I know what you might be thinking: "Why do I need to daily confess my sins when God has forgiven my sins once and for all through the death and resurrection of Jesus?"

When you trusted Jesus as Lord and Savior, you entered into a covenant relationship with your Heavenly Father. You are His child, and that will never change. However, being His child does not change the fact that you sin. The Apostle Paul was one of the greatest followers of Jesus to ever live, but he was keenly aware of his own daily struggle with sin. Paul wrote:

[18]For I know that nothing good dwells in me, that is, in my flesh. For I have the desire to do what is right, but not the ability to carry it out. [19]For I do not do the good I want, but the evil I do not want is what I keep on doing. [20]Now if I do what I do not want, it is no longer I who do it, but sin that dwells within me (Romans 7:18-20).

Thankfully, the Holy Spirit will convict you when you sin, but you will always struggle with sin. Remnants of your old sin nature are still present, and you will battle with your old nature until Jesus calls you home to be with Him. The penalty of your sins has been taken away, but you are a work in progress who still deals with the presence of sin in your life. Therefore, continual confession of sin and seeking God's help to turn from sin is always necessary.

As a Christian, your sin does not change your position before God, but your sin does affect your fellowship with God. In some ways, it's like a marital relationship. Staci is my wife, and only death can change our marital union. She married me for better or for worse, and worse seems to creep up quite a bit in a marital relationship. I sin against my wife often, but because we entered into a covenant relationship, my sin does not change the fact that I am her husband. She does not threaten divorce every time I do something to offend her. In fact, she has never threatened divorce and never will. We entered our marriage with the understanding that divorce would never be a possibility for us. That gives both of us much security in our relationship. I never have to worry about Staci walking out on me because I did something dumb, and if by slight chance Staci ever did choose to walk out on me, I'd simply go with her. She's stuck with me.

While Staci will never divorce me when I offend her, my offenses do affect intimacy within our marriage. My sin hurts my wife, and her sin hurts me. Our sin strains our relationship until one of us asks forgiveness, and the other willingly grants forgiveness. For the sake of intimacy within our marriage, confession is necessary almost daily. When we are continually confessing how we have offended each other and granting forgiveness for those offenses, we actually grow in intimacy. However, if we do not confess offenses quickly, and if we do not forgive quickly, intimacy wanes, and distance in our relationship grows.

Likewise, nothing can separate you from God's love (Romans 8:37-39). You are in a covenant relationship with God, but sin will affect your intimacy with God if you do not confess it. You sin daily, so daily you need to seek God's forgiveness. John writes, "If we confess our sins, he is faithful and just to forgive us our sins and to cleanse us from all unrighteousness" (1 John 1:9). If you confess your sin before God, He will always forgive your sin. He never holds a grudge against you, and He never withholds His forgiveness. You will continue to enjoy fellowship with

God and growing intimacy with Him as you deal with your sin daily. So, for the sake of your own soul, do not let sin hinder your walk with the Lord.

When you fail to confess your sin, over time, you will find yourself not desiring intimacy with God. I've seen it over and over again in the life of believers. I've seen believers so excited about their walk with the Lord as they make progress in their spiritual growth. Then, all of a sudden something happens in their lives. Maybe they get caught up in something they know dishonors the Lord. Or, someone offends them, and they cannot forgive. They get eaten up with bitterness. Those believers who once craved intimacy with God no longer desire to spend time with other believers, spend time in God's Word, or spend time in prayer. I've seen sin destroy a believer's spiritual progress. The longer you dwell in your sin, the less you will crave intimacy with the Lord. Thankfully, the more you grow in intimacy with the Lord the more you will also grow to hate sin just as God hates sin.

YOU NEED TO SEE THAT GOD USES REPENTANT PEOPLE.

After Isaiah experienced the sweet relief of grace and forgiveness, God called him to go to the people of Judah and declare His message. Isaiah was more than willing to go. How could he say "No!" when God had shown him so much grace. Likewise, how can you say "No!" to the God who has shown you and continues to show you so much grace?

Our God is holy, and He uses people who regularly confess and turn from their sins to accomplish His work in the world. God wants you to be holy so that as you live your holy life before unholy people, they might see the Savior at work in you and through you. Our holy God expects us to be different than the rest of the world so we can reach the world. This was the whole point, for example, of the Book of Leviticus. God established a holiness code for the Hebrew people so they would know how to live distinctively different lives from the pagan nations that surrounded them. It was God's desire to bless the nations through the distinctively different lives of His people.

Peter writes: "[14]As obedient children, do not be conformed to the passions of your former ignorance, [15]but as he who called you is holy, you also be holy in all your conduct, [16]since it is written 'You shall be holy, for I am holy'" (1 Peter 1:14-16). When Peter encourages his readers to be holy, he actually quotes from Leviticus to remind believers that God's desire for followers of Jesus is the same as it was for the Hebrews of the Old Testament. God desires for His people to be holy because God uses holy people to reach the world!

It's simple: your sin affects your daily relationship with God, and your sin also hinders your ability to be used effectively for the Kingdom of God. You know that God wants to use you for

His Kingdom purpose. Do not let sin hinder what God wants to accomplish through you. Paul writes:

⁵Put to death therefore what is earthly in you: sexual immorality, impurity, passion, evil desire, and covetousness, which is idolatry. ⁶On account of these the wrath of God is coming. ⁷In these you too once walked, when you were living in them. ⁸But now you must put them all away: anger, wrath, malice, slander, and obscene talk from your mouth. ⁹Do not lie to one another, seeing that you have put off the old self with its practices ¹⁰and have put on the new self, which is being renewed in knowledge after the image of its creator (Colossians 3:5-10).

You need to confess your sin to God. You also need to put it to death. You need to repent of your sin. The word repentance simply means to turn from your sins. God does not want you to confess sin and then return to the very sin you confessed! Instead, God wants you to confess your sins and stop sinning. He wants you to turn from that sin you confessed and choose to live differently. For you, that probably means that you need to go to war with a particular sin and put it to death. For the sake of your intimacy with your heavenly Father, and for the sake of your usefulness in His Kingdom, ask the Holy Spirit to help you put your sin to death.

In your group, reflect on the following questions:

1. God showed His holiness to Isaiah. Why was it so crucial for Isaiah to see and experience the holiness of God? How can you better experience the holiness of God regularly?

2. When Isaiah is confronted with his unholiness, he says, "Woe is me!" What do you think he meant when he said that?

3. Why do we need daily confession if Jesus has forgiven our sins once and for all? How have you seen your sin affect your daily relationship with God?

4. How does sin not only affect our relationship with God but also our effectiveness for His Kingdom? How have you seen your own sin affect effectiveness for the Kingdom of God?

Model the Word

1. In your group, talk about how you can do a better job of helping each other fight and overcome sin. What should accountability look like in your group?

2. In your group, talk about daily confession. What does it look like to have a time of daily confession? How do you do it?

Share the Word

1. Why is the holiness of God important in evangelism? How would you share with an unbeliever about the holiness of God?

2. How would you explain the difference between being forgiven once and for all because of the death and resurrection of Jesus and the need for daily confession to an unbeliever?

Pray the Word

1. As a group, spend time praying for one another asking God to show you how to do a better job of holding each other accountable.

2. Ask God to help you have a better understanding of His holiness and spend time praising Him for His holiness.

3. Ask God to reveal to you any sins that you need to confess to Him and turn from.

Daily Bible Reading

Day 1: Romans 3-4
Day 2: Romans 5-6
Day 3: Romans 7-8
Day 4: Romans 9-10
Day 5: Romans 11-12

12. Grow in the Fruit of the Spirit

Know the Word
Read Galatians 5:16-26

1. What do you see? (Observation)

2. What does it mean? (Interpretation)

3. What do you do? (Application)

4. How should you pray?

While I was in seminary, I lived in Franklinton, Louisiana for a little over two years. Franklinton is a small town of several thousand people about an hour north of New Orleans. It is a rural community historically known for dairy farming. While there weren't many dairies left when I lived there, it was still a highly agricultural area. Many who lived in the area had parents and grandparents who farmed. While there weren't many farmers in my congregation, there were many seasoned gardeners. It seemed like everyone in my congregation had a large vegetable garden. Gardening was a way life, and gardening was always the topic of conversation. Every Sunday when we gathered for worship, men and women would talk about what they planted, what was growing and what was not growing, and how the weather affected their crops.

I was raised in the city; not on a farm. My family didn't grow vegetables in our backyard. Instead, my mother went to the grocery store to buy our vegetables. However, in Franklinton, I wanted in on the action. I wanted to be able to talk with my congregation about gardening, vegetables, and the weather. So, I planted my first garden. I had a church member come to the parsonage located right next to the church to till up a large plot of land for my garden. I went to the local Feed and Seed and bought all kinds of seedlings. (Before I planted my garden, I didn't even know what a Feed and Seed was.) I planted green beans, corn, squash, cucumbers, eggplant, and several other vegetables. Every day, I walked down to my garden and checked on my vegetable plants. It was amazing watching them grow. On days when it did not rain, I watered the garden. When the weeds started to grow, I quickly removed them. After a month or so, my vegetable plants began to bring forth vegetables! And, honestly, that's what I expected to happen. After all, I planted, watered, removed weeds, and cared for my garden to the best of my abilities. My plants did what they were supposed to do: they grew.

As a follower of Jesus, God expects you to grow, and why shouldn't you? He has done everything necessary to bring forth a harvest of fruit in your life. He has placed His Spirit within you, He has put you in the church, and He has given you His Word. However, you know like I do that spiritual growth is difficult because we often let the "weeds" take over.

God wants to bring forth a harvest of fruit in your life. The harvest of fruit that God wants to bring forth in your life is what the Apostle Paul calls the fruit of the Spirit. The fruit of the Spirit are heart qualities that should characterize you as a follower of Jesus. Developing Christlike character (the fruit of the Spirit) is key to becoming a healthy follower of Jesus.

If you want to God to grow the fruit of the Spirit within you, the weeds have to go! In Galatians 5:19-21, Paul describes the works of the flesh. The works of the flesh are the weeds that inhibit growth in the Spirit. As you look at the list of the works of the flesh that Paul describes in Galatians 5:19-21, there's probably a work of the flesh that you struggle with. For example, maybe you don't struggle with physical adultery, but perhaps your heart is producing lust continually. Perhaps you're struggling with an out of control temper. Perhaps you are always envious of what other people have. Maybe you struggle with idolatry – you have given something other than God first place in your life. I don't know what it is for you, but I know our hearts are always producing works of the flesh.

The works of the flesh are destructive. They are life-taking; not life-giving. You have seen firsthand how the works of the flesh hinder your walk with the Lord, destroy your relationships with others, and ultimately destroy you. Nothing of ultimate good comes from the works of the flesh. Sure, in the moment, that temper tantrum tends to relieve some of your frustration, but in the long run, that tantrum destroys you and hurts the people you love. Sure, the momentary sexual pleasure seems worth it, but long term, that sexual pleasure you sought outside of marriage is so hurtful. You've seen how the works of the flesh destroy your life.

The weeds have to go! You have to get rid of the works of the flesh and replace them with the fruit of the Spirit. Let me give you three ways to combat the works of the flesh so you might grow in the fruit of the Spirit.

1. DEPEND ON THE SPIRIT

Note that Paul calls the fruit the fruit of the Spirit. The Holy Spirit is ultimately responsible for your spiritual growth. That should come as a great relief to you. Paul wrote in Philippians 2:12-13:

*12Therefore, my beloved, as you have always obeyed, so now, not only as in my presence but much more in my absence, work out your own salvation with fear and trembling, 13**for it is God who works in you,** both to will and to work for his good pleasure." (Emphasis mine.)*

The problem is that we are extremely independent people who don't want to depend on anyone for anything. So, we look at our Heavenly Father and say to Him, "I can do it myself. If I try hard enough, I can be more patient. If I really work at it, I can be more loving."

It just doesn't work that way. You know it because you have tried to be more patient and more loving in your own power. Instead of trying to become who God wants you to be in your own power, just ask God to help you grow. Ask God for His power to work in you to develop the fruit of the Spirit in your life. Daily, come before God and tell Him that you can't do it on your own. Daily confess to God that you need His help. Daily be in the Bible and daily put yourself in accountable relationships within the local church. These are simple ways to express your dependency on the Spirit to grow you in the fruit of the Spirit.

Also, notice that Paul uses the singular word fruit and not plural fruits when he describes these nine character qualities. That's because you can't pick and choose which character qualities you want to grow in and which ones you don't. You can't say, "Well, I want to be more faithful, but I don't want to have any self-control." No, instead, the goal is for you to grow in each of these character qualities.

2. TAKE PERSONAL RESPONSIBILITY

While ultimately the Holy Spirit is responsible for your spiritual growth, that does not mean you are without responsibility. Notice Galatians 5:24, "And those who belong to Christ Jesus have crucified the flesh with its passions and desires." You have a responsibility to put to death daily the works of the flesh that hinder your growth in the fruit of the Spirit. Think again about what Paul writes in Philippians 2:12-13: "…work out your salvation with fear and trembling…" Yes, it is God at work within you, but your responsibility is to cooperate with that work. How are you going to grow in the fruit of the Spirit if you resist the work of the Spirit instead of cooperating with His work?

How do you take responsibility for your spiritual growth? First, you are responsible for pursuing a relationship with Christ. In my marriage, I am in a covenant relationship with my wife. We have made a commitment to our marriage until death do us part, but if I want to enjoy my relationship with my wife to the fullest, I must daily pursue an intimate relationship with her. It's a daily choice, and in your relationship with Christ, you must make a daily choice to pursue Him.

Second, you are responsible for putting off. Paul writes in Ephesians 4:20-24:

[20]But that is not the way you learned Christ!— [21]assuming that you have heard about him and were taught in him, as the truth is in Jesus, [22]to put off your old self, which belongs to your former manner of life and is corrupt through deceitful desires, [23]and to be renewed in the spirit of your minds, 24 and to put on the new self, created after the likeness of God in true righteousness and holiness.

Put off your old self. Obviously, the Spirit of God helps you put off the old self, but it's your responsibility to make a conscious choice not to gratify the desires of the flesh. You have to make a choice to pull the weeds of sin that have grown in your life. You have to make a choice to go to battle with sin and crucify the flesh. You know the areas of your life where you still struggle, and you know how those areas of sinful behavior are hindering the growth of the fruit of the Spirit within you.

Third, you are responsible for putting on. Paul first instructs believers to put off, but that's only half of the equation. You must put on the new self. Again, the Spirit helps you, but you have to make the conscious decision to live in a way that pleases God. You see, it's entirely possible to put off without putting on. For example, it's possible to put off stealing, drinking, cussing, or cheating on your spouse without choosing to put on peace, joy, faithfulness, and self-control. You can stop a specific behavior that displeases the Lord without putting a Christ-honoring habit in its place. When you put off without putting on, you will likely replace that old sinful habit with a judgmental heart rather than a heart that is pliable to the work of the Spirit. For example, when you put off anger without replacing it with joy, you'll look at other angry people and think, "Why can't you just stop being angry? I did. What's your problem?"

Yes, God is ultimately in charge of your spiritual growth, but you are responsible to cooperate with the work of His Spirit. How are you doing? Are you cooperating with the work of the Spirit in your life? Are you seeing God grow you in the fruit of the Spirit?

3. PUT YOUR EYES ON JESUS

Growing in the fruit of the Spirit requires dependency on the Spirit's work while at the same time cooperating with the Spirit's work. As you cooperate with the Spirit's work, you must put your eyes on Jesus. After all, the Spirit grows you in the fruit of the Spirit by applying the work of Jesus to your life. It is only through the death and resurrection of Jesus that you are able to come into the family of God and experience the Spirit living inside of you to grow you in the character of Christ.

If you think about it, Jesus is the epitome of the fruit of the Spirit. Because He is perfect love, He gave His life for us. Because He is perfect joy, He suffered knowing that real joy for Him was found in restoring us to the Father. Because Jesus is perfect peace, He provided a way to bring us into a relationship with the God we had rebelled against. Because He is perfect patience, Jesus puts up with our immaturity and patiently molds us into who He desires us to be.

Because He is perfect kindness, Jesus extends grace and mercy to us even when we are unkind to Him. Because He is perfect goodness, He showers us with blessings we do not deserve. Because He is perfect faithfulness, Jesus never took His eyes off the plan of God and went to the cross even when it would have been easier to give up. Because He is perfect gentleness, He comes to us in our sin and brokenness and does not condemn us. Instead, He makes us new. Because He is perfect self-control, He never sinned so that He could be the sacrifice for our sins, and so that His perfect life could be applied to our broken, sin-filled lives.

Jesus perfectly embodies the fruit of the Spirit, and our growth in the fruit of the Spirit is contingent on our growth in Jesus Himself. When we grow in our understanding of the Gospel, we will grow in our love for Jesus. As we grow in our love for Jesus, we will love as He loves. We will understand real joy. We will strive for peace with others. We will be patient with difficult people. We will show kindness to those who do not deserve it. We will seek opportunities to do good for others. We will be faithful to the Lord. We will be gentle in the way we minister to those who are broken in sin, and we will be self-controlled as we battle against sin. The Gospel is the fuel that ignites the growth of the fruit in us because when we have experienced Jesus, we want to be like the one who has saved us.

God is far more interested in who you are becoming than what you are doing. His desire is for you to become like His Son because when you become like Jesus by growing in the fruit of the Spirit, you will begin to do those things that God wants you to do. What about you? Are you growing in the fruit of the Spirit?

In your group, reflect on the following questions:

1. Why do you think it is so important to pursue growth in the fruit of the Spirit? How do you think pursuing the fruit of the Spirit will affect the way you serve the Lord in the local church? How do you think pursuing the fruit of the Spirit will affect the way you interact with your family and friends?

2. Think about how the Spirit is responsible for your spiritual growth. In what ways do you need to grow in your understanding of how the Spirit works in your life? What needs to change in your life to allow the Spirit to have control of your life?

3. How can you better cooperate with the Spirit's work in your life? What spiritual disciplines do you think you need to improve in that will help put you in a position to experience the Spirit's work in your life?

4. Think about Ephesians 4:20-24. What do you need to put off? What do you need to put on?

Model the Word

1. In your group, look at the list of the Christ-like character qualities in Galatians 5:22-23. Over the past year, which of these qualities have you seen growth in? Which qualities do you need to experience growth in?

2. In your group, talk about how you can hold each other accountable in growing in the fruit of the Spirit.

Share the Word

1. How would you explain the works of the flesh to an unbeliever without sounding like a hell, fire, and damnation preacher?

2. How could you use what Paul wrote in Galatians 5:22-23 to point someone to Jesus?

Pray the Word

1. As a group, spend time praying for growth in the fruit of the Spirit.

2. As a group, pray about those things you need to put off and those things you need to put on.

3. Pray that you would cooperate with the work of the Spirit in your life, and ask God to reveal areas in your life that you are not allowing Him to have control of.

Daily Bible Reading

Day 1: Romans 13-14
Day 2: Romans 15-16
Day 3: Philippians 1-2
Day 4: Philippians 3-4
Day 5: Ephesians 1-2

13. Grow in Obedience to God's Commands

Know the Word
Read 1 John 2:1-14

1. What do you see? (Observation)

2. What does it mean? (Interpretation)

3. What do you do? (Application)

4. How should you pray?

Be honest. You know you don't like it when someone tells you what to do even when you know it's for your own good. My wife and I went on our first cruise for our tenth anniversary. It was a great trip. Since we had never been on a cruise before, we had no idea what to expect. On the day of our trip, we arrived early, checked in, and began to wander around the boat. As we walked around, a voice came over the loudspeaker requiring everyone on the boat to report to their appropriate muster station for a muster drill. It was our first cruise. We didn't know what a muster station or a muster drill was, so we frantically began asking people to help us understand what was going on. Eventually, we made our way to our muster station for the mandatory drill. The staff scanned our cruise card as proof that we attended the mandatory drill. As soon as we sat down, we heard people complain. No one was happy. We heard things like, "How dare the cruise line take thirty minutes out of our vacation to make sure we would know what to do in case of an emergency!" The cruise line was ensuring our safety. It was wise and right for the cruise line to make us endure a muster drill, but very few people were excited about it. We don't like being told what to do, even if it is for our own good.

It's probably true that many people stay away from the Christian faith because they are convinced that God is a celestial drill sergeant trying to force us to do what we don't want to do. After all, the Bible is full of rules, commands, and regulations. Why would we want to follow God's rules? What's in it for us? On top of that, there's literally hundreds of commandments in the Bible. Even if we wanted to, how can we possibly keep them all? For the unbeliever, and even for the believer, it can seem like God just wants to zap all the fun out of life.

The truth is, God is not a celestial drill sergeant who wants to zap all the fun out of your life. He is a loving Father who knows what is best for His children. He has given you commands for your own good so you might grow into the person He desires you to be. If you are a follower of Jesus, you should not view the commands of God as rules that you have to keep in order to be a "good Christian." Instead, you should view the commands as a gift from God. God has given His commands so you might know what honors Him and so you might know how to express your love for Him. For the Christian, we don't obey the commands of God because we have to but because we want to. We want to obey God because we're convinced that God knows what is best for us, and because we want to honor Him as an expression of our love for Him. As you think about the commands of God, reflect on the following realities.

GOD GIVES COMMANDS AS AN ACT OF HIS LOVE.

Late in his life, the apostle John wrote 1 John, and it is a beautiful letter that reminds the church of the power of love. John witnessed the love of God first hand. He was one of Jesus' closest disciples. In John's Gospel, John referred to himself as the disciple whom Jesus loved (John 21:20-21). Now, when he writes 1 John, John wants believers to understand the most fundamental truth of the Christian faith: God is love (1 John 4:8). In love, God gave His Son as a sacrifice for our sins, and in love, God has given us commands so we might know how to honor Him.

When you think of the commands of God, you probably think about the Ten Commandments in Exodus 20:1-17, and rightly so. However, if you were a Jew, the Ten Commandments were just the tip of the iceberg. The Jews counted 613 commands in the Old Testament that they had to obey. You can imagine how burdensome and how impossible it seemed to try to remember and keep 613 commands! By the time of Jesus, the religious leaders had developed even more commands to help people keep the 613 commands of the Old Testament. It was so laborious! If you were a religious Jew, you might have thought of God as a cruel taskmaster who had unreasonable expectations for His people.

However, the early disciples of Jesus didn't see God as a cruel taskmaster at all. Instead, they saw God as a loving Father who sent His Son to do what no one could do for themselves. No one could possibly keep all the commands of God, but Jesus did. He was perfect in every way, and He completely obeyed His heavenly Father. Jesus Himself said, "Do not think that I have come to abolish the Law or the Prophets; I have not come to abolish them but to fulfill them" (Matthew 5:17).

Jesus came because we could not keep the commands of God. So, He kept the commands for us. The apostles certainly knew they needed Jesus to do for them what they could never do on their own. When Paul reflects on his experience with the commands of God, he writes:

7What then shall we say? That the law is sin? By no means! Yet if it had not been for the law, I would not have known sin. For I would not have known what it is to covet if the law had not said, "You shall not covet." 8But sin, seizing an opportunity through the commandment, produced in me all kinds of covetousness. For apart from the law, sin lies dead. 9I was once alive apart from the law, but when the commandment came, sin came alive and I died. 10The very commandment that promised life proved to be death to me. 11For sin, seizing an opportunity through the commandment, deceived me and through it killed me. 12So the law is holy, and the commandment is holy and righteous and good (Romans 7:7-12).

Even though Paul knew he could never keep all the commands of God, Paul knew the commands of God were good. For Paul, what was so good about the commands of God is that they showed him he was not good. The commands were a constant reminder to Paul that he desperately needed a Savior.

God does not desire for you to sin and break His commands, but you are going to because you are far from perfect. However, you can know that when you do sin as a follower of Jesus, you are already forgiven because you have an advocate in Jesus Christ. In other words, Jesus has pleaded your case before the Heavenly Father. He has presented the Father with His perfect life in exchange for your sinful life. The One who is perfect is your propitiation (1 John 2:2). He has satisfied God's demand for justice by dying the death you deserve and rising again from the dead. Yes, you will break God's commands, but you can rest assured that if you are a follower of Jesus, you will never be condemned for breaking God's commands because Jesus has paid the penalty for your sins.

God's commands are good because God's commands show you your sin and your need for a Savior. God's commands are also good because when you live out His commands, life is better. That's common sense. Again, you're never going to live out God's commands perfectly in this life, but the more you grow in your relationship with Jesus and let the Holy Spirit work in you and through you, the more you will grow in your obedience to God's commands.
The more you grow in obedience to the commands of God, the better life will be. Think about the Ten Commands. Life is better when you do not steal. Life is better when you do not commit adultery. Life is better when you do not murder or lie. Life is better when you honor your father and mother. You've probably noticed before that the Ten Commandments are vertical and horizontal. The first four deal with how we relate to God (vertical), and the final six deal with how we relate to other people (horizontal).

Simply put, if you live God's way, obviously, you are going to have a better relationship with God, but you are also going to have better relationships with people. No wonder when Jesus was asked what the greatest command was, He responded by saying that the greatest command is to love God with the entirety of your being and to love your neighbor as yourself. Further, Jesus said that the entirety of the Law and Prophets depend on these two commandments. (See Matthew 22:36-40.)

Do you see? Because God loves you, He gave you commands for your good. He gave you commands so you could see your need for a Savior, and He gave you commands so you could know how to relate rightly to Him and to others. God did not give us commands to burden us. Instead, He gave us commands to help us.

GOD DESIRES YOUR OBEDIENCE AS EVIDENCE OF YOUR LOVE FOR HIM.

John writes, "And by this we know that we have come to know him, if we keep his commandments" (1 John 2:3). John recorded Jesus saying something very similar in John 14:15: "If you love me, you will keep my commandments." You are not saved by what you do but being saved will affect everything you do. When you begin to understand how much you are loved, you can't help but desire to honor the One who has given everything for you by giving everything for Him. Because you desire to please your loving, heavenly Father, you keep His commands.

John is really clear. If you do not keep God's commands, you are not His disciple. Instead, you are a liar (1 John 2:4). He then goes on to say, "…whoever says he abides in him ought to walk in the same way in which he walked" (1 John 2:6). How did Jesus walk? He lived a life of full devotion to the Father by walking in wisdom and moral purity. Are you a follower of Jesus? If so, you will never be perfect in this life, but you should be growing daily in your ability to walk as Jesus walked. Your desire to obey God and live like Jesus is the evidence that you love Jesus and have given your life to Him.

James makes a similar argument. He writes:

[14]What good is it, my brothers, if someone says he has faith but does not have works? Can that faith save him? [15]If a brother or sister is poorly clothed and lacking in daily food, [16]and one of you says to them, "Go in peace, be warmed and filled," without giving them the things needed for the body, what good is that? [17]So also faith by itself, if it does not have works, is dead. [18]But someone will say, "You have faith and I have works." Show me your faith apart from your works, and I will show you my faith by my works. [19]You believe that God is one; you do well. Even the demons believe—and shudder! (James 2:14-19)

You can say you believe in Jesus all day long, and maybe you've had a spiritual experience where you prayed a sincere, emotional prayer to express your devotion to Jesus. Maybe you have attended church for years. Maybe you've even been baptized and have served in various ministries. However, if you are not obeying the commands of God, your faith is dead. You do not really love the God you claim to love if you are not obedient to Him. So, ask yourself the difficult questions. Are you consistently growing in your obedience to what God has commanded? Are you consistently saying no to sin and yes to what He desires from you?

GOD DESIRES YOUR OBEDIENCE AS EVIDENCE OF YOUR LOVE FOR OTHERS.

God's commands are vertical and horizontal. Notice again what John writes. He explains that he's not giving a new commandment. Instead, John is reminding his readers of the basics of the faith. Your love for God not only gives you a desire to obey Him, but your love for God also gives you a desire to love others as He has loved you. How do you love others in the same way that God loves you? Paul Tripp, Christian author and pastor, has an excellent definition of love. He writes: "Love is willing self-sacrifice for the good of another that does not require reciprocation or that the person being loved is deserving."[1]

Think about that definition. It's easy to love people who are deserving of love, and it's easy to love people who love you in return. However, the love of Christ goes far beyond loving deserving people because no one is deserving of the love of Christ! Yet, even though no one is

---

[1] Paul David Tripp, *What Did You Expect?* (Wheaton, IL: Crossway Publishers, 2010), 188.

deserving of the love of Jesus, He chooses to love us anyway. John writes, "We love because he first loved us" (1 John 4:19). Jesus has always loved you, but you have not always loved Him. He loved you when you were not reciprocating His love.

If you are a believer, you are commanded to love others in the same way that you have been loved. It's not easy, and it requires much sacrifice. However, when you consider how loved you are by Jesus, how can you not show that same love to others? John is clear. Your love for others is an act of worshipful obedience to God, and if you are not willing to love, then you do not know love. If you do not love, you are in darkness.

Again, when you consider how much you are loved, you can understand why the greatest commandment is to love God with everything you are, and you can understand why the second is like it: love your neighbor as yourself. If you would focus on devoting your life to grow in your love for God, then you will begin to obey His commands willingly. When you love God, it becomes easier to reject idolatry, put sin to death, and love your fellow man. Do you want to keep the commands of God? Start with love.

In your group, reflect on the following questions:

1. Jesus summarized the entire law into two commands: love God and love others. How does devotion to God help you to fulfill the commands of God? Think about your relationships with other people. In what ways do you need to grow in obedience to Jesus' command to "love your neighbor as yourself?"

2. John writes, "Whoever says, 'I know him' but does not keep his commandments is a liar, and the truth is not in him…" (1 John 2:4) What do you think John means?

3. How have you viewed the commands of God? As burdensome rules to keep or as an expression of God's love because He knows what's best for you? How has this lesson challenged your thinking about the commands of God?

4. What is legalism? How can Christians prevent turning the commands of God into legalistic practices? How can we infuse grace into the commands of God?

Model the Word

1. In your group, talk about what commands of God you've struggled with. How have you grown in your obedience to the commands of God? What has helped you grow in obedience?

2. Think about the greatest commands: love God and love others. How do you need to grow in your love for other people? How do you think growing in your love for God will help you love other people?

Share the Word

1. How would you explain the commands of God to an unbeliever without sounding like you a moralistic, legalistic religious person?

2. How would you explain the greatest commands (loving God and loving others) to an unbeliever?

Pray the Word

1. As a group, spend time praying that you will grow in your devotion to the Lord and your love for others.

2. Pray specifically for the obedience of each person in your group. What commands are you struggling with? Ask God to help your group members walk in obedience.

3. Pray for your local church. Pray that your local church would be focused on devotion to the Lord and teaching others how to love others in the way Christ loves.

Daily Bible Reading

Day 1: Ephesians 3-4
Day 2: Ephesians 5-6
Day 3: Colossians 1-2
Day 4: Colossians 3-4
Day 5: Philemon 1

14. Grow in Forgiveness

Know the Word
Read Matthew 18:21-35

1. What do you see? (Observation)

2. What does it mean? (Interpretation)

3. What do you do? (Application)

4. How should you pray?

YOU NEED FORGIVENESS.

When you gave your life to Jesus Christ, whoever it was that shared the Gospel with you, whether it was a pastor, a family member, or a friend, told you that you needed your sins to be forgiven. Maybe at the time, you didn't even know you needed forgiveness, but as the Spirit of God began to stir your heart, you realized it. You realized that you had rebelled against the God who loves you, and you were overwhelmed that God would graciously extend His love to you in spite of what you had done. When you placed your faith in Jesus, you became keenly aware of your need for forgiveness.

When we realize the depths of our sin, we long for forgiveness because we know the damage our sin has caused. After David had an illicit affair with Bathsheba, he wrote a heart-wrenching psalm of repentance. He recognized how much damage his sin had done to his family and his nation, but ultimately, he recognized how much damage his sin had done to his relationship with God. David wrote:

³For I know my transgressions, and my sin is ever before me. ⁴Against you, you only, have I sinned and done what is evil in your sight, so that you may be justified in your words and blameless in your judgment" (Psalm 51:3-4).

David recognized that at the root of his sin problem was dissatisfaction with what God had given him. After all, God raised him up to be the king of the most prosperous nation on the face of the planet. God gave David favor with his people, and God empowered David to defeat his enemies. But, when David looked at Bathsheba with lust and summoned her to his home, he was, in essence, saying to God through his actions, "What you have given me is not good enough. I want more." You do the same thing when you choose to sin. In your sin, you say to a good, loving, and gracious God, "I want more than what you have given me."
We discussed at length the need for daily confession and repentance in a previous lesson. However, let's once again be reminded that God does not take our sin lightly. Consider Psalm 5:4-6:

⁴For you are not a God who delights in wickedness; evil may not dwell with you. ⁵The boastful shall not stand before your eyes; you hate all evildoers. ⁶You destroy those who speak lies; the Lord abhors the bloodthirsty and deceitful man.

Psalm 11:5-7 is just as stern:

⁵The Lord tests the righteous, but his soul hates the wicked and the one who loves violence. ⁶Let him rain coals on the wicked; fire and sulfur and a scorching wind shall be the portion of their cup. ⁷For the Lord is righteous; he loves righteous deeds; the upright shall behold his face.

God has no toleration for unrepentant sinners. His wrath burns against all who rebel against Him. The bad news is that we are sinners, and we cannot do anything about it apart from a work of the Holy Spirit. Sin is a part of our nature. We can't help but sin apart from the Spirit's help. Because of our sinful rebellion against God, we deserve to be destroyed. The good news is that God has chosen to extend His love to those against whom His wrath burns. In Romans 5:6-8, Paul writes:

⁶For while we were still weak, at the right time Christ died for the ungodly. ⁷For one will scarcely die for a righteous person—though perhaps for a good person one would dare even to die— ⁸but God shows his love for us in that while we were still sinners, Christ died for us.

You deserved to be destroyed. God's wrath burned against you. However, God chose to love you in spite of your sin. God didn't choose to love you because of anything you did but because He is gracious and merciful. In His grace and mercy, He gave His Son who died in your place. The Father punished His perfect Son so you could be forgiven of your rebellion against the God who created you. You have been brought into an intimate relationship with God, and you have been given the gift of the Holy Spirit who indwells you and empowers you.

If you have surrendered your life to Jesus Christ, you are completely forgiven of your sins. Instead of God destroying you, He is making you new, and He does not hold one sin that you have ever committed or ever will commit against you. Jesus fully paid the penalty of your sin. He took your punishment for you. David writes in Psalm 103:11-12:

¹¹For as high as the heavens are above the earth, so great is his steadfast love toward those who fear him; ¹²as far as the east is from the west, so far does he remove our transgressions from us.

In the Book of Hebrews, God says about His people, "For I will be merciful toward their iniquities, and I will remember their sins no more" (Hebrews 8:12).

God has completely removed your sin, and He doesn't even remember your sin! To be sure, God doesn't forget anything. He is all knowing. God remembers exactly how you rebelled against Him. He remembers that you were once an object of His wrath. However, because of the death and resurrection of Jesus, God treats you as if He doesn't remember your sin. He treats you as if it never happened. When you stand before the God of all creation on Judgment Day, you will not be judged for your rebellion against God because in Christ your sin has been cast as far as the east is from the west.

If you want to be in a right relationship with the God who created you and loves you, you need your sins forgiven, and that's precisely what God has done. He has forgiven your sins completely. While you still need to daily confess and repent of your sins to experience daily intimacy with your heavenly Father, your daily sin doesn't change the reality that all of your sins have already been forgiven. (See Lesson 11.)

YOU NEED TO GIVE FORGIVENESS.

In Matthew 18:21, Peter asked an important question. How many times should you extend forgiveness? When Peter asked Jesus this question, he was generous in the way he asked. "As many as seven times?" (Matthew 18:21) No rabbi in Jesus' day would have taught someone to forgive seven times! The maximum a rabbi would teach a person to forgive was three times.[1] Peter thought he was being gracious with his question, and then Jesus floored Peter with His answer: seventy-seven times. Now, Jesus wasn't giving Peter an exact number of times to forgive someone. Jesus' point was simple. Keep forgiving. Forgive over and over again. Let's be honest, people are ruthless. As the saying goes, "Fool me once, shame on you; fool me twice, shame on me." Shouldn't there be a limit on forgiveness? After all, you can't let someone hurt you over and over again, can you? Jesus continued to answer Peter's question with a parable that makes a startling point: God puts no limits on forgiveness, and neither should you.

The truth is, God has been gracious to His children, but His children are not that gracious to other people. We can't seem to let go of the hurts that others have caused us. We hold on to bitterness. We use our words to tear down those who hurt us, and over the long haul, our relationship with God suffers because of our inability to forgive in the way that Christ forgave. When Jesus taught His disciples how to pray, He taught them to seek God's forgiveness with the understanding that as they experienced God's forgiveness, they would, in turn, extend forgiveness to those who had wronged them (Matthew 6:14). After the Lord's Prayer, Jesus made a shocking statement about forgiveness:

[14]For if you forgive others their trespasses, your heavenly Father will also forgive you, [15]but if you do not forgive others their trespasses, neither will your Father forgive your trespasses (Matthew 6:14-15).

---

[1] Leon Morris, *The Gospel according to Matthew*, The Pillar New Testament Commentary (Grand Rapids, MI; Leicester, England: W.B. Eerdmans; Inter-Varsity Press, 1992), 471.

Is Jesus saying that the forgiveness we receive from God contingent upon our willingness to forgive other people? That's what Jesus is addressing with Peter in Matthew 18:21-35. I imagine when Jesus told this parable Peter was appalled by the actions of the wicked servant, and he should have been. Jesus told the story to demonstrate how absurd it would be for someone who has experienced such lavish grace to withhold grace from someone else. It just doesn't make sense.

For those of us who have experienced the grace of the Father, we will imitate His grace. We won't perfectly imitate His grace, but we will do our best to show grace to others in the same way grace has been shows to us.

If you are not willing to forgive someone who has hurt you, it's probably that you have not really experienced God's forgiveness. To put it bluntly, if you are not at all willing to forgive, you are not a child of God. God's children imitate their Father. You look most like your Father not when you attend church every Sunday or perform some kind of religious duty; instead, you look most like your Father when you graciously extend mercy and forgiveness. If you are an unforgiving person, you are giving evidence that you have rejected the forgiveness of the Father. I'm not saying that you will never struggle to forgive people. You may regularly struggle to forgive people because people will genuinely hurt you. It is difficult to forgive people who have hurt you tremendously. However, if you are a child of God, you will constantly ask God to help you forgive even when it is difficult.

How can you know if you have experienced the forgiveness of Christ in such a way that you desire to forgive others? Let me give you a few ways you can know you are a forgiving person who has been changed by God's grace.

A FORGIVING PERSON LIVES AS IF HE IS DEAD.

Paul writes in Galatians 2:20:

I have been crucified with Christ. It is no longer I who live, but Christ who lives in me. And the life I now live in the flesh I live by faith in the Son of God, who loved me and gave himself for me.

When someone offends you, your gut reaction is to think you have the right to be angry with the person who hurt you. However, if you have surrendered to Christ, you don't have any rights. You don't have the right to be angry. You don't have the right to retaliate, and you don't have the right to withhold forgiveness. You are dead to yourself. You are dead to the rights you think you have, and you are alive in Christ to live for what He alone wants for your life.

When someone hurts you, Christ commands you to forgive that person. It's really as simple as that. You can try to make excuses or give reasons as to why you can't forgive someone, but all

of your excuses and reasons are inadequate. You need to do what Christ has called you to do. Obey Christ because you your life belongs to Him.

A FORGIVING PERSON EXAMINES HIS OWN HEART.

A forgiving person will be quick to recognize his or her own imperfections. You are far from perfect, and throughout your life, you have hurt many people. Why would you withhold forgiveness from someone when you have been just as guilty of hurting others yourself? Choosing to withhold forgiveness from someone else is quite hypocritical when you consider your own imperfections.

You might object immediately when you are challenged to forgive someone who has hurt you. You might say something like, "But you don't know how bad I've been hurt! You don't know the pain that I'm going through." I would never take your pain lightly, and if you are having a hard time forgiving someone, I know the depth of your hurt makes forgiving the person who hurt you seem like an impossibility. However, whenever forgiving someone seems impossible, remember the forgiveness of our Lord. He was rejected by humanity. As He went to the cross, He endured being spat upon, endless mockery, humiliation, and torturous beatings. Those who applauded His miracles and listened intently to His teachings turned on Him in His final moments. Although Jesus experienced rejection and humiliation, as He hung on the cross, He prayed to the Father, "Father, forgive them, for they know not what they do" (Luke 23:34).

Ultimately you need God's help to forgive. Apart from His help, you cannot forgive as He does. When someone wrongs you, immediately take your hurt to the Lord. Maybe you should pray something like, "God, you know my pain, and right now I cannot see past my pain. I need your help. Help me see past my hurt so that I can forgive. Help me to see the person who hurt me as you see her. Help me not to carry bitterness. Instead, help me to be kind and tenderhearted just as you are kind and tenderhearted to me."

If you seek the Lord's help, be assured that He will give you the ability to forgive.

A FORGIVING PERSON EXAMINES HIS ATTITUDE TOWARDS THOSE HE SAYS HE HAS FORGIVEN.

Words are cheap. It is easy to say, "I forgive you." Maybe when you've told that person that you forgave her, you said something like, "I forgive you, but I'll never forget what you've done to me." Is it really forgiveness to hold on to a grudge? When you make a statement like that, essentially you are saying, "I'm saying the words, but the reality is I'm not forgiving you. I'm going to hold your sin over your head and remind you of the pain that you have caused me as often as I can."

As we've already discussed, God remembers your sin no more. In the same way, when you forgive, you are to remember the sin someone committed against you no more. I know it is impossible to forget what someone has done to you, but if you are going to imitate the forgiveness Christ has extended to you, you will treat the person who has sinned against you as if the sin never happened. Besides, if you hold on to grudges and become bitter, not only will you make the person who sinned against you miserable; you will also make yourself miserable. Why live in misery? Why not experience the freedom that comes in forgiving someone else? Why not restore relationships instead of allowing relationships to stay broken and destroyed?

Forgiveness requires that you trust God. You have to believe that His way is better than your way. You have to trust that imitating Him is always the wisest course of action. Forgiveness also requires selfless love. Isn't it true that one of the reasons we don't forgive is because we are just too in love with ourselves? We think we should be treated a certain way, and if we are mistreated, then whoever harms us must pay for how they abused us. The essence of self-love is to expect everyone else to bow and cater to you instead of you humbling yourself for the sake of others. Forgiveness requires that you love others, even those who hurt you, more than yourself. The only way to love those who offend you is to immerse yourself in the God who loves you in spite of how you have grieved Him.

As you ask God to forgive you of your sins, also ask Him to give you a heart of forgiveness like His. Holding on to past offenses and bitterness will stifle not only your relationship with the person who has hurt you, but it will also stifle your relationship with the Lord. Do not hold on to hurt any longer. Because of who you are in Christ, freely grant forgiveness to those who have hurt you. Maybe you have hurt someone. What is stopping you from confessing your offense to the person you have hurt and seeking his or her forgiveness? Do not let pride or selfishness hinder you from restoring relationships you have damaged. You will never regret choosing to forgive or asking for forgiveness, but you will often regret having an unforgiving heart.

In your group, reflect on the following questions:

1. Read Matthew 6:14-15. What does Jesus mean? Does God really choose to withhold forgiveness from us when we do not forgive others?

2. Why has God chosen to forgive us? How has this lesson changed or helped your understanding of forgiveness?

3. Why do you think forgiveness is such an issue for believers? Why do we struggle to give and receive forgiveness?

4. How does Jesus' parable in Matthew 18 help you to understand God? Yourself?

Model the Word

1. In your group, talk about times that you've had to grant forgiveness to someone else. Have you struggled to forgive? Why or why not?

2. Is there anyone that you need to forgive right now? How can your group hold you accountable to obey God's Word in the area of forgiveness?

Share the Word

1. Why is a right understanding of forgiveness so important when you share the Gospel?

2. How would you explain forgiveness to someone who is without Christ?

Pray the Word

1. As a group, spend time thanking God for His forgiveness.

2. If there are unconfessed sins in your life, ask God to reveal those to you, and confess them.

3. Pray that God would cultivate in you a heart of forgiveness towards others.

Daily Bible Reading

Day 1: 1 Timothy 1-2
Day 2: 1 Timothy 3-4
Day 3: 1 Timothy 5-6
Day 4: 2 Timothy 1-2
Day 5: 2 Timothy 3-4

15. Grow in Your Speech

Know the Word
Read James 3:1-12

1. What do you see? (Observation)

2. What does it mean? (Interpretation)

3. What do you do? (Application)

4. How should you pray?

I've heard James called "The Proverbs of the New Testament," and you can easily understand why. James is an interesting letter that is full of practical wisdom. James does not give us robust theology in the same way that Paul does. Instead, James focuses on helping believers to live out the Gospel in practical ways. Even though James was the half-brother of Jesus, he doesn't even talk about Jesus all that much in his letter. However, James sounds like Jesus, and the presence of Jesus is in every verse of this short letter. When I read through this letter, I can't help but think of the similarities between James' letter and what Jesus taught in the Sermon on the Mount. James is full of wisdom for believers, and he has a lot of wisdom to give us when it comes to how we use our words.

Let's be honest. Our speech gets us into all kinds of trouble. We say things we know we shouldn't say. We gossip, we lie, and we make promises we can't keep. We complain, we insult, we curse, and we yell and scream. We use our words in all kinds of destructive ways. No wonder James tells us that our tongues are a deadly poison! We need to hear James' message, and more importantly, we need to heed James' message.

James isn't the only New Testament writer to write about how we use our speech. Paul writes to the church at Ephesus, "Let no corrupting talk come out of your mouths, but only such as is good for building up, as fits the occasion, that it may give grace to those who hear" (Ephesians 4:29). How would your life be different if you used your words to build people up rather than tear people down? What if you were less critical of people? What if you didn't gossip as much? What if you didn't lie so much? What if you didn't lash out in anger so much? Learning to allow the Spirit to help you to take control of your speech is crucial to your discipleship. As you reflect on James 3 think about the following truths.

WORD PROBLEMS ALWAYS STEM FROM A HEART PROBLEM.

Do you want to know if you're growing as a disciple of Jesus? Examine the way you use your speech. The way you talk is a good indicator of what God is doing in your life. Jesus had some pretty stern words for the way the Pharisees used their words. Jesus said:

33Either make the tree good and its fruit good, or make the tree bad and its fruit bad, for the tree is known by its fruit. 34You brood of vipers! How can you speak good, when you are evil? For out of the abundance of the heart the mouth speaks. 35The good person out of his good treasure brings forth good, and the evil person out of his evil treasure brings forth evil. 36I tell you, on the day of judgment people will give account for every careless word they speak, 37for by your words you will be justified, and by your words, you will be condemned (Matthew 12:33-37).

Jesus used a simple metaphor with the Pharisees. A good tree produces good fruit, and a bad tree produces bad fruit. When you deliver that sarcastic comment, you might think it's just a joke. Or, you might be quick to say, "I really didn't mean that." However, Jesus is quick to point out that the words that come out of your mouth are a reflection of what's inside of you. At the root of your sinful, hurtful speech is a heart problem you need to deal with.

We have a tendency to blame our sinful speech on things outside of us instead of admitting that we have a problem that's deep inside of us. For example, if I had a better job, I wouldn't complain so much about my lack of money. If my kids obeyed me, I wouldn't yell at them so much. If they fixed the traffic flow problems in Charleston, I wouldn't scream insults at the guy who cuts me off in traffic. From my perspective, I don't have a problem. Everyone else has a problem. However, from God's perspective, I am the one with the problem! The problem is not outside of me, it's inside of me. My disrespectful kids, my lack of a seven-figure salary, and the traffic flow problems in Charleston don't change my responsibility to honor God with my speech.

If you struggle with your speech, own it. You have a heart problem that you have to start dealing with. The sooner you are honest with yourself, the sooner you can begin to put to death those heart attitudes that affect the way you use your words.

WHATEVER CONTROLS YOUR HEART WILL CONTROL YOUR WORDS.

If word problems stem from your heart, then whatever controls your heart will control your words. Further, if you are continually using your words in a way that dishonors the Lord, then it is evident that you are not allowing the Holy Spirit to control your life. The way you speak is an indicator of what your heart is clinging to.

Years ago, Staci served as the Vacation Bible School director of our church. It was a challenging role. She was responsible for recruiting workers, providing them with the resources they needed, training them, and making sure that our Vacation Bible School ran efficiently to achieve the goal of helping children know the love of Jesus. Our Vacation Bible School attracted several hundred children, so directing Vacation Bible School was no small task. During Vacation Bible School season, I could expect our home to be filled with VBS supplies as Staci sorted through the supplies to determine what would be used for the upcoming VBS.

One year, I took an international mission trip a couple of weeks before our church's upcoming VBS. As the trip ended, I was ready to get home. I was ready to sleep in my bed and eat regular food. We had a red-eye flight back to Atlanta, and then we took a van for the two-hour ride home. Finally, after twenty-four hours of travel, I walked into my home around two-o'-clock in the morning. When I walked in my home, all I could see was VBS stuff all over my house. I didn't want to come home to VBS stuff. I wanted to come home to a nice, clean house. After not seeing my wife for ten days, my first words to her were not, "I missed you. I love you. It's good to be home." Rather, my first words were, "It looks like VBS vomited in our house." That was not my best moment, but at that moment, my words revealed that my heart was clinging to a selfish desire for everything to be my way.

Be honest. What is your heart clinging to? Is your heart clinging to pride? If so, you will continuously use your words to build yourself up in front of others. You will talk about your accomplishments, or how great your life is so other people will give you the accolades you so desperately want. Is greed controlling your heart? If so, you'll use your words to manipulate other people to get what you want. Is jealousy controlling your heart? If so, you'll use your words to hurt people who are not making you the first priority in their lives. Is insecurity controlling your heart? If so, you'll use your words to gossip about others in an attempt to make yourself look better in the eyes of others. Consider the way you've used your words lately. Think about the way you talk. What does your speech reveal about what's really controlling your heart?

CHRIST MUST CONTROL YOUR HEART IF YOU ARE GOING TO HAVE VICTORY OVER YOUR SINFUL SPEECH.

The only hope to gain control of your tongue is Jesus Himself. Paul David Tripp, author and pastor, reminds us that our tongues will only be tamed when our hearts are controlled by the rule of the King.[1] Jesus is your only hope to find victory over your sinful speech because He is the only one who has ever lived who never struggled with a speech problem. The Apostle Peter wrote:

He committed no sin, neither was deceit found in his mouth. When he was reviled, he did not revile in return; when he suffered, he did not threaten, but continued entrusting himself to him who judges justly (1 Peter 2:22).

Every word Jesus spoke was purposeful and used to accomplish the will of the Father. The One who spoke perfectly and lived perfectly gave His life as a sacrifice for people who cannot control their mouths. He rose from the dead proving that He is your conquering King who can free you from your sin – even your sin of corrupt speech. It's a simple reality. If you have surrendered your life to Jesus, your mouth belongs to Him.

Have you ever noticed how we have a tendency to hold people up who "speak their mind?" You've heard people talk abrasively, and you've probably said, "He's just speaking what's on his mind." Speaking your mind should not be your goal. Instead, your goal should be to speak

---

[1] Paul David Tripp, *War of Words* (Phillipsburg, NJ: P&R Publishing, 2000), 101.

the mind of Christ. How do you let Christ control your speech in such a way that you speak His mind rather than speaking your own mind? Let me give you four ways to begin allowing Christ to control your speech.

1. PUT YOURSELF THROUGH AN HONEST EVALUATION.

Do you want to submit to Christ's rule over your words? Then, it's time to be honest. When's the last time you have confessed your sins of speech to the Lord? Maybe an honest evaluation would include asking a trusted friend or your spouse a simple question: "Based on my words, what would you say controls my heart?" That might be a painful exercise, but it may really help you uncover sin that is lurking deep in your heart.

2. FILL YOURSELF WITH THE WORD.

What you fill yourself with will eventually come out of you. If you fill yourself with Jesus and His Word, you eventually will find yourself speaking truth and love instead of lies and gossip. I know studying God's Word is a time-consuming discipline, but you are not going to experience a change in your speech unless you are spending time with your Savior. The more you continue to put the sinful influences of this world into your heart, the more it's going to affect your heart and your speech.

3. THINK BEFORE YOU SPEAK.

Think before you speak. Seems simple enough, right? However, if you're like me, you don't think near enough before you speak. You just speak. You have no filter. Whatever comes to your mind finds its way out of your mouth, and you have seen the damage that's done. Before you speak, ask yourself some simple questions. 1) Does what I want to say reveal my desires or God's desires? In other words, are your words revealing a selfish heart or a heart that genuinely wants to see the will of God accomplished? 2) Am I going to help build a relationship, or am I going to damage a relationship by what I want to say? You can't take back your words once you speak them. The excuse, "I didn't mean to say that" doesn't really cut it once you've hurt someone with your words. 3) Am I going to hurt the reputation of Christ and His church or am I going to help the cause of Christ and His church by saying what I want to say? If you are a follower of Christ, you are a representative of His Kingdom. Your words can significantly hurt the cause of Christ.

4. ALWAYS REMEMBER THE GOSPEL.

You are not perfect. You never will be in this life. Only Christ is perfect, and He loves you even when you fail in your speech. Because of the cross, your sinful speech has already been forgiven. Do not condemn yourself every time you slip back into a sinful speech pattern. Instead, seek God's forgiveness yet again and keep trusting the Spirit of God to grow you in this area. I am sure that the more you seek to surrender your speech to the rule of the King, the more you will see growth in this area of your life.

In your group, reflect on the following questions:

1. How does James 3 help you understand the nature of your words?

2. Look at the three different illustrations James uses to discuss the destructive nature of the tongue. Why are these illustrations so fitting?

3. Read James 3:7-8. If these verses are true, why should we even try to control our words?

Model the Word

1. In your group, talk about what controls your heart and how you see that reflected in your speech.

2. How can your group hold each other accountable for your speech?

Share the Word

1. How have you seen your speech or the speech of someone else hinder the work of the Gospel?

2. How has this studied challenged the way you use your words as a representative of Christ and His church?

Pray the Word

1. As a group, spend time thanking God for Jesus who has already forgiven us of our speech problem.

2. Ask God to help you to use your words in a way that is consistent with Ephesians 4:29.

3. Ask God to help you think before you speak.

Daily Bible Reading

Day 1: Titus 1-2
Day 2: Titus 3
Day 3: Matthew 1-2
Day 4: Matthew 3-4
Day 5: Matthew 5-6

16. What is the Church?

Know the Word
Read Acts 2:42-47

1. What do you see? (Observation)

2. What does it mean? (Interpretation)

3. What do you do? (Application)

4. How should you pray?

The Book of Acts is the compelling story of the birth of the church, and if you think about it, there is no organization on the face of the planet that has brought about as much change in society as the church. In our culture, many will criticize the church and speak about how Christianity has been the cause of wars, oppression, and social injustice. While the church certainly isn't perfect, can you think of any organization on the face of the planet that has brought about as much good in society as the church? In the Sermon on the Mount, Jesus told His followers that they were salt and light in this world (Matthew 5:13-16), and throughout the centuries that's indeed what the church has been. This movement that started with a small group of disciples in Jerusalem has grown into a movement of countless followers of Jesus who have impacted the world. In the name of Jesus, followers of Jesus have fed the hungry, cared for widows and the sick, started schools, started hospitals, brought about social change, and so many other positive things in our world. Can you imagine how much darker the world would be without the church?

When you placed your faith in Christ, you became a member of the most significant and most powerful organization on the face of the planet. You became a member of the church, empowered by Jesus Christ Himself, to accomplish His purpose in this sinful and broken world. Don't take for granted your membership in the local church. You need the church, and if you are working through this material in a discipleship group, you have already discovered how much you need the church! The discipleship group that you are meeting with regularly has been pouring into your life and helping you grow in Christ. Not only do you need the church, but the church also needs you. According to God's design and purpose, He has uniquely created you and gifted you to further His Kingdom through the local church. As a member of a local church, you are a part of a worldwide movement to help other people discover the joy that is found inside a relationship with Jesus as you bless the world with love and good deeds, and as you open your mouth and share the hope that is within you. As you think about the significance of the church, I simply want to help you answer two questions.

1. WHAT IS THE CHURCH?

So, what exactly is the church? The Bible gives us several analogies to help us understand the unique nature of the church. The church is described as the body of Christ (1 Corinthians 12:12-14), the bride of Christ (Ephesians 5:31-32), the family of God (1 John 2:12-14), and stones that God is using to build into holy temple (Ephesians 2:20; 1 Peter 2:5). Each one of those analogies is rich, and we could do a whole study on each of these analogies.

In the New Testament, the word translated church in our English Bibles is the Greek word ekklesia. The word ekklesia simply means gathering or assembly. The church is the gathering of a particular people – people who have publicly confessed Jesus Christ as Lord and have committed their lives to live under the rule and authority of Jesus Christ.

Undoubtedly, you've read the phrase kingdom of God or kingdom of heaven in the New Testament. When you think of a kingdom, you probably think of a specific people in a specific location at a specific time in history. Maybe you think of the British monarchy and its storied history. Perhaps you think of some fairy tale with a kind and benevolent king who rules over his land. Regardless, when you think of a kingdom, you think of a king ruling over a specific group of people at a specific time in history in a specific place. However, when Jesus spoke of the kingdom of God, he was not speaking of a physical location or a particular period of time. When Jesus spoke of the kingdom of God, He spoke of the reign and rule of God over His people. Bible scholar George Ladd wrote:

"The kingdom is primarily the dynamic reign or kingly rule of God, and derivatively, the sphere in which the rule is experienced. In biblical idiom, the kingdom is not identified with its subjects. They are the people of God's rule who enter it, live under it, and are governed by it. The church is the community of the kingdom but never the kingdom itself. Jesus' disciples belong to the kingdom as the kingdom belongs to them; but they are not the kingdom. The kingdom is the rule of God; the church is a society of men."[1]

God's kingdom is not confined to a time or place. Instead, God's kingdom exists wherever there are people who are submitted to His rule and reign. I know it's hard to believe, but when you go to Walmart on your way home to pick up a few groceries, God's kingdom is in Walmart, because undoubtedly walking up and down the aisles of Walmart are people who are submitted to the reign and rule of Christ. There might only be a handful of believers walking the aisles, but they are there, filling their carts with groceries. Because Christ-followers are in Walmart, the kingdom of God is present in Walmart, but in Walmart, the kingdom is invisible. Here's my point: we can't always see the kingdom of God. We don't always know who's in the kingdom and who's out of the kingdom, but we know the kingdom is present. Wherever people are submitted to the reign and rule of Christ, the kingdom is present.

The church is the gathering of the citizens of God's kingdom. The church and the kingdom are not the same, but they are intimately connected. The kingdom is the invisible rule and reign of God over His people at all times and in all places. The church is the visible expression of the kingdom on earth as followers of Christ gather to live out the values of the kingdom of God in the community. Obviously, not everyone who gathers in the church is a true follower of Jesus, but the church is made up of followers of Jesus who have submitted to the reign and rule of Jesus. When you gather with your local church, you can see who belongs to the kingdom, and in the church, we experience together what it means to live under the reign and rule of our King.

---

[1] George Ladd, The Blessed Hope (Grand Rapids: Eerdmans Publishing Company, 1956), 111.

2. WHY DOES THE CHURCH GATHER?

As you studied Acts 2:42-47, you saw some reasons why the early church gathered together. Two thousand years after the establishment of the church, we gather for the same reasons:

WE GATHER TO WORSHIP.

As the early church gathered, every person was in awe (Acts 2:43). Why wouldn't they be in awe? God was saving people left and right, and miracles were regularly occurring. You can be sure that when the early church gathered, they worshiped. They praised God for what He was accomplishing in the lives of people. When we gather, we gather to worship. We gather to praise the King who has allowed us to enter His Kingdom through the sacrifice of Jesus. We worship because we see the evidence of God's work in our lives and in the lives of others. We worship because God alone is deserving of our worship.

WE GATHER TO BE TAUGHT THE WORD OF GOD.

The Bible is central in our gatherings as a church because we believe that in the Bible God reveals His redemptive plan and how we are to live in light of His redemptive. The Bible is more than a book about God. According to Paul, the Bible has been breathed out by God so we might know Him and how to live in a relationship with Him. Paul further explains that the Bible is profitable not only for teaching, but also to point out sin in our lives, to offer correction from that sin, to train us in righteousness, and to equip us for every good work (2 Timothy 3:16-17). You need to gather with the body so you can be with other believers who will help you to learn the Bible and apply it to your life. Sure, you can read the Bible on your own, and you should. However, you will always grow best when you gather with other believers to learn and apply the Bible. You need to sit under the teaching of wiser and more mature teachers who can help you understand the Bible.

WE GATHER FOR FELLOWSHIP.

If you grew up in a Baptist church in the south as I did, fellowship meant eating fried chicken (the Baptist bird) in the Fellowship Hall after a Sunday morning worship service. While I have great memories from those times together as a church family, true fellowship is not just sharing a meal together. Real fellowship is living out the values of the Kingdom of God together. Genuine fellowship is caring for each other by ministering to needs. Real fellowship is holding each other accountable in our spiritual growth. Real fellowship is learning how to forgive each other and getting past petty offenses. Genuine fellowship is learning to love each other in spite of our differences. Real fellowship is praying together for each other and for the expansion of the Kingdom. Real fellowship is serving our community and our world together for the sake of the Gospel.

WE GATHER TO REMEMBER THE WORK OF JESUS.

The early followers of Jesus gathered to "break bread" together. In other words, they shared the Lord's Supper together. You probably know that in the local church we regularly share the Lord's Supper together, and we regularly observe baptism. These are the two ordinances that Jesus has given to the church to help us remember His work. Whenever someone places his or her faith in Christ, that person is baptized. Baptism is a visual declaration of what has happened in that new believer's life. When that new believer goes into the water, he is saying, "Jesus has washed me of my sins. I'm dead to my old self, and when I come out of this water, it is a picture of the new life that God has given me." Whenever you see someone baptized, it should remind you of when you placed your faith in Christ. More importantly, every time you see someone baptized, it should remind you that Jesus died in your place so you might have the opportunity to experience a new life.

The church often celebrates Lord's Supper or communion. Right before the death of Jesus, He shared a Passover meal with His disciples. When He shared this meal, he gave unleavened bread to His disciples and told them that the bread represented His body. He gave them a cup of wine and told them that the wine represented His blood (See Luke 22:14-23). From that point on, whenever they took of the Passover meal, they weren't to remember the sacrifice that was made for the Hebrew people in Egypt when the angel of death passed over their homes before God set the Hebrews free (Exodus 12). Instead, they were to remember the death of Jesus. Because of His death, our Heavenly Father has "passed over" our sins.

The next time you see a baptism or share in the Lord's Supper, don't take it lightly! Baptism and the Lord's Supper are two precious pictures that God has given the church to remember the sacrificial work of Jesus Christ. The reality is you need to remember the work of Jesus because it is so easy to take for granted what Jesus has done for you!

WE GATHER TO SCATTER.

You noticed how Acts 2:42-47 ended. "And the Lord added to their number day by day those who were being saved" (Acts 2:47). Why were people being saved? Because after meeting together, early believers were going back into the temple to testify about what God was doing in the lives of people through the death and resurrection of Jesus. The early church was sharing the Gospel! While the church is the gathered assembly of God's people, the visible manifestation of the kingdom of God on earth, God does not intend for the church to stay in holy huddles isolated from the world. Instead, God intends for the church to scatter into our community and our world to proclaim the Gospel of Jesus Christ. We gather to worship and to be equipped so that we might scatter to make a lasting impact in our communities with the Gospel of Jesus Christ.

Never take the church for granted! The church is the most powerful organization on the face of the planet because the church is full of kingdom citizens who are empowered by the Spirit of God to take the Gospel to the ends of the earth so that all might know that the God of all creation is worthy of worship! Don't take the church for granted because without the witness of the church, you would not be a follower of Jesus. Don't take the church for granted because without the faithfulness of the church, you would be stunted in your spiritual growth.

In your group, reflect on the following questions:

1. How does Acts 2:42-47 help you to have a better understanding of the church?

2. How does Acts 2:42-47 challenge you in the way that you relate to the church?

3. Why do you think we struggle to live out what we see in Acts 2:42-47?

Model the Word

1. In your group, talk about the impact the church has had on your life.

2. Based on what you read, how would you explain the difference between the kingdom of God and the church to a new believer? Why is the distinction important?

Share the Word

1. People who are far from God are very skeptical of the church. How would you explain the significance of the church to someone who is not a believer?

2. What would you say to someone who says, "I don't need to be a part of the church to be a Christian?"

Pray the Word

1. As a group, pray for your church. Pray that your church will function in a way that is consistent with Scripture.

2. Ask God to help you have the right expectations of your church and ask God to help you serve your church faithfully.

Daily Bible Reading

Day 1: Matthew 7-8
Day 2: Matthew 9-10
Day 3: Matthew 11-12
Day 4: Matthew 13-14
Day 5: Matthew 15-16

17. The Ordinances of the Church

Know the Word

Read Romans 6:1-11 and Mark 14:12-22

1. What do you see? (Observation)

2. What does it mean? (Interpretation)

3. What do you do? (Application)

4. How should you pray?

I can't think of anything more powerful than witnessing a new believer being baptized or sharing in the Lord's Supper as a family of faith. Over the years, I've witnessed countless baptisms and shared in the Lord's Supper many times. However, several years ago, I saw baptism and experienced the Lord's Supper in some very unique and powerful ways.

On a short-term mission trip to Russia, I traveled with a local, Russian pastor and a team of Russian and American believers to a rural town south of the city of Volgograd. Only a handful of believers lived in this town, and on this day, a new believer wanted to follow through with believer's baptism. In this particular town, there was no pastor or local church. This group of believers regularly gathered to pray and worship, but they did not call themselves a "church" because they did not have an ordained pastor to lead them. The group was mostly made up of women. Since there was no pastor to lead them, they would not observe baptism or Lord's Supper because it was their conviction that they needed an ordained pastor to administer the ordinances of the church. So, when we arrived in this town, there were several of us who were ordained pastors. Finally, these believers could observe the ordinances of the church!

We went down to the river, and the Russian pastor who traveled with us took an elderly lady by the hand and escorted her into the river. She had been saved for some time but had not been baptized. The lady must have been in her late seventies. In the presence of brothers and sisters in Christ who gathered to witness her baptism, this elderly lady publicly professed her faith in Jesus Christ. Many people passed by that day and witnessed her baptism. The vast majority of people who walked by and saw her baptism were not followers of Jesus. In an area where Christians are often ridiculed and persecuted because of their faith, this older woman testified to the world that Jesus was her Savior. It was a beautiful and emotional moment that I will never forget.

Later on, we gathered with these believers and shared the Lord's Supper. It was an equally powerful moment. Some of these believers had not taken the Lord's Supper in several years. In Russia, we took the Lord's Supper a bit different than we do here in the states. We passed a loaf of bread around. Everyone tore off a piece of bread. Then we passed around a big chalice full of wine, and everyone drank from the same cup. It was a bit different sharing the same cup of wine with everyone. Who knows how many germs we passed around! However, what a powerful moment. I couldn't help but cry as I watched my brothers and sisters in Christ remember the death of Jesus. While language and thousands of miles separate me from my Russian brothers and sisters, that moment served as a vivid reminder of our unity in Christ.

Baptism and the Lord's Supper are not empty rituals we observe on a Sunday morning to fill the time. We call baptism and the Lord's supper ordinances because they were ordained by Jesus as symbolic reminders of the Gospel for the church to observe regularly.

We believe that baptism and the Lord's Supper are symbolic. Some faith practices wrongly teach that these two ordinances confer grace on those who participate in them. However, baptism does not save us, nor are we given special grace by God when we take of the Lord's Supper. Instead, these two ordinances serve as visual reminders of settled spiritual realities. Think of the pictures that you have hanging on the walls of your home. In our living room at home, we have pictures hanging on our wall of both Luke and Hudson from when they were younger. They are beautiful pictures, and every time I look at those pictures, I remember their more youthful days. I remember exactly where we were when the pictures were taken. I remember what we were doing. I remember what it was like to have toddlers running around. Those pictures take me back to something that happened in the past.

Similarly, the same thing happens every time I witness a baptism or take the Lord's Supper. The person being baptized is taken back to the moment that she gave her life to Jesus. Her baptism is a picture of what Christ did in her life when she trusted Him as Lord, and as I witness her baptism, I'm taken back to the moment I trusted Jesus. Every baptism I witness reminds me of when I placed my faith in Jesus. When I take the Lord's Supper with my church family, I remember the sacrifice of Jesus on the cross. I remember the punishment that He took upon Himself in my place. Baptism and the Lord's Supper are pictures of the work of Christ, and every time I see a baptism or take the Lord's Supper, I remember the work of Christ in my life. But not only do I remember the work of Christ in my life, every time I witness a baptism or take the Lord's Supper, I remember that I belong to a family of believers who are committed to Jesus. The ordinances are potent images. Let's think for a moment about what these powerful images teach us.

BAPTISM: A PICTURE OF NEW LIFE

The word baptize means to plunge, dip, or immerse. When John baptized Jesus in the Jordan river, he immersed Jesus in the water. Immersion is essential because of what it represents. Also, baptism follows a person's conversion experience because it symbolizes the work of salvation in the life of a believer. Because baptism means to immerse, and because baptism follows a conversion experience, infant baptism is not consistent with Scripture. While some churches have theological reasons for why they baptize infants, we do not believe that this is the teaching of Scripture. If you experienced baptism as an infant, carefully consider what Scripture teaches about baptism.

In Romans 6:1-11, Paul explains what baptism symbolizes. Paul explains that we are baptized into the death of Jesus (Romans 6:3-4). When someone goes under the baptismal waters, it's a picture of death and burial. When the candidate for baptism goes under the water, it is a picture of going down into the grave. Why such a morbid picture? Paul tells us in

Romans 6:6, "We know that our old self was crucified with him in order that the body of sin might be brought to nothing, so that we would no longer be enslaved to sin."

When you placed your faith in Jesus Christ, you died to your former way of life. You renounced a life of sin and death and exchanged that life for peace with God and a life of righteousness through a relationship with Jesus Christ. When you experienced baptism, it was a picture of the death of your old life, and when you came out of the waters, it was a picture of the new life that Christ has given you. Paul wrote in Ephesians 2:4-6:

4But God, being rich in mercy, because of the great love with which he loved us, 5even when we were dead in our trespasses, made us alive together with Christ—by grace you have been saved 6and raised us up with him and seated us with him in the heavenly places in Christ Jesus…

You have been made alive by the grace of God, and when you came out of the baptismal waters, it was a picture of how, as an act of grace, Jesus raised you from your spiritual death and gave you new life.

Your baptism is not only a picture of what happened in your life (your conversion experience). Your baptism is also a picture of what is going to happen in your life. Paul writes in Romans 6:5, "For if we have been united with him in a death like his, we shall certainly be united with him in a resurrection like his." God has given you spiritual life, and your baptism symbolized that reality. But, God has also promised you resurrection life. What baptism symbolizes, resurrection from the dead, will one day be a physical reality for you. One day Christ will return, and when He does, all those who have died in Christ will be raised from the dead physically and will live with Him forever. Baptism is a vivid reminder that sin and death no longer rule over the life of the believer. Instead, Jesus, the life-giver, rules and reigns over the life of the believer. If you are a baptized believer of Jesus Christ, every time you witness a baptism, you should rejoice for the person who is being baptized, and you should remember your baptism and rejoice over what God has done in your life as well.

We believe baptism is an act of obedience that identifies us with Jesus and His Church. At the beginning of the Gospels, John baptized Jesus, even though Jesus did not need to be baptized. When Jesus came to John to be baptized, John hesitated. He said, "I need to be baptized by you, and do you come to me?" (Matthew 3:14) Jesus never sinned. He did not need a baptism that symbolized death to His former way of life. However, the baptism of Jesus was significant because, in His baptism, Jesus identified with us. The One who is fully God reminded us in His baptism that He is one of us. Jesus was not guilty of any sin, but He placed Himself among the guilty. He went to the cross and took the guilt of the world upon Himself. Paul writes, "For our sake he made him to be sin who knew no sin, so that in him we might become the righteousness of God" (2 Corinthians 5:21). Jesus identified Himself with us in His baptism, and when we are baptized, we identify ourselves with Jesus. Through baptism, we are publicly declaring that we belong to Jesus. Not only do we publicly declare our identity with Jesus through our baptism, but we also announce our public identity with His church. In baptism, we are saying that we belong to the people of God.

Before Jesus ascended into heaven, He commanded His disciples to go into all the world to spread the good news of the Kingdom, and He commanded His disciples to baptize new believers. Jesus said:

[18]All authority in heaven and on earth has been given to me. [19]Go therefore and make disciples of all nations, baptizing them in the name of the Father and of the Son and of the Holy Spirit, [20]teaching them to observe all that I have commanded you. And behold, I am with you always, to the end of the age (Matthew 28:18-20).

Baptism is not optional for the believer. Jesus commanded that His followers be baptized as a way of identifying with Him. If you have not experienced baptism, I strongly encourage you to follow through with baptism. It is an act of obedience, and it is so important in your walk with Jesus because, for the rest of your life, it will serve as a visual reminder of the work that Jesus has done in your life. It is so vital because your baptism will publicly identify you with Jesus and your church. Don't put it off. Talk with your discipleship group about any fears or hesitations you have about baptism. It's likely that in your group, there are members who once shared those hesitations. Your group members can probably help you work through those fears and hesitations. Talk to your pastor. I'm sure your pastor would love the opportunity to explain baptism to you further, and I'm sure your pastor would love the opportunity to baptize you. Do not hesitate in your obedience to the Lord.

LORD'S SUPPER: A PICTURE OF THE ULTIMATE SACRIFICE

Every year, the Jewish people looked forward to sharing the Passover meal as a family. God initiated the Passover meal in Exodus 12 for the Hebrews as an annual reminder of how He brought them out of Egypt. During this sacred meal, the father stood before his family and led them through a four-course meal. The Passover meal was a time of teaching, and as the meal began, a child would ask his father the same question every year: "Why is this night different from all other nights?" After the child asked this question, the father would tell the story of the first Passover.

Everything on the table symbolized something that taught the family about the Hebrews' affliction and God's deliverance. The green vegetables on the table reminded the family of the life that God had given His people. The bitter herbs on the table reminded the family of the harsh slavery the Hebrews experienced in Egypt. The unleavened bread on the table reminded the family of the haste in which the Hebrews ate the first Passover meal as they prepared to leave Egypt. The mixture of fruit, nuts, and honey symbolized mortar and bricks and reminded the family of the harsh work the Hebrews endured in Egypt. The family feasted on a roasted lamb. As they ate the lamb, they remembered the blood of the lamb that was applied to the doorposts of the Hebrew homes in Egypt.

The meal consisted of four courses, and at one point in the meal, the father would lift the unleavened bread and say to his family, based on Deuteronomy 16:3, "This is the bread of affliction which our fathers ate in the land of Egypt. Let everyone who hungers come and eat; let everyone who is needy come and eat the Passover meal."

Each course of the meal ended with a cup of wine. The four cups of wine that concluded each course of the meal represented the four promises God made to the Hebrews in Exodus 6:6-7: 1. to bring them out of affliction, 2. to deliver them from slavery, 3. to redeem them, and 4. to make them His own people.

You can imagine the shock of the disciples on that fateful Thursday evening when Jesus shared a Passover meal with them and radically changed the meaning of the Passover meal for everyone who would follow Him. Jesus took the bread and said to them, "From now on, when you take the bread, it is a reminder of my body given for you." In other words, when Jesus held up the unleavened bread before His disciples, He was essentially saying to them, "I am the bread of affliction. I am the One who will suffer for you."

Then, after taking the bread, He took the cup and told His disciples that the cup represented the blood He would shed for them that would usher in a new covenant for God's people. Through Jesus' shed blood, all of the promises of God, represented by the four cups of wine that Jews drank during the Passover meal, would find their fulfillment in Him. On that Thursday night before His death on the cross, Jesus forever changed the meaning of the Passover.

As believers, we do not celebrate the Passover Meal. We celebrate the Lord's Supper. In our churches, we regularly observe the Lord's Supper to remember the ultimate sacrifice that Jesus made for us when He died on the cross. Like baptism, the Lord's Supper is symbolic. Briefly, let's think about what the Lord's Supper symbolizes.

1. The Lord's Supper symbolizes the death of Jesus. The broken bread symbolizes the body of Christ pierced for our transgressions (Isaiah 53:5). The cup represents the blood of Jesus poured out for us. Paul wrote, "For as often as you eat this bread and drink the cup, you proclaim the Lord's death until he comes" (1 Corinthians 11:26).

2. The Lord's Supper symbolizes our participation in the benefits of Christ's death. When you eat the bread and drink the cup, you are saying that you have applied the benefits of Christ's death to your life. He died to forgive you of your sins, and when you take the Lord's Supper, you are declaring that you are forgiven because of the sacrifice of Jesus.

3. The Lord's Supper symbolizes spiritual nourishment. Jesus said, "I am the bread of life" (John 6:35). When you take the Lord's Supper, it is a reminder that Jesus alone satisfies our deepest longings.

4. The Lord's Supper symbolizes the unity of believers. We take the Lord's Supper together as a church family to remind ourselves that Jesus died for His Church. When we take the Lord's Supper, we remember that regardless of our backgrounds, we are now one in Christ. He has made us a family.

Baptism and Lord's Supper are significant in the life of the church because of what they symbolize and communicate to the Church. The next time you witness baptism, rejoice in what God has done in the life of the person being baptized and remember the Gospel. The next time you take Lord's Supper, remember the Gospel and give thanks for the sacrifice of Jesus.

In your group, reflect on the following questions:

1. Why is it important to understand that baptism and the Lord's Supper are symbols? Why do you think it is significant that God gave us baptism and the Lord's Supper as symbols of the work of Jesus?

2. What did you learn in this lesson about baptism and the Lord's Supper that you have not thought about before? How did this lesson enhance your understanding of these two ordinances?

3. Why is it not appropriate for unbelievers to take the Lord's Supper?

4. Personally, how can you do a better job of observing the ordinances? Why do these ordinances matter for you?

Model the Word

1. In your group, take turns explaining the significance of baptism.

2. In your group, take turns explaining the significance of the Lord's Supper.

Share the Word

1. When you share the Gospel with someone, is it important to talk about baptism? Why or why not? At what point should you talk about baptism in a conversation with someone who is lost?

2. Imagine that you bring a lost friend to a worship service on a day that the Lord's Supper is being observed. How would you have a conversation with your lost friend about the Lord's Supper and why it isn't appropriate for your friend to partake of the Lord's Supper?

Pray the Word

1. Pray that every time your church observes the ordinances of the church it would remind your church of the work of Christ.

2. Pray for each your group members to have opportunities to share the Gospel.

Daily Bible Reading

Day 1: Matthew 17-18
Day 2: Matthew 19-20
Day 3: Matthew 21-22
Day 4: Matthew 23-24
Day 5: Matthew 25-26

18. Why God Has Placed You in the Church

Know the Word
Read 1 Corinthians 12:1-31

1. What do you see? (Observation)

2. What does it mean? (Interpretation)

3. What do you do? (Application)

4. How should you pray?

Have you ever noticed how much emphasis we Christians put on having a personal relationship with God? When you came to faith, it was a personal decision that you made for yourself, and since coming to faith, you have been encouraged to grow in personal intimacy with God. As part of this discipleship series, you have been working on developing a personal time with the Lord each day as you have been developing the disciplines of personal Bible study and personal prayer. You've been working on developing your own time with the Lord. As you've been working on your personal time with the Lord you have undoubtedly seen growth in your walk with the Lord.

While it is essential to develop a personal relationship with the Lord, your relationship with the Lord wasn't meant to be private! My father is from Illinois. During the Vietnam War, he was drafted and stationed at Fort Gordon right outside of Augusta, Georgia. While he was in Augusta, he met my mother and never went back to Illinois. I grew up in Augusta, which meant I didn't see my father's side of the family very much. We would make the trip to Illinois every few years, but those short trips were not enough for me to build solid relationships with my dad's side of the family.

When I was in seminary, my paternal grandfather died. I flew to Illinois to meet my parents and attend my grandfather's funeral. I didn't know much about my grandfather's faith. I knew he attended church, but I didn't know if he had ever made a decision to follow Jesus. Before the funeral, I pulled my grandfather's pastor to the side and asked him if my grandfather possessed saving faith. I wanted to know if my grandfather followed Jesus. The pastor responded to my questioning by saying, "Faith is a very personal and private matter." Say what? No, it's not! If you are genuinely a follower of Jesus, people know it, and indeed, your pastor should know it! Your faith in Christ was not intended to be lived in isolation. Instead, God intends for you to live out your faith in community with other believers. In fact, if all you focus on in your faith is having a "personal" relationship with Jesus, you will discover that your growth in Jesus will quickly be stunted. No wonder the author of Hebrews wrote: "[24]And let us consider how to stir up one another to love and good works, [25]**not neglecting to meet together**, as is the habit of some, but encouraging one another, and all the more as you see the Day drawing near" (Hebrews 10:24-25, emphasis mine).

The fact of the matter is that while we claim to be followers of Christ, we don't think much of what it means to be a part of His church. Many Christians regularly "neglect to meet together." It's not that we don't like attending church, but if something better comes along like a weekend trip, a sporting event, or warm weather, we'll neglect the body of Christ for whatever seems better at the moment. Please understand, I am not trying to be a legalist who says, "You're not a good Christian if you do not attend church every time the doors are open," but I am saying that your spiritual growth is directly proportional to your commitment to be involved with a local body of believers. Don't believe me? Quit being involved in your local church for a while and see what happens in your walk with the Lord. As we think about our relationship to the local church, I want to remind you of two fundamental truths: (1) you need the church and (2) the church needs you.

1. YOU NEED THE CHURCH.

There are numerous reasons why you need the local church, and perhaps you can think of some reasons why you need the local church that are not listed below. However, consider the following reasons why you need the local church.

YOU NEED THE LOCAL CHURCH TO LEARN.

Sure, you can learn the Bible on your own. The Holy Spirit lives in you, and He is more than able to lead you to know the truth. However, in God's design, He desires for us to do are best learning and growing in community. In the previous lesson we discussed Acts 2:42-47. In Acts 2:42, when the church was established, Christ followers devoted themselves to the apostles' teaching. They willingly put themselves under the teaching of the men who had actually been with Jesus. Bottom line, in the church there are so many people you can learn from. God has spiritually gifted people in your church with the ability to understand and explain the Word well. You can learn from those who have lived out the Word in their daily lives. You can also learn from those who have struggled and persevered in their faith.

YOU NEED THE LOCAL CHURCH TO BE TRAINED.

In 1 Corinthians 12:4 Paul writes, "Now there are varieties of gifts…" As you read 1 Corinthians 12, you read about some of the spiritual gifts that God gives His children. However, 1 Corinthians is not the only letter in the New Testament that discusses spiritual giftedness. You can also find spiritual gifts listed in Romans 12:6-8 and a list of leadership gifts in Ephesians 4:11. No book in the New Testament gives an exhaustive list of spiritual giftedness, but the point is clear: every believer is spiritually gifted.

What is a spiritual gift? A spiritual gift is not something that you were born with, but something that you were born again with. In other words, when you placed your faith in Jesus Christ, the Spirit of God spiritually gifted you for ministry in and through the local church. A spiritual gift is not a natural ability. For example, being a good musician or a good cook is not a display of spiritual giftedness. Being a good communicator is not necessarily evidence of a specific spiritual gift. These are all abilities that you develop over time. Perhaps you were born with some natural talents or a personality that has driven you to develop specific talents and abilities, but those talents and abilities you possess are not spiritual gifts.

A spiritual gift is a supernatural ability that may be related to your natural abilities, but it may not be related to your natural abilities at all. For example, you may be a wonderful cook, and you may really enjoy having people over for dinner. Your passions and natural abilities might be related to a spiritual gift of hospitality. You may be a teacher, and you may have a passion for explaining difficult concepts to people in a simple way that they can understand. Your natural ability and passion to teach may relate to the spiritual gift of teaching. Then again, it may not since the spiritual gift of teaching is specifically related to helping people understand Scripture. Even though you are a gifted teacher, you may not be a gifted teacher of the Bible. On the other hand, you may hate standing in front of people and explaining something, but God has saved you, and now all you want to do is help people to understand Scripture. Maybe God has gifted you with the spiritual gift of teaching, and you couldn't be more surprised!

How do you know your spiritual gift, and how do you know how to use it? That's where the church comes in. For me, I discovered my spiritual gift in the local church. I was given opportunities to teach and preach, and as I took advantage of those opportunities, I discovered that I was really passionate about teaching and preaching the Bible. I couldn't see myself doing anything else, and as I took advantage of those opportunities, people within the church would come alongside of me and affirm what God was doing in my life. People would say things like, "What you said tonight really helped me understand God's Word better." Or, "I can see you serving as a pastor of a church someday." On top of that, I had pastors who came alongside of me and taught me how to develop and deliver sermons. I discovered my spiritual gift and learned how to use it within the local church.

God used those opportunities and the affirmation of other people to confirm in me a spiritual giftedness of teaching and preaching. For you, as you begin to take advantage of ministry opportunities in your church, you are going to discover what you are passionate about and what you do well for the Kingdom. Other believers are going to come alongside of you and confirm what God is doing in your life. So, jump in and serve!

A healthy church will not only help you discover your spiritual giftedness; a healthy church will also train you in how to use your spiritual gift. Not only do you need to be trained to use the spiritual gifts God has given you, but you also need to be trained in a variety of other ways. You need to be trained in sharing the Gospel, in how to study the Bible, in how to pray, in how to give, in how to discern the will of the Spirit, and you need training in a variety of other areas as well. According to Ephesians 4:12, God has placed spiritually mature leaders in the church to equip you for the work of the ministry. The local church should be a hub of discipleship – a training ground so that Christ followers may learn to serve the Lord well.

I know you might not know your spiritual giftedness. Perhaps an online spiritual gifts inventory might help you think through your possible spiritual giftedness. However, if you are closely connected to other believers in your local church, why not ask them what they see in you? They might be able to tell you exactly how they see God working through you. Other believers might be able to help you identify your passions and giftings. The more closely connected you are to the body of Christ the more other mature believers can speak into your life and help you discover precisely how God has gifted you for ministry.

YOU NEED THE LOCAL CHURCH SO YOU CAN BE LOVED PROPERLY.

Maybe you have had some bad church experiences. In the past, you may have been a part of a local church that hurt you tremendously. Maybe someone gossiped about you or betrayed you. Unfortunately, churches have a pretty bad reputation for destroying their own, but this is not the way it's supposed to be! The church is supposed to be the one place on earth that you can know that you will find real love and forgiveness. The church is supposed to be the one place on earth where you can experience authentic community. Jesus said:

[34]*A new commandment I give to you, that you love one another: just as I have loved you, you also are to love one another.* [35] *By this all people will know that you are my disciples, if you have love for one another (John 13:34-35).*

The church should be the place where you turn to receive the spiritual care that you need, and the church should be the place that shows the world genuine love in action.

2. THE CHURCH NEEDS YOU.

You need the church, but the church also needs you. Let me give you several reasons why the church needs you:

THE LOCAL CHURCH NEEDS YOU SO IT CAN FULFILL ITS MISSION.

According to Paul, the church works best when every member of the body is using his or her spiritual giftedness to further the ministry of the church. Without each member using his or her spiritual giftedness to further the ministry of the church suffers. Many of our local churches struggle today because individual Christ followers do not see how integral they are to the work of the ministry. For too long churches have depended on professional, seminary trained ministers to do the work of the ministry, but that is not the biblical model. The biblical model is every believer serving out of his or her giftedness to see the Gospel go forward through the local church.

THE LOCAL CHURCH NEEDS YOU SO DISCIPLES CAN BE MADE.

Your local church is full of people who need to grow in Christlike maturity, and there simply aren't enough pastors who can individually invest in every single person in the church so that individual believers can be equipped and discipled. As a follower of Jesus, you share in the responsibility of equipping believers to become fully surrendered followers of Jesus. Paul wrote to Timothy, "You then, my child, be strengthened by the grace that is in Christ Jesus, 2 and what you have heard from me in the presence of many witnesses entrust to faithful men, who will be able to teach others also" (2 Timothy 2:1-2). A generation of Christ followers is coming up behind you who need your godly influence over their lives desperately so they might know how to walk by faith. Paul also wrote to Titus:

¹But as for you, teach what accords with sound doctrine. ²Older men are to be sober-minded, dignified, self-controlled, sound in faith, in love, and in steadfastness. ³Older women likewise are to be reverent in behavior, not slanderers or slaves to much wine. They are to teach what is good, ⁴and so train the young women to love their husbands and children, ⁵to be self-controlled, pure, working at home, kind, and submissive to their own husbands, that the word of God may not be reviled. ⁶Likewise, urge the younger men to be self-controlled (Titus 2:1-6).

THE LOCAL CHURCH NEEDS YOU SO THE WORLD MIGHT SEE THE POWER AND LOVE OF GOD ON DISPLAY.

Remember what Jesus said in John 13:34-35. The world knows that you are a disciple of Christ by your love – especially by how you love other people. This world is so broken, and people need to see that there really is hope. When a broken world sees real love on display, it can't help but be attracted. What kind of impact could we have on this world if we focused on building Christ-centered, hope-filled, encouraging relationships within the church? The church needs you to live well and love well. The church needs you to not harm the reputation of Christ through lack of commitment, constant complaining and criticism, and a refusal to live at peace with your brothers and sisters in Christ. Instead, the church needs you to further the cause of Christ through a commitment to the local body, a commitment to the mission of the church, and a commitment to love others as Christ loves you.

Because the church is made up of imperfect people, the church will always be imperfect. However, the church is God's plan to reach the world with the Gospel of Jesus Christ. Let us take our commitment to the church seriously, and let us strive to use our spiritual giftedness to further the ministry of the local church for the sake of the Gospel.

In your group, reflect on the following questions:

1. How does 1 Corinthians 12:1-31 help you have a better understanding of the role of the church?

2. How would you define spiritual giftedness? What do you think is your spiritual giftedness?

3. Why do you think God has chosen to use you the church as His plan to reach the world with the Gospel?

Model the Word

1. In your group talk about spiritual giftedness. What spiritual gifts do you see present in the lives of your group members?

2. When have you seen the church you are a part of live out what Paul describes in 1 Corinthians 12:1-31? What effect did that have on the lives of the members of the church? What effect did that have on the local community?

Share the Word

1. Do you think a lost person can clearly see the love of Christ in your local church? Why or why not? How would you respond to a lost person who makes the statement: "I'd never be a part of a church because the church is full of hypocrites?"

2. How might God use your particular spiritual giftedness to reach someone who is far from Christ?

Pray the Word

1. As a group, continue to pray for your church. Pray that every member of your church will operate out of his or her spiritual giftedness, and pray that every member in your church will seek to be unified with the body of Christ.

2. Ask God to help you use your spiritual giftedness well for the sake of His Kingdom.

Daily Bible Reading

Day 1: Matthew 27-28
Day 2: Hebrews 1-2
Day 3: Hebrews 3-4
Day 4: Hebrews 5-6
Day 5: Hebrews 7-8

19. Why God Has Placed Leaders in the Church

Know the Word

Read 1 Peter 5:1-5

1. What do you see? (Observation)

2. What does it mean? (Interpretation)

3. What do you do? (Application)

4. How should you pray?

When I was twenty-four years old, a church of about twenty-five people in the small town of Franklinton, Louisiana called me to pastor their church. At the time, I was living over six hundred miles away from Louisiana in my hometown of Augusta, Georgia. New Orleans Seminary had a campus in Atlanta, so once a week I drove to Atlanta to take classes from 9:00 in the morning to 9:00 at night. The drive was getting old, and I was not going to be able to reach my educational goals by attending seminary in Atlanta, so I decided to move to the New Orleans area. My pastor, who was a New Orleans graduate, connected me with the church in Franklinton, and before I knew it, a U-Haul truck was in front of my apartment loading up all my earthly possessions.

I still remember my first day in Franklinton. After several church members helped me move in, there I was, all alone, getting ready to begin my journey as a pastor. At twenty-four years of age, I was in no way prepared to lead a congregation of people who were old enough to be my grandparents. I can remember thinking things like, "What do I do now? How do I start?" I knew I was supposed to preach every Sunday, but what else was I supposed to do as a pastor? Maybe you've wondered what your pastor does during the week. Does a pastor actually do anything during a week? Or, does he only work on Sundays? Does a pastor do anything besides preaching and occasionally perform weddings, funerals and make hospital visits? Why has God given pastors to the church?

After two decades of ministry, I've learned much about pastoral ministry both from Scripture and experience, and I can tell you that while a pastor's primary responsibility is preaching and teaching the Word of God, that's not all a pastor does. However, before we dive into what a pastor does, let's think about who a pastor is.

WHO A PASTOR IS.

If you've been in the church for a while, you know there are all kinds of leaders in the church. In a church, you'll find worship leaders, children's leaders, student leaders, small group leaders, discipleship group leaders, and leaders of a variety of other ministries. In fact, leadership development is a part of the discipleship process. As you continue your discipleship process, you will grow as a leader who is more than able to lead others to grow in intimacy with Jesus Christ. The local church is full of potential leaders.

While the local church is full of leaders, the Bible describes two types of leaders in particular that are necessary for the church to function well: elders and deacons. Elders are not necessarily elderly people, but instead, elders are spiritually mature people that are entrusted with the oversight of the local church. In the New Testament, three Greek words describe the role of the elder: *presbuteros* (elders), *poimainō* (pastor or shepherd), and *episkopeō* (overseer). All three of these words are used interchangeably to describe the office of pastor or elder.

A pastor is someone who oversees the work of the church. Different churches have different approaches to the office of pastor. Some churches have one pastor, while other churches have multiple pastors with one pastor that acts as a lead or senior pastor who does most of the preaching and is responsible for the overall oversight of the church. Other churches have a board of elders that are made up of some pastors/elders who are seminary trained and receive a salary from the church while the other elders may not be seminary trained and do not receive a salary from the church. Regardless of the church structure, the pastor is charged with overseeing the local church while understanding that ultimately Jesus is the head of the church. (Colossians 1:18).

Deacons, on the other hand, are not given the responsibility of overseeing the overall ministry of the church. Instead, they are given the responsibility of serving the church. If you look at all the times deacons are referenced in the New Testament, you will never find a specific job description for deacons. However, the word deacon means servant. So, the local church, at the discretion of the elders, has the freedom to use deacons however they think best for that particular church. While each church sets aside men to serve in the office of deacon, everyone should aspire to be a deacon in the sense that everyone should want to be a servant of God's people. In reality, the men that serve in the office of deacon should be setting the example for the rest of the church as to what it looks like to serve the church faithfully.

When Paul writes to his young protégé, Timothy, he writes about the kind of men that can serve as pastors and deacons (1 Timothy 3:1-13). Interestingly, in these verses, Paul doesn't really give a job description of either pastors or deacons other than stating that a pastor must be able to teach (1 Timothy 3:2). Instead, Paul focuses on the character qualities of pastors and deacons. It would be helpful for you to read this passage and consider the type of men that can serve as pastors and deacons. It's evident from what Paul writes that God is far more concerned with the character of leaders than He is concerned about the leader's abilities. If you think about it, the character qualities that should be characteristic of pastors and deacons should be characteristic of every believer. Believers should be able to look to pastors and deacons as an example of God-honoring lives.

Simply put, both pastors and deacons lead the way in setting an example of Christ-like character, but the pastors are the one set apart by the church to teach and lead the congregation. That's who a pastor is, now let's think about what a pastor does.

WHAT A PASTOR DOES.

So far, we've established that a pastor preaches and provides oversight for the church. Is there anything else a pastor does? Paul Alexander and Mark Dever have helped me think through the role of a pastor. In their book, The Deliberate Church, they describe three primary obligations of a pastor. The Bible uses the metaphor of a shepherd to describe a pastor, so according to Alexander and Dever, the primary obligations of a pastor are to lead the flock to graze, guide the flock, and guard the flock.[1]

1. LEAD THE FLOCK TO GRAZE.

People need to know the Word of God, and God has charged pastors to preach the Word of God. Paul wrote to Timothy:

[1]*I charge you in the presence of God and of Christ Jesus, who is to judge the living and the dead, and by his appearing and his kingdom: [2]preach the word; be ready in season and out of season; reprove, rebuke, and exhort, with complete patience and teaching. [3]For the time is coming when people will not endure sound teaching, but having itching ears, they will accumulate for themselves teachers to suit their own passions, [4]and will turn away from listening to the truth and wander off into myths. [5]As for you, always be sober-minded, endure suffering, do the work of an evangelist, fulfill your ministry (2 Timothy 4:1-5).*

Paul could have instructed Timothy to spend his time a lot of different ways. He could have instructed Timothy to spend all his time out in the community visiting sick people, visiting the prisons, or spending time in people's homes. Being in the community with people is indeed an essential part of the ministry. However, if people are going to have a right understanding of who God is, they need a correct understanding of His Word. So, Paul's primary instruction to Timothy was to preach the Bible faithfully. Timothy was to help his people graze on the riches of the Word of God.

You need your pastor to spend time studying the Bible and praying so that He might help your local church have a right understanding of who God is. Indeed, you can understand the Bible apart from your pastor. You can read the Bible for yourself, read books about the Bible, listen to podcasts, and seek out all kinds of resources to help you understand the Bible. However, God has entrusted the pastor of your local church with the job of making sure that when the entire congregation gathers each week, they get a steady diet of the Word of God.

---

[1]Paul Alexander and Mark Dever, *The Deliberate Church* (Wheaton: Crossway Books, 2005), 94-95.

2. GUIDE THE FLOCK.

We've already discussed that the role of a pastor is to guide the flock. Just as a shepherd directs his sheep in the direction they need to go, a pastor directs his congregation in the way it needs to go. A pastor leads his congregation. A pastor leads by charting a course for the ministry, casting vision, developing strategy, etc. Biblically speaking, the primary way the pastor leads the church is by equipping followers of Jesus to do the work of the ministry. Often, when we think of of pastoral leadership, we think that the pastor leads best when he does the work of the ministry, but that's simply not what the Bible teaches! It's not the job of pastors to carry the burden of performing all the work of the ministry. It's not the job of the pastor to visit every sick person, lead every program, or even preach every message! Instead, it's the job of the pastor to ensure that every member of his congregation is adequately equipped to use his or her gifts and abilities to do the ministry that God has given that local church. Paul wrote:

[11]And he gave the apostles, the prophets, the evangelists, the shepherds and teachers, [12]to equip the saints for the work of ministry, for building up the body of Christ, [13]until we all attain to the unity of the faith and of the knowledge of the Son of God, to mature manhood, to the measure of the stature of the fullness of Christ, [14]so that we may no longer be children, tossed to and fro by the waves and carried about by every wind of doctrine, by human cunning, by craftiness in deceitful schemes (Ephesians 4:11-14).

The best way a pastor can lead is by developing other leaders. A pastor leads by helping people discover their unique giftedness and by assisting people to use their unique giftedness in the life of the church. Your pastor should be faithfully preaching the Word, and your pastor should be active in discipling other believers so that they might live out the calling God has placed on their lives. You can be a huge help to your pastor by allowing him and encouraging him to fulfill Ephesians 4:11-14.

3. GUARD THE FLOCK.

If you read the New Testament carefully, you'll notice that false teaching abounded in the early church. You can understand why. The church was just getting started, and the New Testament was still being written. People were trying to understand the implications of the death and resurrection of Jesus, and many were getting it wrong. So, many of the New Testament letters address false teaching and call the readers to beware of false teaching. For example, Paul warned Timothy about false teaching that was prevalent in Ephesus:

[3]As I urged you when I was going to Macedonia, remain at Ephesus so that you may charge certain persons not to teach any different doctrine, [4]nor to devote themselves to myths and endless genealogies, which promote speculations rather than the stewardship from God that

is by faith. ⁵The aim of our charge is love that issues from a pure heart and a good conscience and a sincere faith. ⁶Certain persons, by swerving from these, have wandered away into vain discussion, ⁷desiring to be teachers of the law, without understanding either what they are saying or the things about which they make confident assertions (1 Timothy 1:3-7).

False teaching pervaded the early church, and it pervades the church today. Throughout the history of the church, all kinds of false teachings have risen, and faithful pastors have had to defend what the Bible actually says about a variety of issues like the nature of salvation, the Trinity, how we worship, etc. You've probably encountered some false teaching in today's church. For example, in the evangelical church, the prosperity gospel has become prevalent teaching, and it is undoubtedly a heretical teaching. Outside of evangelical churches, different cults have their own spin on Jesus. Jehovah Witnesses teach that Jesus is not God. Mormons teach that Jesus is a god, and you can become a god as well and inherit your own universe if you live the right way.

You need to be aware of false teachings. You also need to know how to defend your faith against false teachings. God has given pastors to the church to guard the flock from false teachers. It is a pastor's job to make sure that his congregation can identify false teaching, and it is a pastor's job to make sure that false teaching does not enter the local church. A pastor often does more than lead the flock to graze, guide the flock, and guard the flock, but these are three obligations that every pastor must fulfill out of love for the people that God has entrusted to his care.

As you think about the pastors that God has placed in your life let me encourage you to pray for them. Pastors need your prayers! Let me also encourage you to support and minister to your pastor. Your pastor is not perfect. He might not preach as effectively as the preacher does at the megachurch down the street. However, that does not mean that God is not using him to feed your soul. Your pastor will make mistakes. Forgive him when he does. Your pastor will also make decisions that you do not agree with. The temptation will be to criticize your pastor or to talk bad about him because you don't agree with him. Fight that temptation. Realize that God has given you a pastor for your good. While there are some immoral, self-centered pastors out there, the majority of pastors are really trying their hardest to care for the flock that God has entrusted them. Pray for your pastor!

In your group, reflect on the following questions:

1. How does 1 Peter 5:1-5 help you have a better understanding of the role of the pastor?

2. What is the difference between a pastor and a deacon? How does your church allow deacons to serve in the congregation?

3. Think about the three obligations that every pastor has. What do you think are the unique challenges a pastor faces as he tries to fulfill these obligations?

Model the Word

1. In your group, talk about a particular pastor or spiritual leader that has influenced your faith.

2. In your group, talk about how you can support the work of your pastors and the work of the church.

Share the Word

1. How would you explain the role of a pastor to someone who is not a follower of Jesus? How can a pastor model the work of Jesus?

2. What are some false teachings that might keep someone who is not a follower of Jesus from coming to faith in Christ?

Pray the Word

1. As a group, pray for your pastors that God might use them for the work of the Kingdom.

2. Ask God to help you support the work of your church and to be an encouragement to your leaders.

Daily Bible Reading

Day 1: Hebrews 9-10
Day 2: Hebrews 11-12
Day 3: Hebrews 13
Day 4: James 1-2
Day 5: James 3-4

20. Creation

Know the Word

Read Genesis 1:1-2:25

1. What do you see? (Observation)

2. What does it mean? (Interpretation)

3. What do you do? (Application)

4. How should you pray?

BIBLICAL THEOLOGY

The Bible is a big book comprised of smaller books, all of which vary in genre, purpose, style, etc. It can be difficult at times to see the connection points between Genesis and Revelation or Psalms and Romans. Every book of the Bible, no matter how long or short, straightforward or complex, is connected in some way or another, and every book ultimately points to Jesus Christ and the saving power of the gospel. One helpful way to see how the Bible is connected is by using biblical theology. To understand biblical theology, we first need to define theology. Theology literally means the study of God (-ology means "the study of "and Theos is the Greek word for "God"). You don't need to be a preacher or theologian to do theology. Actually, everyone is a theologian in some sense. If you've ever opened and read the Bible, you have studied God. And while you may never be an academic who dedicates his or her life to know God as deeply as possible, you can certainly be equipped with the tools to know Him as deeply as you possibly can. You already have some of the tools necessary for the task. We've spent the past 19 weeks learning about how to be a disciple of Jesus, how to read the Bible, how to pray, and what the Christian life should look like. Over the next 14 weeks, you will be equipped to do biblical theology.

What is biblical theology? It differs from systematic theology (you may have heard of this) and historical theology (maybe not as much). Systematic theology is a highly structured and organized approach that attempts to discover what the whole Bible says about a given topic. For example, we could ask, "What does the Bible say about the church?" Using systematic theology, we would find all the verses about the church, organize them, and attempt to figure out what and how God wants us to think about the church today. Historical theology is an attempt to figure out what the church has believed about a given topic and how the church has interpreted the Bible throughout history. In this sense, we would look at how Christians from Paul to the present day have thought about and understood what the Bible says about the church, and allow those results to guide us in how we think about it today. Biblical theology is tricky to define because there are varying views about what exactly the discipline is. People often use the term to refer to entirely different things. For our purposes, biblical theology is the study of how the diverse parts of the Bible fit together to form a unified and cohesive story. This practice focuses on common themes that are present throughout Scripture. Biblical theology, in the way we are using it, isn't better or worse than systematic or historical theology. Each works together to provide a robust understanding of who God is and what He has done for us in Christ. Biblical theology, however, will help you think about the story of the Bible holistically, and provide a solid foundation as you learn more about systematic and historical theology. It's foundational for doing theology, and, remember, everyone is a theologian.

Each week, you'll look at passages where some of these themes are most clear. While we can't address every theme, we'll try to focus on the big ones. You'll notice as you get further into the story that the authors return to and build upon a few foundational themes. Therefore, pay close attention these first few sessions. If you can begin to think well about the first few chapters and books of the Bible, figuring out the latter parts becomes a lot easier. As with any study, humility is vital. Don't expect to get through these sessions and have the whole Bible figured out. God's Word is inexhaustible! This is simply a starting point, and we hope it will lead to a lifelong study and love of God's Word. Let's jump into this beautiful story.

CREATION: GENESIS 1-2

Every good book or story has introductory information that is vital for understanding what follows; the Bible is no different. Genesis 1-11 provides an introduction to the rest of the Bible. A lot of time and ground is covered in these 11 chapters, and the story slows down a bit with the introduction of Abraham in chapter 12. Some of the most important themes in Scripture come from these chapters, and most of those show up in the first three. If you can grasp what's going on in Genesis 1-3, the rest of Scripture starts to make a lot more sense. We'll look at Genesis 3 next week. Genesis 1-2 depict the beginning. It's here we see God's original design and intention for humanity. There are a lot of questions we could ask about these chapters, whether scientific, philosophical, or theoretical. Those questions are fine to ask, but our focus is on the story. The first question you may ask is this: "Why are there two creation accounts?"

Let's start there.

WHY TWO CREATION ACCOUNTS?

It may seem strange that there are two different creation accounts, or maybe you have never questioned it but are now since we brought it up. On a surface level, it may just be that Genesis 1 is an overview and Genesis 2 provides more specific details, but that doesn't seem to quite get at what's going on. The first creation account is found in Genesis 1:1-2:3. The word "God" appears 35 times in those verses. "God" is translated from the Hebrew word Elohim. Elohim simply means divine being and can be used generically to refer to any god or gods. Ancient cultures near Israel had concepts for "god" and would use "Elohim" to refer to their respective deities. In the second creation account from 2:4-24, the language changes to "the LORD God" and is used 11 times. When "LORD" is in all capital letters in your Bible, it's translated from the Hebrew word Yahweh. Yahweh is the proper name for the God of Israel.

There are numerous points we could make about the word Yahweh, but to know Yahweh's name, you must be in a relationship with Him. Whereas Elohim can be generic, Yahweh is incredibly specific. Therefore, when Yahweh Elohim (LORD God) is used, it's a specific reference to the all-powerful, loving, merciful, creating, and redeeming God of Israel. The one true God. Why does this matter? Anyone, especially when Moses was writing, could read the first chapter of Genesis and agree with it. Although there are people today who deny the existence of God, the vast majority of people throughout history have agreed there is some deity who made everything around us. Each religion differs on who that god(s) is, his or her specific characteristics, qualities, whether or not he can be known, etc., but most affirm there is something or someone responsible for creating the universe. This doesn't mean there are no important Christian elements in Genesis 1 (we'll look at that below), but Moses uses a generic term for "god" to get any reader's attention, to draw them in and get them hooked. Notice what happens in chapter 2. Moses moves from very broad "God (Elohim)" to very specific "the LORD God (Yahweh Elohim)." Essentially, Moses is saying something like this: "We all agree that some god made all of creation, right? Well, let me tell you exactly who that God is. It isn't whatever gods you've been worshipping in Egypt or Babylon. No, the God who made everything is Yahweh, the God of Israel. He's a creating God, a personal God, and a relational God. He's the God we (Israel) know. And guess what? You can know Him, too." It's from this vantage point that Moses sets the stage for the rest of the story. Let's look at some specific themes in these two chapters.

THE LAND

Remember, just because Moses uses generic language for "God" in chapter 1, it doesn't mean that it isn't the Christian God who is doing the creating work. What exactly is God doing in chapter 1? He's certainly creating all things—plants, animals, people—but He goes about it in a very specific way. God could have simply spoken one word, and the garden of Eden would have been complete. But that isn't what we see Him do. On the first two days, God separates the light from the darkness and creates an expanse in the waters. Notice what happens on day three: God brings forth dry land from the waters, and it is on this day He sees it as good for the first time. The land isn't passive in the work that takes place over the next days. Where do the plants come from? The land. Where do the animals come from? The land. God isn't personally crafting each plant and animal and placing them in exact spots. God speaks, and the land produces and provides. But, for whom is the land providing?

God doesn't haphazardly create a good land that produces and provides. He creates it for a purpose. God desires for humans to dwell in the land He's prepared for them. It's only when He creates man and woman that God sees His creation as very good. It's essential for us to grasp this concept, because, as we move forward in the story, the theme or idea of the land becomes increasingly important. We must always remember why the land is important. Yes, it provides; yes, it produces; yes, it's abundant and bountiful. However, the land is chiefly important because it is the place God has prepared for His people to dwell in His presence, which is where we turn next.

PRESENCE OF GOD

In my estimation, this is one of the most helpful and impactful themes to trace throughout the Scriptures. Why is the garden of Eden so important, so wonderful, and so beautiful? It may be because before the fall, there is no sin or shame. There is no sickness or death. The garden provides food and water. It's a lush place teeming with life. Adam and Eve have an unbroken relationship, and everything seems close to perfect. All of those things are great, but none of those things in themselves are why the garden is very good. The garden is so important because it is where the presence of God dwells with His people. It's where God and humanity fellowship with one another. In a sense, it's where heaven and earth meet. All of the good things listed above are contingent upon God's presence. In the presence of God, there is no sin, shame, or death. The whole story of the Bible is about God reconciling His people to Himself in Christ Jesus so they can be back in His presence forever. Keep this theme in mind, especially as we move toward the tabernacle, temple, the coming of Jesus Christ, and the Holy Spirit. Next week we'll look at what happens when humanity is no longer in God's presence.

GOD'S INTENTION TO SPREAD THE GARDEN

In Genesis 1:28, God tells the humans to, "Be fruitful and multiply and fill the earth and subdue it, and have dominion over the fish of the sea and over the birds of the heavens and over every living thing that moves on the earth." The garden of Eden was in a defined place (see 2:10-14); it didn't cover the whole earth. Outside of the garden was the wilderness (a theme we'll look at next week). The wilderness was untamed and dangerous. God's desire was for Adam and Eve to take what was in the garden to the ends of the earth. They were to fill the whole world with worshipers of God, subduing the wilderness, and spreading the presence of God to all places. As you know, they didn't get very far in this task, but we'll pick this idea up again as we move along through the story.

MAN FROM THE DUST

This is a minor theme, but it's helpful to understand what's going on as God creates Adam. Whereas the rest of life on earth arose from the land in response to God's words, God takes part of the land (the dust) and forms a human Himself. Humans have a close connection to the land. They come from it, they are instructed to subdue and interact with it, and ultimately, they return to it (Gen. 3:19). It's only when God breathes (spirit) into the dust that it becomes a living thing. Before the breath (spirit) of God, man is dead; after the breath of God, man is a living thing. Man is also completely passive in this work. God chooses to bring dead things to life; it is His work and His doing, which becomes vitally important when we get to God bringing the spiritually dead to life. Man is also set apart because of the breath of God. The plants and animals are living creatures, but not in the same way humans are. Humans are meant to rule over creation in worship and obedience to God.

WORSHIP AND OBEY IN THE GARDEN TEMPLE

The idea of worship and obedience may not initially jump off the pages as you read through Genesis 2, but it's there; we just have to dig into the text a bit to see it clearly. Genesis 2:15 says, "The LORD God took the man and put him in the garden of Eden to work it and keep it. And the LORD God commanded the man, saying, 'You may surely eat of every tree of the garden, but the tree of the knowledge of good and evil you shall not eat, for in the day you eat of it you shall surely die.'" There are several important things to note here.

First, the phrase "work it and keep it" is an interesting translation (don't worry, we won't be doing a lot of translation work as we go through these sessions, but in certain spots it's necessary, and this is one of those spots). The Hebrew words are *'abad* (work) and *shamar* (keep). Both of these Hebrew words have a range of possible translations (we know because of how they are used elsewhere in Scripture and other Hebrew writing). 'Abad can be translated "work," "serve," or "worship," depending on the context. And shamar can be translated "watch," "protect," or "obey," again, depending on the context. What's really interesting is that when this word combination is used elsewhere in Scripture, it gets translated "worship and obey," rather than referring to simply caring for a garden. It's a much weightier combination in this sense. It is specifically used to describe the duties Levitical priests had in the tabernacle and temple (Num. 3:7-8, 8:25-26; Lev. 18:5; 1 Chron. 23:32; Ezek. 44:14), which, as we will see in a few weeks, is where the presence of God dwells among His people. The garden of Eden, then, acted as a temple where God's people could freely worship and obey Him.

Second, we must ask: why is translating these Hebrew words this way important? Adam and Eve's job was not merely to be gardeners. Yes, God did command them to subdue the earth and spread the garden of Eden throughout the world. However, their main job, and much more important job, was to worship and obey God. Obedience is an act of worship. How do we worship God? In a lot of ways, but all of them are acts of obedience, whether it be reading the Bible, praying, singing songs of praise, living lives of faithfulness and godliness, etc. To obey God in every area of our lives is to worship Him. This helps make sense of why God immediately gives Adam a command to follow. To be obedient to God, Adam needed a command to obey. Adam's act of worship was contingent upon him following the command not to eat from the tree of the knowledge of good and evil, and we know he failed at that pretty quickly.

As we move forward, the idea of a "garden temple" will appear over and over. Eden is both a garden and a temple. As a garden, it provides food and a place for people to live and prosper.

As a temple, it is where God's people can worship and obey Him. The design God gives Israel for the construction of the tabernacle and temple is meant to reflect the garden of Eden. The prophets speak of a time when God will dwell with His people in a garden or garden city. Ezekiel prophecies of a future garden temple. And in Revelation, John describes the same idea. Hold on to this idea of God's people worshiping and obeying Him in a garden temple. All of those images are meant to draw our attention back to God's original design in Eden and cause us to look forward to the new and better Eden.

MARRIAGE MANDATE

The final thing we'll look at from this text is Adam and Eve's union. If you read 2:18-24, you'll notice the story is actually kind of strange. We can't separate Adam's interaction with the animals from God providing him a wife. As a kid, you may have been taught that God brought all the animals to Adam and he was able to name them whatever he wanted, but that's not what's going on. Adam wasn't acting as the first scientist, providing a taxonomy of all living creatures. Nor was Adam just randomly choosing what the animals names would be. Remember, this is prior to the fall, so Adam hasn't been impacted by sin, which means his mind hasn't been affected by sin either. When the animals approach him, he simply knows what they are. This may sound strange to you, but think about it: Adam didn't have to learn language, he just spoke. He didn't have to learn how to walk; he just walked. And he didn't have to learn what the animals were; he just knew.

When he finished with the animals, he realized there was nothing like him. All the other animals had things like themselves, but for Adam, there was no one. There was no other human to be in relationship with him, and God said that wasn't good for him; therefore, God made Eve, his wife. It was with this woman that Adam was to fill the earth and subdue it, spreading the glory of God across the world. Next week we'll look at how this immediately goes wrong, but marriage is an important theme for us to understand because it ultimately points toward the relationship between Christ and the church. It points toward a perfect groom who works to make his bride spotless.

CONCLUSION

Ok, take a deep breath. We covered a lot of ground this week. You may have learned some of that before, or you may not have heard any of it at all. You may be thinking, "I would have never gotten all those things because I don't know Hebrew, Greek, or have any of the resources to figure this stuff out." Whatever the case, it's ok! I didn't know any of this stuff before someone taught me, and I still don't know Hebrew and Greek! But now it's all ingrained in my head, and every time I teach it to others, it becomes more solidified. And that's what's going to happen for you. Once you teach these things to someone else and help them figure out what the Bible teaches, it's going to become more and more familiar to you. This is the process of discipleship. Learning God's Word is a lifelong endeavor. Each week won't have this much content, but I want you to feel equipped and have the resources to teach these things to others.

In your group, reflect on the following questions:

1. What is biblical theology (in the way we are using it) and how does it differ from systematic theology and historical theology? What may be a helpful benefit of using biblical theology?

2. As you read Genesis 1-2 what are the differences and similarities between the two accounts. Why do you think we have the two accounts and not just one?

3. What stands out to you most from these two chapters? What themes or ideas discussed above help you think well about Genesis 1-2?

Model the Word

1. Take time for each group member to explain one of the themes found in Genesis 1-2 and why that theme is important.

2. How would you go about teaching this text to someone else? If you had a friend who wanted to understand Genesis 1-2 better, where would you start? What would you point out to them?

Share the Word

1. Think about reading these chapters from the perspective of an unbeliever. How could you use Genesis 1-2 to share the gospel or begin a gospel conversation? How could some of the themes we discussed help you as you share the story of Jesus Christ?

2. How can beginning with God's original design and intention for humanity be a helpful way to have a gospel conversation? Why is creation an important element of the gospel?

Pray the Word

1. As a group, spend time praying for each other to have a better understanding of God's Word.

2. Thank God for His creating work. Thank Him for creating the people in your group and for creating a way for us to know Him and be in relationship with Him.

3. Pray a prayer of anticipation. As Christians, we long for the day when we are with God face to face in new creation. Tell God how much you look forward to spending eternity with Him in His presence.

Daily Bible Reading

Day 1: James 5
Day 2: 1 Peter 1-2
Day 3: 1 Peter 3-4
Day 4: 1 Peter 5
Day 5: 2 Peter 1-2

21. Sin

Know the Word

Read Genesis 3:1-24

1. What do you see? (Observation)

2. What does it mean? (Interpretation)

3. What do you do? (Application)

4. How should you pray?

Last week we looked at some major themes from Genesis 1-2, such as the Land, the Presence of God, and Eden as a Garden Temple. Remember, these themes will show up over and over as you read through the Bible. This week is the fall of man. Despite God's intention for His people to dwell in His presence in the place He prepared for them, Adam and Eve quickly disobeyed the one command God gave them. The Bible doesn't specify how much time elapsed between the creation of man and woman and their fall, but it likely wasn't long.

Genesis 3 depicts quite an interesting scene. A crafty serpent comes to Adam and Eve and deceives them. Rather than obeying God, Adam and Eve desire to be like Him, knowing good and evil. For Adam and Eve, however, knowing good and evil is the worst thing that could happen to them. Upon taking the fruit of the tree, sin enters into the world. Their eyes are opened to their nakedness, and they feel shame. Adam and Eve make clothing out of fig leaves to cover their shame. As God walks through the garden in the cool of the day, Adam and Eve hide from Him. The time of fellowship with God they once loved is gone. As God confronts the humans, Adam blames Eve and Eve blames the serpent. God declares a series of curses (mostly) and blessings (one) on the serpent and humans. The scene ends with God driving the humans out of the garden.

God's good design quickly goes awry. In Genesis 4-11, we see how rapidly and devastatingly sin moves through and affects humanity. Genesis 3 seems bleak and hopeless. However, there is much within this chapter that provides hope for the rest of the story. Let's look at a few themes from Genesis 3 that will not only help us to understand this chapter better but also to understand the rest of Scripture.

THE SERPENT

Who is this serpent? Though Moses doesn't directly identify the serpent as Satan, other texts provide clarity on its identity. John writes, "And he seized the dragon, that ancient serpent, who is the devil and Satan, and bound him for a thousand years, and threw him into the pit, and shut it and sealed it over him, so that he might not deceive the nations any longer, until the thousand years were ended. After that he must be released for a little while" (Rev. 20:2-3). Notice that John also refers to Satan as a dragon. The biblical authors use a range of words to compare Satan to a serpent, dragon, or beast.

The serpent was one of the many beasts of the field. Last week, one of the themes we looked at was God's intention for humans to spread the garden across the whole earth (Gen. 1:28). The humans were supposed to have dominion over the beasts of the field and all creeping things. In Genesis 3, rather than ruling over the beasts of the field, they allow a beast of the field to rule over and deceive them. After they are deceived, the humans act like and resemble the beasts of the field more so than the God of the garden. Genesis 4 immediately tells a story of two brothers acting like beasts of the field, ensuing in murder and the destruction of God's creation rather than the multiplication of it. As you continue through the story, keep in mind this idea of Satan as a deceptive serpent, dragon, or beast (bonus material: "Devil" means "tempter" and "Satan" means "accuser").

SIN

Sin is a word we often use but rarely define. The Bible calls a lot of things "sin" and uses a lot of synonyms of the word such as transgression, iniquities, evil, etc. Most simply, sin means to miss the mark. In both Hebrew and Greek, it's used as a term for accuracy when throwing spear or rock (see Judges 20:16). If one "missed the mark," he didn't hit the center of the target. This definition is quite helpful when thinking about sin or sins. It doesn't matter if you miss the target by an inch or a mile—a miss is a miss. In spear throwing, it might matter who is the closest to center, but when it comes to the holiness and perfect standard of God, a miss is a miss. And any miss in relation to God, no matter how close or far, results in death. It's easy to think that Adam and Eve's sin wasn't that bad. It wasn't like they committed murder; they ate a fruit! How extreme their sin was didn't matter—they missed the mark of God's holy standard.

Think about this: Moses couldn't enter the promised land because of his sin. He didn't kill anyone. He didn't commit adultery. He didn't even steal. He struck a rock twice with his staff instead of simply speaking to it so water would come out. That may seem extreme, but it missed the mark of what God told him to do, which was to only speak for the rock to provide water (see Num. 20:1-13). King David, on the other hand, committed adultery and had the woman's husband murdered in battle (see 2 Sam. 11)! Those seem like extremely different variations of sin, and they are, but both Moses and David missed the mark of God's holy and perfect standard. Ultimately, Moses and David were unfaithful to God. Anything that misses the mark is sin. This definition of sin should be helpful as you read through the story. Some of God's people are going to commit much worse acts than others, but they are all going to miss the mark.

In Genesis 3, we see that sin affects three different relationships. First, sin affects the relationship between God and humans. After Adam and Eve sin, they are immediately ashamed to be in the presence of God, and they try to hide from Him. Ultimately, God kicks them out of the garden because they cannot be both in sin and in His presence. We talked about the importance of the presence of God last week. Keep in mind the relationship between sin and the presence of God as we move forward. Second, sin affects the relationship between humans. Adam immediately blames Eve for their wrongdoing, and Eve blames the serpent. Humans don't want to take accountability for their sin, and the immediate outpouring of sin in Genesis 4 results in the murder of a human by a human. God's desires that humans work together to spread His presence over the whole world, instead they are constantly against one another. Third, sin affects the relationship between humanity and creation. One of God's curses toward Adam is that the ground will no longer produce abundantly for him. Rather, he will earn his food by the sweat of his brow. Sin affects every area and relationship of our lives. Think about these relationships as we move forward.

FIRST GOSPEL

Though Genesis 3 seems bleak, it's actually full of promise and hope, and it's all centered around Genesis 3:15. God promises the serpent, "I will put enmity between you and the woman, and between your offspring and her offspring; he shall bruise your head, and you shall bruise his heel." You may be thinking: that doesn't seem so hopeful! However, Genesis 3:15 is actually the first bit of good news after the fall. If you want to be fancy, you can call this verse the protoevangelium. If you want to be a normal English-speaking person, just call it the first gospel (proto means first, evangelium means gospel). This is the first verse of a future hope for sinful humanity.

God promises the serpent that an offspring or seed will come from the woman who will bruise the head of the serpent, and the serpent will bruise his heel. Depending on the translation you are reading, that word bruise may also be translated crush or strike, which more accurately embodies the force of the word. The offspring of the woman is going to crush the head of the serpent, even though the serpent will strike His heel. It is this offspring who will save humanity from the serpent and restore them to a right relationship with God. The question, then, is this: Who is the offspring of the woman who will crush the head of the serpent and reconcile humanity to God? The rest of the story is in response to this question. As you continue through the Bible, notice how important offspring or seed is. Every character in the biblical story should cause us to ask: Is this the promised one who will crush the serpent?

SALVATION/ATONEMENT

The ideas of salvation and atonement don't immediately jump off the page as you read Genesis 3. However, this chapter sets the framework for how God will forgive and save His people moving forward. Once Adam and Eve sinned, they knew they were naked and felt shame. To cover their sin and shame by their own efforts, they made clothing made out of fig leaves. Notice, however, what God covers them with later in the chapter. After God declares the curses and blessing, Moses writes, "And the LORD God made for Adam and for his wife garments of skins and clothed them" (Gen. 3:21). God killed an animal(s) and used the skins to cover Adam and Eve. God atoned for their sin. If they were going to live, something had to die. Atonement literally means reparation or satisfaction for wrongdoing. In Genesis 3, God sets the standard for how He will handle the sin of humanity. In an act of mercy, God allows Adam and Eve to live, but God is just, and sin must be paid for. Therefore, animal blood is shed in place of Adam and Eve, and it is through the atonement of an animal's death that Adam and Eve live. Notice also that Adam and Eve were not able to cover their sin by their own efforts. Atonement is only a work God can do.

God atones for Adam and Eve's sin, but there is still a problem: humanity is inherently different after sin. Sin is a massive problem for these people, and they can no longer dwell in the presence of God in their sinful state. Moreover, God doesn't want them to be in a sinful state forever, so He drives them out of the garden. Moses writes:

[22]*Then the LORD God said, "Behold, the man has become like one of us in knowing good and evil. Now, lest he reach out his hand and take also of the tree of life and eat, and live forever—"* [23]*therefore the LORD God sent him out from the garden of Eden to work the ground from which he was taken.* [24]*He drove out the man, and at the east of the garden of Eden he placed cherubim and a flaming sword that turned every way to guard the way to the tree of life (Genesis 3:22-24).*

God showed Adam and Eve mercy by atoning for their sin. God shows Adam and Eve grace by kicking them out of the garden. Why is that an act of grace? Isn't Eden where the people want to be? Well, yes, but notice what could happen: if Adam and Eve got their hands on the fruit of the tree of life, they would live forever in their sinful state. God promised He was going to fix humanity's problem (Gen. 3:15), but that won't happen if the humans eat of the tree of life. It's better for humans to live in a broken, sinful state, and eventually die rather than living forever with the problem of sin. Throughout Scripture, God is at work to save His people and redeem them to Himself, even if it isn't always apparent.

WILDERNESS

Wilderness is not mentioned in this chapter, so why are we focusing on it? Think back to last week when you read about God's intention to spread the garden. Eden was a defined place. God commanded Adam and Eve to be fruitful, multiply, and subdue the whole earth. The earth needed to be subdued because outside of the garden things were wild. In the garden, things were peaceful, and creatures lived in harmony. Outside of the garden, everything was chaotic, and creatures lived in contention with one another. God's desire was for the humans to spread the peace, joy, and life inside the garden to everywhere outside of it. Therefore, when God cast Adam and Eve out of the garden, He sent them into a dangerous world. He sent them away from His presence. In the wilderness, they would be tempted to despise God and follow after their own desires in ways they couldn't have imagined in the garden. Wilderness is always in stark contrast to the presence of God.

CONCLUSION

Genesis 3 is a heartbreaking chapter that is also filled with much hope. Genesis 1-3 sets the stage for God's miraculous rescue of humanity. The rest of the story is about God providing the way for his people to return to His presence in the place He has for them. Hopefully this has helped you to understand the importance of these three chapters. The biblical authors will repeatedly return to these themes, so it's vital for us to understand them and recognize them when they show up in the story.

In your group, reflect on the following questions:

1. What stands out most to you about Genesis 3?

2. What is something new you learned about this chapter and its importance to the story of the Bible?

3. What themes or ideas above help you think well about this chapter?

Model the Word

1. Take time for each group member to explain one of the themes in Genesis 3 and why it's important for understanding the chapter.

2. How would you teach this text to someone else? If you had a friend who wanted to understand this chapter, where would you start? What things would you point out to them?

Share the Word

1. Think about reading this chapter from the perspective of an unbeliever. How could you use Genesis 3 to share the gospel or begin a gospel conversation? How could some of the themes in Genesis 3 help you as you share the story of Jesus Christ?

2. How can beginning with sin and brokenness be a helpful way to have a gospel conversation? Why is sin an important element of the gospel?

Pray the Word

1. As a group, spend time praying for each other to have a better understanding of God's Word.

2. Thank God for His promise to save His people. Thank Him for forgiving you of your sin.

3. Pray for opportunities to share the gospel with others. Pray that the Spirit will open their eyes to the truth of God's Word and their need for salvation.

Daily Bible Reading

Day 1: 2 Peter 3
Day 2: Jude 1
Day 3: John 1-2
Day 4: John 3-4
Day 5: John 5-6

22. Covenant

Know the Word
Read Genesis 12:1-9 and Genesis 15:1-21

1. What do you see? (Observation)

2. What does it mean? (Interpretation)

3. What do you do? (Application)

4. How should you pray?

Genesis 1-11 covered the prehistory of the Bible. It set the framework of God's design, humanity's fall, and the broken human state which God promised to save and redeem. In Genesis 11, we see the famous story of the Tower of Babel. All people on earth spoke one language, and, rather than spreading across the whole earth as God originally commanded (Gen. 1:28), the people gathered into one place to build a great city and name for themselves. God intervened, made them speak different languages so they were confused, and spread them over the face of the whole earth. One way or another, God was going to ensure that people multiplied and filled the earth. But there is a problem: how will these newly formed nations be saved and redeemed? The answer comes in Genesis 12. We'll look at Genesis 12 in more detail below, but notice how God promises Abram that through him all the nations of the earth will be blessed. God is at work through Abram and his descendants to bless all the families of the earth. He makes a covenant with Abram. Actually, God makes several covenants throughout Scripture. Let's look at what a covenant is and why it's an important theme in Scripture.

WHAT IS A COVENANT?

If *covenant* is a word you're unfamiliar with, don't worry: it's probably not a term you use in your everyday life—most of us don't. It is a word, however, that was significantly important in Israel's history and that of the surrounding nations. A covenant is, "A compact or agreement between two parties binding them mutually to undertakings on each other's behalf. Theologically (used of relations between God and man) it denotes a gracious undertaking entered into by God for the benefit and blessing of humanity, and specifically those who by faith receive the promises and commit themselves to the obligations which this undertaking involves."[1] Now, that may sound a bit convoluted, so let's break it down.

Between humans, a covenant can be any agreement that both parties intend to uphold. For example, when two people get married, they make a covenant to be faithful to one another for better or for worse, until death. It's the responsibility of both parties to uphold the covenant. But, as you know from the high divorce rate in our country, humans make covenants or agreements all the time they can't or don't keep. In the context of the Old Testament, covenants were unalterable or binding in nature (we'll see how that plays out below). Covenants were taken extremely seriously. Moreover, when someone made a covenant, it was typically a stronger party making an agreement with a weaker party for their protection or benefit.

Therefore, when God made covenants with His people, the supreme, sovereign, and perfect ruler of the universe promised the protection and overall good of the ones with whom He

---

[1] G.L. Archer Jr, "Covenant," in *Evangelical Dictionary of Theology*, ed. Walter A. Elwell (Grand Rapids: Baker Academic, 2001), 299.

made the covenant. God swore to keep the covenants by His own name and nature. He swore by himself to keep the promises He made. Covenants were not, however, God simply making promises with no intent of response from His people. Covenant always implies relationship. God entered into covenants with people. When He promised to do a thing, it was expected that the other person(s) would uphold his end of the covenant as well, which was faithfulness and obedience. The idea of covenant is key to understanding the promises of God and how they unfold in Scripture.

Keep a couple of things in mind as we think about covenants. First, none of the covenants God makes are in contradiction with ones He's made before. There is no covenant for one people that isn't effective or applied to people who come after. This is particularly important to remember when we get to the New Covenant. Think back to Genesis 3:15: Jesus was always "Plan A." God didn't continue to make new covenants because the previous ones weren't good. The covenants are progressive. As God continues to reveal Himself to His people, He reveals a little more about the plan of salvation. He gives Abraham a little information, Moses a little more, David a little more, and we see the fullness of His salvific work in the person of Jesus Christ. As the story moves forward, God progressively reveals more about what He is doing to save and bless the nations. Think of it this way: the new covenant, centered on Jesus Christ, is the fulfillment and fullness of the covenants with Noah, Abram, Moses, and David. Second, the covenants below are not all the ones God makes, but they are the major ones. Third, covenant is not as much a biblical theme as it is the framework into which the themes fit. If you can grasp the idea of covenant, the relationship between the Old and New Testaments begins to make a lot more sense. Covenant helps with our "big-picture" understanding of the Bible.

THE COVENANT WITH NOAH

The first time covenant is used in the Bible is in the story of Noah. Moses writes, "But I will establish my covenant with you, and you shall come into the ark, you, your sons, your wife, and your sons' wives with you" (Gen. 6:18). In Genesis 6, sin and corruption affected humanity to the point where people only thought and did evil all the time. God promised to wipe humanity from the earth in order to start over, all except for Noah and his family. Noah found favor in God's sight, and God promised to protect Noah so that through him, humanity could continue and have a fresh start. Also, someone needed to be protected so that the promise of Genesis 3:15 would remain true. Someone from the line of Adam and Eve had to survive for the promised offspring to come.

The covenant with Noah is interesting, because, although this is the first mention of covenant, it points back to a covenant God already made. Most translations read, "I will establish my covenant with you," which gives the impression that it is a new thing God is doing. However, the most accurate translation reads, "I will confirm my covenant with you," which implies a covenant has already been made and God is reaffirming His intention to keep it. Notice how similar the language of the story of Noah and the flood (Gen. 6-9) is to that of the story of Adam and creation (Gen. 1-3). Both are told to be fruitful and multiply; both are told to rule over creation and subdue it; both are called to be faithful to God. Noah is supposed to serve as the new Adam, proving faithful where Adam failed. However, Noah quickly falls short and sins against God (Gen. 9:18-28).

Something to note about this covenant is that God promises never to flood the earth and destroy mankind again, regardless of how evil man gets moving forward. God binds Himself to His promises, and humans receive the benefit of living without fear being destroyed again by a great flood. Covenant always implies relationship, but the terms of this agreement and fulfillment are by God Himself. God promises that His original covenant with Adam and creation will continue forward. God will see to it that an offspring comes to save and redeem fallen humanity, despite how bad that humanity may get.

THE COVENANT WITH ABRAHAM

There is much we could look at here, but this will provide a simple overview of God's dealings with Abraham. There isn't just one instance where God makes and reaffirms promises He made to Abraham. The major interactions between God and Abraham regarding covenant are found in Genesis 12, 15, 17, and 22. In Genesis 12, God makes promises to Abram. In 15, God makes a covenant with Abram. In 17, God changes Abrams name to Abraham and gives the sign of circumcision to affirm the covenant. And in chapter 22, God tests Abraham, sees that he is faithful, and assures the reward of the promises and covenant by oath. Since we are primarily focusing on covenant, we'll only briefly look at Genesis 12 and 15.

While they may not seem like it initially, Genesis 12:1-9 are some of the most important verses in the whole Bible, and how you understand them will dictate how you understand the rest of the story moving forward. Remember, God scattered the nations over the face of the earth at the Tower of Babel, and God intends to redeem humanity to Himself through an offspring. Therefore, God chooses Abram to be the one through whom the offspring will come. God makes several promises to Abram: (1) God will make Abram a great nation; (2) God will bless him; (3) God will make his name great; (4) God will bless those who bless him; (5) God will curse those who curse him; and, this is important, (6) God will bless all the nations through him. That's quite the list of promises! The immediate response from Abram is obedience (12:4-6). In verse 7, God affirms His promises, and in verses 8-9, Abram shows more obedience.

God's intention is to create a great nation out of Abram so that all the nations of the earth will be blessed. It's through Abram the promised offspring will come. Abram and his descendants

(Israel) will be blessed to be a blessing to others. Abram will be made great, not for his own sake, but for the sake of God's name and the salvation of the nations. The nations God scattered in Genesis 11, He promises to save in Genesis 12. So how does covenant relate to these promises? Look at Genesis 15.

Abram believes God will keep his promises, but there is one problem: if Abram will have many descendants, he needs an offspring so his family can continue, but he has no son. God promises Abram will have his very own son from whom descendants will come that outnumber the stars. Moreover, God affirms His promise of a great land in which His people will dwell. And to affirm His promises, God makes a covenant with Abram. It's at this point that the details of covenant become quite clear.

Whereas God confirmed the covenant with Noah, God cuts a covenant with Abram. What's the difference? This is a point in the story where God is revealing something new about His plan to save and redeem His people. This is a new covenant in the sense that it reveals information about God's plan that was previously unknown. It's the same in the sense that it doesn't at all contradict the covenants made with Adam and Noah. Here we see the progressive nature of God's covenants.

So, what does it mean to cut a covenant? In this instance, God is the initiating party, which means He is affirming to Abram that He will follow through on His promise of both an offspring and a land. To cut the covenant, animals were cut in half and set on two different sides of an area, creating a lane or space in which one of the parties could walk or pass through. When passing through the two halves of the animals, the initiating party was effectively saying, "Let me be killed and cut in half in this same way if I do not keep the promise I am making you." That may seem kind of morbid today, but that is how serious these covenants were.

The amazing thing about this account is that God is the one initiating the covenant. As Abram was in a deep sleep, he saw a smoking fire pot and flaming torch pass between the animals that had been cut in half. Both of these items most likely represent the presence of God, which is often associated with fire. (See Exodus 13:21-22.) Abram could be assured that the promises God had made him to this point would absolutely come to fruition. We know, as Abram did, the God of the universe cannot be killed and torn apart like animals. Therefore, the only option was for God to keep His promises. Abraham's job was to trust that God would actually keep His promises. Again, covenants always require more than one individual making a promise; the other individual has to trust and believe those promises will be upheld, but it's God who is making the promises and fully intends to keep them, no matter the cost.

THE COVENANT WITH MOSES/ISRAEL

After the Exodus from Egypt, God appeared to Moses and Israel at Mount Sinai. In two weeks we'll look more closely at what all is going on when God gives Moses the law, but, for the purposes of this week, we need to understand that another covenant is made with Israel at Sinai. This is often referred to as the Mosaic covenant, or, as Paul refers to it, the old covenant (2 Cor. 3:14). It's this covenant that Jesus and the New Testament authors look back to and reflect upon most frequently. While the Mosaic covenant can be a bit complex, and it's easy to get lost in all the laws, rules, and sacrifices, at the heart of the covenant is God's grace and His desire for the obedience of His people. Moses writes:

3The LORD God called to him [Moses] out of the mountain saying, "Thus you shall say to the house of Jacob, and tell the people of Israel: 4You yourselves have seen what I did to the Egyptians, and how I bore you on eagles' wings and brought you to myself. 5Now therefore, if you will indeed obey my voice and keep my covenant, you shall be my treasured possession among all peoples, for all the earth is mine; 6and you shall be to me a kingdom of priests and a holy nation. These are the words that you shall speak to the people of Israel" (Exodus 19:3-6).

The Mosaic covenant is interesting because it is conditional. Now, that word may make you feel uncomfortable, but remember that no new covenant can nullify the promises of a previous covenant. The covenant with Moses doesn't change anything about the promises God made to Adam, Noah, and Abraham; all of those promises will come true. The Mosaic covenant is a fuller description of God's plan of salvation. Why, then, is it conditional? It's not conditional based on the nature of salvation. God already saved Israel from Egypt and fully intends to use them to bring to fruition His previous promises. The conditional aspect of the covenant is whether or not these people—Israel—will become God's treasured possession, a kingdom of priests, and a holy nation. Israel will only receive those blessings if they are obedient to the Mosaic covenant. Well, as the story progresses, we see they aren't at all obedient to the covenant, so keep in mind those promises and how and to whom they get applied moving forward.

THE COVENANT WITH DAVID

The Covenant with David is referred to as the Davidic covenant. Again, we'll look at this in more detail in a few weeks, so just keep in mind that God does, in fact, make a covenant with David concerning the future kingdom and future king. The keystone text for this covenant is 2 Samuel 7. In this passage, God promises David that a king will come from his line who will establish the kingdom and will reign on the throne forever. While the word covenant isn't used in 2 Samuel 7, it is used in other texts which refer to God's promise to David as a covenant such as 2 Samuel 23:5, Psalm 89 and 132, and 2 Chronicles 13:5.

THE NEW COVENANT

Though several of the prophets speak of a future covenant God will make with His people, Jeremiah most clearly refers to it as the new covenant:

31Behold, the days are coming, declares the LORD, when I will make a new covenant with the house of Israel and the house of Judah, 32not like the covenant that I made with their fathers on the day when I took them by the hand to bring them out of the land of Egypt, my covenant that they broke, though I was their husband, declares the LORD. 33For this is the covenant that I will make with the house of Israel after those days, declares the LORD: I will put my law within them, and I will write it on their hearts. And I will be their God, and they shall be my people. 34And no longer shall each one teach his neighbor and each his brother, saying, "Know the LORD," for they shall all know me, from the least of them to the greatest, declares the LORD. For I will forgive their iniquity, and I will remember their sin no more (Jeremiah 31:31-34).

"New" doesn't mean that the "old" wasn't beneficial or good. The new covenant is not at odds with the old covenant. The new covenant is the fulfillment of the old covenant. If you think that the new covenant sounds like it points to Jesus Christ, you're absolutely right! Jeremiah, Isaiah, and Ezekiel all prophesy of a time when one will come who can establish the new covenant (everlasting covenant, covenant of peace, the promise of a new heart and spirit) and reconcile God's people to Himself. An offspring will come who can make the new covenant possible. A new and better Adam, a new and better Abraham, a new and better Moses, and a new and better David will come who can not only uphold His end of the covenant but also fulfill all the previous covenants and bring their many promises to fruition

CONCLUSION

We covered a lot today. Hopefully, this helped you better understand the importance of covenant throughout the Bible. These covenants are vitally important and find their fulfillment in Christ. If we don't have a grasp on these covenants and why they are so important for the Old Testament authors and readers, it becomes more difficult to understand how they apply and are fulfilled in the New Testament. Keep the covenants in mind as we move forward.

In your group, reflect on the following questions:

1. What stands out to you most about Genesis 12 and 15?

2. What is something new you learned about these chapters and their importance to the overall story of Scripture?

3. What themes or ideas above help you think well about these chapters?

Model the Word

1. Take time for each member to explain the importance of one of the covenants mentioned above and why it is important for understanding the Old Testament.

2. How would you teach Genesis 12 and 15 to someone else? What aspects or ideas would you emphasize?

Share the Word

1. Think about reading these chapters from the perspective of an unbeliever. How could you use them to share the gospel or begin a gospel conversation? How can the idea of covenant be helpful to you as you share the gospel with others?

2. Why is it helpful to understand God's covenants with Adam, Noah, Abraham, Moses, and David? How does Jesus fulfill the promises made in these covenants?

Pray the Word

1. As a group, spend time praying for each other to have a better understanding of God's Word.

2. Thank God for His faithfulness to his covenants and promises. Reflect on what it means that we serve a God who cannot and will not break his promises to his people.

3. Pray for opportunities to share the gospel with others. Pray that God will give you boldness to share with those in your family and at your job.

Daily Bible Reading

Day 1: John 7-8
Day 2: John 9-10
Day 3: John 11-12
Day 4: John 13-14
Day 5: John 15-16

23. Exodus

Know the Word
Read Exodus 12:33-51; 13:17-22; 14:1-31

1. What do you see? (Observation)

2. What does it mean? (Interpretation)

3. What do you do? (Application)

4. How should you pray?

Last week we looked at several of the more important covenant's God made in the Old Testament. This week, we'll look at one of the most important stories in the Old Testament, and the Bible as a whole: Israel's Exodus from Egypt. Why is this event so important? The Exodus is God's most salvific work in all of the Old Testament. God shows His power, grace, and mercy to an undeserving people through miraculous acts, freeing them from bondage and leading them into life as His covenant people. He also makes a distinction between those who are His people and those who are not, and He does so in a very particular way, which we'll look at below. As you continue through the story, notice how often God draws Israel's attention back to the Exodus. Time and time again, God will remind Israel of how He saved them from the Egyptians by His mighty hand and power, and He will call them to holiness in response to their salvation.

CONTEXT

To better understand the Exodus, we need some context. In Genesis 15, God made a covenant with Abraham and affirmed His promise that from him would come a great nation that would bless all other nations. Tucked within that great promise, however, was God's declaration that Abraham's decedents would be servants to a foreign nation for 400 years. God would not allow them to stay in bondage forever, and He promised Abraham his decedents would indeed return to the land God promised them. As the story progresses, Abraham's family grows. He had Isaac, who had Jacob, who had twelve sons. One of Jacob's sons—Joseph—was sold into slavery by his brothers and became a servant in Egypt. God's sovereign hand was with Joseph, and He caused him to prosper and become second in command to Pharaoh. Because of a severe famine, all of Joseph's family was able to move to Egypt and live in the best of the land. Once Joseph died, Abraham's descendants became great in number. A Pharaoh rose who didn't know Joseph and was worried the Israelites would become too numerous and may overtake the Egyptians. Therefore, he forced them into hard slave labor.

Although they were oppressed, the Israelites became even more numerous, and Pharaoh decreed that all sons born to the Israelites should be killed. It's at this point we are introduced to Moses. His mother put him into a basket and floated him down the Nile river. Pharaoh's daughter found him and saved his life. Though Moses grew up in the house of Pharaoh, he knew he was an Israelite and wanted to help his people. After attacking an Egyptian who was beating a Hebrew worker, Moses fled from Egypt and became a shepherd in the land of Midian. As Israel cried out for God to free them from bondage, God remembered His promises to Abraham and set out to save Israel from Egypt. As Moses was tending to his family's flock, God appeared to him in a burning bush, and He told Moses that He would use him to free Israel from Egypt. It's at this point the details of the Exodus begin to unfold. Let's look at some of those details and see how they will help us both understand this story and the story moving forward.

PHARAOH VS. GOD

With the introduction of a new Pharaoh in the book of Exodus, Moses presents us with the most objectively evil character in the biblical story to this point. Is he ultimately more evil than the serpent? Well, no, but we don't have much information about the serpent yet; he was only present in one chapter. Pharaoh, however, is certainly in the line of evil stemming from the serpent. The first 18 chapters of Exodus are dedicated to the interactions between Pharaoh and God. Pharaoh/Egypt becomes somewhat of an archetype for evil rulers that will proceed him in the biblical story, and he is the antithesis of what a ruler should be in God's kingdom. What Pharaoh desires for Israel and what God desires for Israel are quite the opposite, and their motivations behind their desires are in stark contrast to one another.

The language of Exodus 1:6-7 should sound familiar:

⁶Then Joseph died, and all his brothers and all that generation. ⁷But the people of Israel were fruitful and increased greatly; they multiplied and grew exceedingly strong, so that the land was filled with them.

Moses intentionally causes us to remember God's covenants with Adam, Noah, and Abraham. Whereas God wanted Israel to be fruitful and multiply, Pharaoh did not. Rather, he wanted their destruction. Instead of preserving life to fill the earth, Pharaoh sought to kill all the sons of Israel by casting them into the Nile. Pharaoh went against God's will for both Israel and all of mankind. And although God's people were multiplying and filling the land, they weren't able to serve the LORD God; instead, Israel was forced to serve Pharaoh.

Pharaohs in Egypt were treated like gods, not simply because of their power, but both they and the Egyptians thought Pharaohs were divine. Egypt also had various other gods, such as the sun god, god of the Nile, god of crops and fertility, etc. The conflict between Pharaoh and God was one of supremacy and power. One major question of the Exodus is this: Which of these two rulers has ultimate authority? In Pharaoh's pride, he fancied himself and didn't even acknowledge the LORD God of Israel: "But Pharaoh said [to Moses], 'Who is the LORD, that I should obey his voice and let Israel go? I do not know the LORD, and moreover, I will not let Israel go'" (Exodus 5:2).

In response, God tells Moses, "'Now you shall see what I will do to Pharaoh; for with a strong hand he will send them out, and with a strong hand he will drive them out of his land.' God spoke to Moses and said to him,

²"I am the LORD. ³I appeared to Abraham, to Isaac, and to Jacob, as God Almighty, but by my name the LORD I did not make myself known to them. ⁴I also established a covenant with

them to give them the land of Canaan, the land in which they lived as sojourners. ⁵Moreover, I have heard the groaning of the people of Israel whom the Egyptians hold as slaves, and I have remembered my covenant. ⁶Say therefore to the people of Israel, 'I am the LORD, and I will bring you out from under the burdens of the Egyptians. And I will deliver you from slavery to them, and I will redeem you with an outstretched arm and with great acts of judgment. ⁷I will take you to be my people, and I will be your God, and you shall know that I am the LORD your God, who has brought you out from under the burdens of the Egyptians. ⁸I will bring you into the land that I swore to give to Abraham, to Isaac, and to Jacob. I will give it to you for a possession. I am the LORD'" (Exodus 6:2-8).

It's from this point that the battle between Pharaoh and God begins. Through the ten plagues and destruction of Pharaoh and his army, God systematically dismantled the gods of Egypt, proving that He was supreme and sovereign over not only Israel but Egypt as well. Pharaoh was only in power because God allowed it. As you move forward in the story, keep the theme of God vs. the kings of the earth in mind. Pharaoh and Egypt act as an archetype for what is to come (think Assyria, Babylon, etc.)

PLAGUES

Have you ever taken time to consider the oddity of the ten plagues? Frogs, locusts, bloody water, and extreme darkness are all a bit strange. Why does God send the plagues He does in the manner He does? God could have chosen any kinds of curses, but He chose these particular ten in order to show His power to Israel, Pharaoh, and all of Egypt. The plagues might even seem a bit unfair to the Israelites and Egyptians. After all, it wasn't all of Egypt that was opposing God; it was primarily Pharaoh. There are several things to remember about the plagues and why God chooses to do these acts.

First, the plagues serve as judgment on Pharaoh and the people, both Israelite and Egyptian. Notice the first three plagues affect everyone, Israel included. Though Israel was God's people and He was at work to save them, they were not innocent. Israel were sinners just as the Egyptians were. No people are exempt from God's judgment. Throughout the Old Testament, God uses plagues, war, and destruction to judge the sin of all people. If you can remember this idea, it will help greatly as you move forward in the Old Testament.

Second, the plagues display God's mighty power. God shows His power over animals, land, weather, and the gods of Egypt. Pharaohs magicians perform some of the same works initially, but even they couldn't keep up with the incredible acts of Yahweh. In the final plague, God shows His power over life itself. By the end of Israel's Exodus, there should be no doubt that the same God who delivered His people is the same God who created all things in Genesis 1-2.

The creator God is also the rescuing God who will stop at nothing to return His people to His presence to praise Him for who He is and what He has done for them.

Third, the plagues represent a distinction between Israel and Egypt. This doesn't mean Israel is innocent; remember, they were affected by the first three plagues. But as the plagues progress, God chooses to keep Israel unaffected in the land of Goshen while Egypt suffers. This distinction is most clear in the final plague. Remember the distinctions God makes between those who are His people and those who are not as we move forward.

HARDENING OF PHARAOH'S HEART

This aspect of the Exodus is one of the most difficult to explain. As you read through Exodus, you will notice that at times, Pharaoh hardens his own heart against God, and at other times, God hardens Pharaoh's heart. What is going on here? How is it fair that God can judge Pharaoh and Egypt when God is the one hardening Pharaoh's heart and causing him to rebel? Is Pharaoh really at fault? Let's look at a few things that will help us understand what is going on here.

First, we must understand why God is doing all of this work. Exodus 6:1-9 and 7:1-6 reveal that God will display His power to both Israel and Egypt. For Israel, God is proving to be the God of their fathers, and the one who has the power to redeem them from slavery. He is showing Himself to be the God of salvation. To Egypt, God is proving to be the only true and sovereign God, and He intends to use Pharaoh to make these purposes known. Israel's salvation, which, remember, means the salvation of all nations, including Egypt, is at stake (Genesis 12).

Second, Pharaoh is not completely passive in any of this work. Pharaoh is an evil ruler who believes himself to be a god; he doesn't want to listen to the God of the Israelites. Several times Pharaoh hardens his own heart. God didn't need to step in during those instances to work in Pharaoh. Pharaoh was simply acting according to his sinful nature and spurning God despite the miracles before him. We must remember that Pharaoh was a sinner who deserved condemnation and death, despite any work God did or didn't do in his heart. He had plenty of chances to repent, but he did not.

Third, there is a mystery between God's sovereign work in the world and man's volitional free will. This isn't the time and place to get into that discussion, and, thankfully, the text doesn't demand it of us. Keep in mind, we are practicing biblical theology, so we want to address these themes as the Bible presents them. Moses, the author of Exodus, doesn't give us a systematic treatment of why God hardens Pharaoh's heart; he simply tells us what God did. Even the Apostle Paul doesn't try to explain the tension. Paul writes in Romans:

¹⁴What shall we say then? Is there injustice on God's part? By no means! ¹⁵For he says to Moses, "I will have mercy on whom I have mercy, and I will have compassion on whom I have compassion." ¹⁶So then it depends not on human will or exertion, but on God, who has mercy. ¹⁷For the Scripture says to Pharaoh, "For this very purpose I have raised you up, that I might show my power in you, and that my name might be proclaimed in all the earth." ¹⁸So then he has mercy on whomever he wills, and he hardens whomever he wills. ¹⁹You will say to me then, "Why does he still find fault? For who can resist his will?" ²⁰But who are you, O man, to answer back to God? Will what is molded say to its molder, "Why have you made me like this? ²¹Has the potter no right over the clay, to make out of the same lump one vessel for honorable use and another for dishonorable use?" (Romans 9:14-21).

Rather than attempting to explain the apparent tension, Paul appeals to God's sovereignty to do as He pleases, whether or not it always makes sense to human minds. The relationship between God's sovereignty and man's free will is a theme throughout Scripture, and it's good for us to wrestle with the tension, but don't allow it to detract you from the story or ultimately from God's work in salvation.

PASSOVER

We've mentioned the tenth plague several times already. It is by far the most important of the plagues, and it is vital for understanding not only what is happening for Israel but also a theme that is one of the most important in all of Scripture. God told Moses that the angel of death would pass over every home in the land of Egypt and kill the firstborn son of every family. Though the Israelites had been set apart from many of the plagues, no one was exempt from this one. This was God's pinnacle act of judgment on the sin of both Israel and Egypt. However, because God was rich in grace and mercy toward Israel, He provided a means for their firstborn sons to be saved. With a very specific set of instructions, God commanded every Israelite home to sacrifice a spotless lamb and spread its blood over the doorposts. As the angel of death passed over the home, he would spare the firstborn son if blood covered the home; if not, however, the angel of death would kill the firstborn son. On the night of Passover, Israel's firstborn sons were spared, and Egypt's were killed, including Pharaoh's. This final plague sent Pharaoh to the brink, and he sent Israel away from Egypt. Every year after this event, Israel celebrated the Passover in remembrance of God's salvation from the punishment of sin and death.

The idea of a spotless lamb covering the sins of God's people is highlighted in the Passover. This isn't the first time the blood of a lamb signifies a salvific act, and it certainly won't be the last moving forward. From Exodus on, the biblical authors will highlight this theme of a spotless lamb that can cover sin. The problem, however, is that no lamb could perfectly cover the sin of Israel, which is why they needed to make sacrifices on a regular basis. The spotless lamb highlighted in the Passover is a foreshadowing of a spotless lamb who will come as a once and for all sacrifice. Jesus is the spotless lamb who came and covered sin for all time, but we still have much more of the story to go before we get to Him.

PASSING THROUGH THE SEA

The importance of Israel passing through the Red Sea may not be initially apparent, but it's quite a significant part of the story. Think about it: even though the Passover made the final distinction between those who are God's people and those who are not, Israel wasn't in the clear just because of the Passover—they still need to get out of Egypt so they can get to the land God promised Abraham and his descendants. Even after losing his own son, Pharaoh regrets allowing Israel to leave and decides to chase after them. Pharaoh and his army chase Israel all the way to the bank of the Red Sea, where Israel immediately complains to Moses and accuses him of bringing them into the wilderness to die. They complained to Moses because he brought them out of slavery; imagine that! They had already forgotten the miraculous event of the Passover.

In His final act of grace and mercy to complete the Exodus event, God parts the Red Sea and allows Israel to pass through on dry ground. In Hebrew literature, the "sea" is often associated with abyss or death. So, whereas Israel should have died passing through the waters of the Red Sea, God allowed them to live. Whereas they normally wouldn't be able to pass through to the other side, God allowed them to pass through and led them to live in his presence. In contrast, God caused the waters of the sea to crash in on the Egyptians, and they all died. Passing through the waters proved to be life for God's people, and death for those who are not. This idea of "passing through the waters of death" is one that is important to remember going forward. Yes, Israel's sin had been covered by the spotless lamb, but they also needed to pass through the waters of death in order to experience life. The New Testament authors will use this idea of "waters of death" and apply it directly to baptism.

EXODUS AS SALVATION

There is no one element of the Exodus that perfectly represents God's saving work. When taken as a whole, however, the Exodus is the most salvific event in the Old Testament. It shows God's love for His people, His mercy and grace, His judgment of sin, and His plan to save a people for His pleasure to bring them into His presence. Moving forward, the biblical authors point back to the Exodus as the chief event and example of God's salvation. Israel is meant to remember how Yahweh saved them from Egypt, but Exodus also points us forward to a much greater salvific work seen most clearly in the person and work of Jesus Christ.

In your group, reflect on the following questions:

1. What stands out to you most about these passages?

2. What is something new you learned about this chapter (and the surrounding context) and its importance to the overall story of Scripture?

3. What themes or ideas above help you think well about the Exodus?

Model the Word

1. Take time for each member to explain the importance of one aspect of the Exodus story.

2. How would you teach these passages to someone else? What aspects or ideas would you emphasize?

Share the Word

1. Think about reading the story of the Exodus from the perspective of an unbeliever. How could you use this story to share the gospel or begin a gospel conversation? How can the ideas the Exodus be helpful to you as you share the gospel with others?

2. Why is it helpful and important to understand the Exodus in light of the whole story of the Bible?

Pray the Word

1. As a group, spend time praying for each other to have a better understanding of God's Word.

2. Thank God for His faithfulness to save and redeem His people. Thank Him that He has saved and redeemed you with a mighty arm and outstretched hand through Jesus Christ.

3. Pray for opportunities to share the gospel with others. Pray that God will give you boldness to share with those in your family and at your job.

Daily Bible Reading

Day 1: John 17-18
Day 2: John 19-20
Day 3: John 21
Day 4: 1 John 1-2
Day 5: 1 John 3-4

24. Law

Know the Word

Read Exodus 19:1-20:21

1. What do you see? (Observation)

2. What does it mean? (Interpretation)

3. What do you do? (Application)

4. How should you pray?

Two weeks ago, we looked at several of the major covenants in the Old Testament. One of those, the Mosaic covenant is particularly important because it's the Mosaic covenant that establishes the formal and legal relationship between God and Israel. It's through this relationship that Israel receives God's law. This week, we'll look at what the law is and why it is so important for both Old and New Testaments. Understanding the law and its place in Scripture is key for moving forward in the story. Thinking wrongly about God's law can lead to thinking wrongly about many other aspects of the Bible. However, thinking rightly about God's law, its importance to all of Scripture, and how it applies to Christians today will help you connect the dots between the first five books of the Bible and the New Testament.

Have you ever started a plan to help you read through the Bible, gotten to the second half of Exodus, into Leviticus, and found yourself suddenly confused, puzzled, and maybe even bored? Let's be honest: once we get to Exodus 19-20 and God gives Israel his laws, things get kind of weird. And certain sections can be mind-numbing to read through. Some laws, like those in the Ten Commandments, make sense, and we still refer to them and abide by them today. On the other hand, commands like the ones found in Leviticus 19:19 can be outright confusing: "You shall keep my statutes. You shall not let your cattle breed with a different kind. You shall not sow your field with two kinds of seed, nor shall you wear a garment of cloth made of two kinds of material" (ESV). I imagine you're wearing clothes right now that are made out of more than one type of material. Are you in sin? Are you disobedient to the commands of the Bible?

Ultimately, the questions we must ask are these: What is law as presented in the Bible? Do the laws of the Mosaic covenant apply to New Testament believers? Should we follow all the laws or only some? Were some laws only meant for the people of Israel? How do we go about picking and choosing the laws we should follow in the New Testament? Just as a disclaimer: these are weighty questions. Time and space won't allow me to cover how everyone has gone about answering those questions (and, if you're honest, you don't want to read all of that). The goal for today is to help you think through biblical law in such a way that it helps your understanding of the whole story of the Bible.

WHAT IS BIBLICAL LAW?[1]

Let's start with the word *law*. What does that mean in our modern context? Law is the system of written rules which a particular country or community recognizes as regulating the actions of its members and which it may enforce by the imposition of penalties. That's a pretty standard definition. The written law may be such that it is illegal not to wear a seatbelt while driving a car. If one is caught without a seatbelt on while driving, that person will face the penalty stated

---

[1] Much of the information and ideas from this lesson were either influenced by or came directly from The Bible Project's work on biblical law. You can find more from them at thebibleproject.com.

by the written law (usually a fine for a certain amount of money). Legislative bodies pass written laws, and the written laws are called *statutes*. Societies that abide by statutes can be called *statutory law* societies.

In statutory law societies, all the laws are written and recorded, so if someone violates the law the courts can look at the written law to make a judgment. Ideally, the laws are written clearly enough so that there is minimal interpretation needed; therefore, judges can rule straightforwardly. If the person was not, in fact, wearing his seatbelt, for whatever reason, he deserves punishment according to the law; it is not up to the judge to interpret why the individual wasn't wearing his seatbelt. The law is clear. America, as you probably recognize, is a statutory law society. Interestingly, however, statutory law societies are relatively new in relation to all societies in world history, especially those in the Old Testament.

Israel, and most (if not all) of the nations surrounding them, was a customary or common law society. In a common law society, there is no strict written code to which authorities or rulers look to make legal decisions. Rather, judges rule according to the principles or ideals of a community. Whereas statutory law societies enact consistent punishments according to a written law (meaning the seatbelt fine is always $25), common law societies don't have a consistent set of standards by which to enact punishments and enforce laws. Instead, judges use subjective interpretation supported by context, testimony, etc.

"But wait," you might object, "Israel's written laws are found in the Old Testament! Isn't that a written code by which they ruled and judged?" Well, not exactly. Let's look at what is going on with those laws. According to Jewish tradition, there are 613 laws found in the first five books of the Bible, which are called the Torah (Genesis, Exodus, Leviticus, Numbers, and Deuteronomy). You may have heard that word before. Often, Torah gets translated as "law," but it actually means to instruct, to teach, to guide. This is a critical distinction. As 21st century Americans, we naturally think about the term "law" within the context of our statutory law system. If we read the Torah with our modern assumptions about law, we'll miss the point of what God wants us to understand as we read through these books.

Think about it: if the only purpose of the Torah is to provide laws, restrictions, and punishments, then it wouldn't make much sense for Genesis to be considered part of "the law." There are no real laws for Israel to follow until Exodus 20. The entirety of the Torah is to provide teaching and instruction to the reader. This is true even of the "laws" God gives to Israel. They are guidelines toward ideals, not necessarily hard and fast rules. The 613 commands are to guide and instruct Israel in the way they should live as a people set apart for God's glory and the blessing to the nations. Now, that may sound strange and even wrong at first glance, but examples are provided below to show how this works. Remember, Israel was a customary or common law society; therefore, when judges made rulings, they didn't look to the 613 commands to see exactly how and if someone violated a specific command, they judged the person based on whether or not they violated the ideals the commands were aimed at meeting. As you read through the Torah, remember that our modern legal context is vastly different from that of ancient Israel. This distinction alone will significantly help you understand the law better, but we shouldn't stop there.

LAW AS COVENANTAL PARTNERSHIP

Why 613? Were those all the laws Israel had? Could Israel really only have 613 laws to instruct them for every part of their society? Those are great questions! The answer is no; those were not all of the laws Israel lived and operated by as a society. The biblical authors are very intentional with how they craft and tell the story of Israel's history. Without getting too convoluted, there are 611 commands in the Torah that fit "thou shall" or "thou shall not." These are explicit commands. God explicitly instructs Israel what to do and what not to do. According to rabbinic tradition, there are two implicit commands that God gives Israel. An implicit command is one that is implied but not plainly expressed. The first is "I am the LORD your God, who brought you out of the land of Egypt, out of the house of slavery" (Exodus 20:2). The implicit command is that one must believe the LORD God to be the God of salvation, the one who created everything, the one who is worthy of love and adoration. The second implicit command is in the Shema, "Hear, O Israel: The LORD our God, the LORD is one" (Deuteronomy 6:4). Again, the implicit command is to believe and confesses the LORD is both the creating and saving God, and that He is one. Add the two implicit commands to the explicit commands, and we arrive at 613 laws.

In Hebrew, the letters of the alphabet are also numbers; each letter has a numerical value. That may seem odd, but the Romans used letters as numbers, which we call Roman numerals today. The Hebrew word "Torah" is comprised of four Hebrew letters. When the numerical value of those letters is added together, you get 611, which is how many explicit commands are in the Torah. Coincidence? Absolutely not (hopefully you're starting to see how deliberate and intentional the biblical authors were as they put this book together; examples like this are all over the Old Testament). Add the two implicit ones and there are 613 commands to instruct and guide Israel, but for what? This is where the covenantal partnership comes in.

The commands in the Torah were not meant to be a "law code" for Israel as a society in the same way we have laws that regulate what we can and can't do in a statutory law society. The commands were the stipulations of a covenant. Remember, a covenant is a contract or agreement which binds two parties together. In the Bible, God enters into covenants for the blessing and benefit of humanity, and, in return, He expects humanity to uphold their end of the agreement, which is expressed by faithful obedience. In this case, God enters into a specific covenant with a specific group of people. If Israel is to be a royal priesthood, a holy nation, and a blessing to all other nations, they have to follow these commands. While some of the commands do affect Israel as a society, they are not meant to be holistic in governing Israel as a society. These commands or "laws" are terms of the covenantal agreement between God and Israel. And, remember, the commands are at aimed at ideals that God desires Israel to live by. Let's look at a few examples to elucidate this idea.

LAW IN THE OLD TESTAMENT

There are many ways to separate the commands of the Torah into different categories. One of the most popular approaches divides the commands into the (1) moral, (2) civil, and (3) ceremonial. According to this approach, the moral commands are for all people for all time; the civil commands governed how Israel was to live as a society; and the ceremonial laws were religious practices particular to Israel. In my estimation, this approach can be helpful, but it misses both the heart of the Torah and its usefulness for Christians today. The approach below is not the only way to think about the commands of the Torah, but I've found it quite helpful.

Rather than thinking about the law as a strict set of rules, some of which are applicable today and some that are not, a better approach may be thinking about them in categories of ideals. All 613 laws can be categorized under the heading of some sort of biblical ideal, which means that obeying the commands themselves is not the ultimate aim. The commands are meant to help Israel be set apart from the nations, trust God, and worship Him in faith. Each law points toward a bigger and more important form of worship and obedience that God desires from His people. We don't have the space to look at all of the ideals the laws point toward, but let's look at a few. Many of the commands in the Torah are about calendar, festivals, holidays, and important religious dates. How can those possibly be useful for New Testament believers? Well, all of the commands concerning the calendar point toward the ideal of the sabbath. What is the sabbath? Most simply, it's a day of rest, but, in the Old Testament, it was more than just a day for people to relax. The sabbath was a day for Israel to look back to creation in worship and praise of God, but it was also a day for Israel to look forward to the future rest they would have with God for eternity. The Scripture recounts how God used six days to create the universe and everything in it and He rested on the seventh day after His work was complete. The number seven symbolizes completion, perfection, and rest in God. Interestingly, all the holidays in the Old Testament are based on patterns of seven. Holidays either take place on the seventh day of the week, for seven days, in the seventh month, or on the seventh year.

The Passover, for example, is a seven-day festival that started the first month of the Israelite calendar. Seven months later, in the seventh month of the year, there are all kinds of important Jewish dates and events, like the Day of Atonement. Every seven years, the Israelites were supposed to allow the land to rest. And every 50 years, they were supposed to celebrate Jubilee, a time when all debts were forgiven and slaves were allowed to return to their land.

Jubilee happened on the 50th year because it was a sabbath of sabbaths. Seven rounds of letting the land rest on the seventh year makes 49 years (7x7—a completion of completions); therefore, the 50th year was a huge celebration that was meant to cause Israel to remember the rest they were supposed to have in God and look forward to the day where they could experience eternal rest and forgiveness. So, when God gives the commands about the calendar, is He just fascinated with the number seven, or is He causing Israel to think about and reflect upon a higher ideal, the ideal of sabbath? The calendar laws pointed toward a greater reality and were meant to cause Israel to reflect on God and desire the future rest He promised.

As you read through the law, you will notice that a lot of the commands are about being clean or unclean. In other words, these commands differentiate between that which is holy and unholy or that which is pure and impure. These are the holiness or purity laws. We can easily mistake some of these laws as arbitrary if we don't remain focused on the ideals of holiness and purity. Next week we'll look at the importance of holiness in the tabernacle/temple, but think back to Genesis 1-2. The garden was special because it's where people could dwell in the presence of God. If man and woman were going to stay in God's presence, they had to remain holy (set apart) or pure. That didn't happen, and God kicked them out of the garden because sin and impurity can't be in the presence of God.

Only one thing can make people holy or pure—that's God. Many things, however, can make people impure. Touching dead bodies, eating non-kosher food, skin conditions, hair and beard conditions, having a child, menstrual cycles, and many other things are listed as causing impurity, which resulted in people having to spend time outside of the camp. Some of these things may seem a bit absurd today, but the commands were not arbitrary. God was serious about His holiness, and He demanded that His people be holy as well. The purity laws, then, were not meant to cause people to suffer needlessly or always be worried about having a skin condition but to amplify both the holiness of God and the necessity to be pure in His presence.

The last ideal we'll look at is sacrifice (these aren't the only three, but are important ones that will help you think about the law). So much of the Levitical law concentrates on how Israel was to go about making sacrifices, often in gory detail. From bulls to rams to birds and lambs, God had very specific instructions about the process of sacrifice. From what we've studied to this point, the overall purpose of sacrifice should be clear. Because of sin, humans deserve death and punishment. Rather than killing humans each time they sinned, God allowed them to sacrifice animals on their behalf. The death humans deserved was transferred to the animal, and the animal's blood covered the people's sin and was a pleasing aroma to God.

An animal, however, could never wholly cover the sin of a human, which is why the sacrifices had to be repeated consistently. God wasn't a bloodthirsty monger who enjoyed the death of His creation. He was compassionate and gracious, and provided His people a means to live and worship Him. The sacrificial laws, then, were meant to show Israel how seriously God took sin, the cost of sin, and His grace and mercy toward them despite their sin. Sacrifice was the how people could continue to prosper and be in relationship with God. It pointed toward a day when sacrifice would no longer be necessary and the need for sacrifice would find its completion in a once-for-all sacrifice.

LAW IN THE NEW TESTAMENT

The law exposes the human condition and shows how desperately we need a savior. Time and time again, Israel failed to uphold the law. When we say Israel failed at keeping the law, we need to be clear about what we mean. Many Israelites went through the motions of keeping the individual commands. By the time of Jesus, the Pharisees had gotten very good at keeping the commands, but that didn't mean they were upholding the law. While they kept the commands, they missed the ideals to which the commands pointed.

So, what were they missing? The answer is faith. God does and always has desired faithfulness from His people. In the Old Testament, Israel's faithfulness was shown by keeping the law, not the individual commands per se, but the ideals to which those commands pointed, things like sabbath, holiness, and sacrifice. When Jesus came along, He didn't come to get rid of the old system; He came to fulfill it (Matt. 5:17-20). He perfectly met all the ideals which the law pointed toward. He was faithful; He was holy; He found his rest in God alone; He understood sacrifice and what that meant for Him and His ministry. Think about it: in several instances, Jesus tells people that the law is actually much more complicated and harder to keep than they think. Whereas murder used to mean killing someone, under Jesus it means hating someone in your heart. Whereas adultery used to mean cheating on your husband or wife, under Jesus it means lusting after someone in your heart. Under Christ, the laws become much harder. Paul refers to this as the law of Christ (Galatians 6:2; 1 Corinthians 9:21).

Since the law of Christ is even harder than that of the old covenant, how can humans possibly keep it? Well, we can't, which is why Jesus Christ kept it on our behalf. Under the law of Christ, the driving principles are faith, hope, and love. Just as in the Torah, the greatest commandments in the New Testament are to love God and love neighbor. The ideals of the law of Christ are the same as the laws of the Torah, and Christ perfectly keeps and completes them. We'll look more at the law of Christ when we get to the New Testament portion of our study.

CONCLUSION

I know that was a lot of information, and there is so much more that we could address about the law. Hopefully, this was helpful and will lead you to learn more about biblical law and how it affects your walk with Christ. Remember these few ideas: (1) There is a major contextual difference between common/customary law and statutory law; the law in the Torah is the former, and our modern Western/American law is the latter. (2) The Torah is not a complete collection of Israel's laws as a society, but are the terms of the agreement between God and Israel in their covenantal partnership. (3) The laws in the Old Testament can be grouped under certain ideals that God wanted Israel to strive toward and remember, some of which are sabbath, holiness, and sacrifice. (4) Jesus Christ does not abolish Old Testament law, rather He fulfills it, and we now live under the law of Christ, which is driven by the principles of faith, hope, and love.

In your group, reflect on the following questions:

1. What stands out to you most about Exodus 19-20?

2. What is something new you learned about these chapters and their importance to the overall story of Scripture?

3. What themes or ideas above help you think well about these chapters?

Model the Word

1. Take time for each member to explain the importance of biblical law and how it can help in reading and understanding the Old Testament.

2. How would you teach Exodus 19-20 to someone else? What aspects or ideas would you emphasize?

Share the Word

1. Think about reading these chapters from the perspective of an unbeliever. How could you use them to share the gospel or begin a gospel conversation? How can the idea of the law be helpful to you as you share the gospel with others?

2. Why is it helpful to understand God's law and His relationship with Israel? How does Jesus fulfill the law?

Pray the Word

1. As a group, spend time praying for each other to have a better understanding of God's Word.

2. Thank God for His law. Thank him that Jesus Christ fulfilled the law and because of Him we can have salvation.

3. Pray for opportunities to share the gospel with others. Pray that God will give you boldness to share with those in your family and at your job.

Daily Bible Reading

Day 1: 1 John 5
Day 2: 2 John
Day 3: 3 John
Day 4: Revelation 1-2
Day 5: Revelation 3-4

25. Temple/Tabernacle

Know the Word
Read 2 Chronicles: 2:1-18; 5:7-14; 7:1-3

1. What do you see? (Observation)

2. What does it mean? (Interpretation)

3. What do you do? (Application)

4. How should you pray?

Last week we learned about biblical law, how it was used in the Old Testament, and how Christians should think about it today. This week we'll look at the major concepts of temple and tabernacle. You'll learn about these two ideas and the role they play in the Old Testament. You will also learn why the temple and tabernacle are themes that are crucial for understanding the overall story of Scripture. The idea of temple/tabernacle is one that runs right through the Bible, beginning to end. Let's see how these themes work.

TEMPLE/TABERNACLE

To understand how these themes operate, we first need to define what exactly the temple and tabernacle were and what the differences and similarities were between them. In the Old Testament, temples and tabernacles were places for people to worship various gods. For Israel, they were places to worship Yahweh, the one true God, and it was the tabernacle that came first. After the Exodus from Egypt, Israel received God's law at Mount Sinai. As Moses was on the mountain, God instructed him to build a tabernacle. The tabernacle was about half the size of the future temple, and it was made out of lighter and different materials. Why? Because Israel needed it to be portable. Remember, when Israel was at Sinai, they were on the long journey to the land God promised them. It would be pretty impractical to build a temple every time they had to move camp, so God gave them a tabernacle they could easily transport.

The temple was much bigger, more elaborate, and, most importantly, permanent. The permanence of the temple is crucial because once it was established in the land, God promised Israel it wasn't going to move. If the temple didn't move, God didn't move, because God's presence was equated with the temple/tabernacle (we'll cover this idea more fully below). When the temple was destroyed, Israel sincerely felt like God had abandoned them because of the close connection between God's presence and the temple. Both temple and tabernacle were where God's presence dwelt, both had specific instructions for who could enter certain areas, both allowed for sacrifice and worship, and both were instrumentally vital to Israel's faith.

THE MEETING PLACE BETWEEN HEAVEN AND EARTH

A helpful way to think about the temple is that it is the location in the Old Testament where heaven and earth most often meet. Think of heaven and earth as two different "spaces" or "dimensions" (stick with me here; it should make more sense in a bit). We understand earth pretty well. It's the space we live in every day. There are land and water, trees, flowers, animals, and people, among other things. Sometimes the earth space is beautiful—like a sunset over the ocean or a mountain range with snowcapped peaks. The earth's beauty is also present in relationships between people—someone helping another in need, caring for the poor, orphan, or widow. Sometimes the earth space is ugly—like an area ravaged by hurricanes, oil spills in the ocean, or massive forest fires. Earth's ugliness also shows up among people—poverty-stricken villages, disease, war, racism, and death. Although the earth has hints of beauty in accordance with how God created the world, sin causes the earth space to be harmful, evil, and unholy.

What about heaven space? What is that like? Most people probably think of heaven as being a place one goes after death, the place where God lives. Heaven has been skewed by our cultural context to be a place with angels floating in clouds, endless buffet lines where you never get full, unlimited football where everyone wins, and the pleasures we want most in life, basically like living at an eternal resort. That's not heaven at all (I mean, God definitely is there, but hear me out)! Heaven is heaven because it's where the presence of God is. When the biblical authors give us insight to "where God is," they often use the imagery of a throne room (Isaiah 6, Revelation 7). In the throne room of heaven, wherever that is, God is present. There is no sin, no shame, no death. In God's presence, there are no effects of sin because there is no sin. Sinful things can't be in the presence of God.

Let's review: in the earth space there is lots of sin, and in the heaven space there isn't and can't be sin. Therefore, heaven space and earth space can't coexist in the same place. Either the earth space has to become holy, or the heaven space has to become unholy. How, then, will God and humans ever be in relationship if these two spaces can't overlap? That's a great question! Think of heaven space as a circle and earth space as a circle. The two can't perfectly overlap, but that doesn't mean they can't touch. Throughout Scripture, we see God come into the earth space without becoming unholy, and that's because the holiness of God is such that it can make anything around it holy. But the problem with God's holiness is that it is kind of like the sun: if sinful beings get too close, they will die. Sinners have to keep their distance (think of Moses at the burning bush). The point where heaven and earth meet is in God's presence on earth. In the Old Testament, God desired to be among His people, but they were sinful, and if they got too close to Him, they would die. Therefore, God created a means by which sinful people could live in proximity to His presence, worshipping and obeying Him. His solution: the tabernacle and the temple.

In both the tabernacle and temple, there was a cube-shaped room where the presence of God dwelt all the time—the holy of holies. Because of the sinfulness of humanity, no one except for the high priest could go into God's presence once a year, and even the high priest could die if he didn't do it correctly. Although this wasn't an ideal situation, it provided Israel relationship, fellowship, and the ability to worship their God. His presence served as their rest, comfort, protection, and salvation. His presence was meant to be the center of their lives, which is why, as Israel camped in the wilderness, they had very specific instructions to build the camp around the tabernacle. It was a sign that the presence of God was at the center of their existence and worship. As mentioned earlier, the tabernacle was always on the move, but when Solomon built the temple, it served as a permanent location for God's people to dwell in His presence.

The temple, however, was never meant to be the ultimate aim or location where heaven and earth met. The only reason there needed to be a temple was because of sin. At creation, God's people dwelt freely in His presence. Adam and Eve were naked and unashamed; they walked and talked with God. The tabernacle and temple were only necessary when sin entered into the world so that God's people could dwell in His presence without dying, although not as they could have in the Garden of Eden. God's presence in the temple wasn't the goal; it pointed to a greater, future reality when God's people could once again dwell in God's presence for eternity, with no dividing wall and no chance to sin. Let's very briefly look at how this works in the Bible.

THE GARDEN OF EDEN AND THE PRESENCE OF GOD

Eden was special primarily because it's where the presence of God was. It was a garden-temple. The unique aspect of this garden-temple was that there were no barriers between people and God because there was no sin. The garden was plentiful and beautiful; it provided everything Adam and Eve needed to flourish. The biblical authors repeatedly draw their reader's attention back to the Garden of Eden. The tabernacle and temple themselves were designed and decorated in such a way as to cause them to, in many ways, reflect a garden, with trees, leaves, flowers, etc. Once God kicked Adam and Eve out of the garden, He placed the cherubim at the east entrance with a flaming sword to keep them from coming back. The tabernacle and temple also faced east, and depictions of cherubim were used to decorate both structures, not simply for the sake of decoration, but to cause Israel to think back to the Garden of Eden and long for the day when they once again would be in a garden-temple with God.

THE TABERNACLE AND THE PRESENCE OF GOD

Once the construction of the tabernacle was complete, Moses writes:

[34] Then the cloud covered the tent of meeting, and the glory of the LORD filled the tabernacle. [35] And Moses was not able to enter the tent of meeting because the cloud settled on it, and the glory of the LORD filled the tabernacle. [36] Throughout all their journeys, whenever the cloud was taken up from over the tabernacle, the people of Israel would set out. [37] But if the cloud was not taken up, then they did not set out till the day that it was taken up. [38] For the cloud of the LORD was on the tabernacle by day, and fire was in it by night, in the sight of all the house of Israel throughout all their journeys (Exodus 40:34-38).

The presence of God is frequently depicted as a cloud or as fire. When you see later references to clouds or fire (as we'll see below), it should cause you to think about the presence of God in the tabernacle or temple and why the author is using those images. This doesn't mean that every time clouds or fire are mentioned it refers to the presence of God, but often it does.

THE TEMPLE AND THE PRESENCE OF GOD

The importance of the temple in connection with the presence of God should be clear by now. In the passages for this week, the author of Chronicles records the building and dedication of Solomon's temple. Notice how in chapter five, a cloud fills the temple once the ark of the covenant enters, and how fire from heaven comes down after Solomon dedicates the temple. These are direct references to God's presence in the temple and among His people. King Solomon reigned roughly from 970-931 BCE, so the temple was built during that time (1 Kings 6), and it was destroyed by King Nebuchadnezzar of Babylon in 587 BCE (2 Kings 25). It lasted about 370 years, which, in comparison to the length of Israel's history, wasn't great. After their exile, Israel longed for a time when the temple would be rebuilt, and they would be back in God's presence.

King Cyrus of Persia allowed some of the Israelites in exile to return to Jerusalem to rebuild the temple and worship God. The books Ezra and Nehemiah record the Israelites returning to rebuild the temple and city wall. Upon laying the foundation for the new temple, many rejoiced; however, the elders who had seen Solomon's temple wept, because the new temple was nothing in comparison to the old, which leads us to an interesting point in the story. Although Israel built a new temple, which lasted until 70 CE, they desired a greater temple, a place for God to dwell among his people as in the days of Solomon's temple. They desired the type of temple described in Ezekiel 40-48 (I highly recommend you check these chapters out).

Ezekiel had a vision of a new and future temple. While space doesn't allow me to go into much detail, Ezekiel saw a glorious temple like one not known before. The glory of God filled this temple, and it was a place where all people could come and worship Him. In chapter 47, Ezekiel describes water dripping out from the temple. The water formed a stream, and then a river, which became massive and eventually flowed into the Dead Sea. As the river flowed, it brought everything to life on both sides—flowers, plants, trees, fruit, and animals. What Ezekiel describes is very much like a garden coming to life by waters of life flowing from the temple, which is filled with the glory of God. We see the idea of a future garden-temple that was present in Eden. Here's the problem: the second, depressing temple was nothing like what Ezekiel describes. So, when, if at all, will we see Ezekiel's temple? Here's where this theme starts to get really neat.

JESUS AND THE PRESENCE OF GOD

In John chapter 1, John writes about the eternal Son of God taking on human flesh: "And the Word became flesh and dwelt among us, and we have seen his glory, glory as of the only Son from the Father, full of grace and truth" (John 1:14). The Greek word that is translated "dwelt" means "to have one's tent, encamp, have a tabernacle." Therefore, the verse could literally and faithfully be translated, "And the Word became flesh and tabernacled among us." Now, any reader with a basic knowledge of the theme of tabernacle or temple will immediately understand the point John is making. Whereas the fullness of the glory of God was once veiled, hidden in the holy of holies, the fulness of the glory of God is now present and active in the person of Jesus Christ. Whereas humans once couldn't come close to the tabernacle because they were unclean and would die, the glory of God has now come close to make them clean and provide life. The presence of God is on full display in the person of Jesus Christ.

THE CHURCH AND THE PRESENCE OF GOD

In Acts 2, the Apostles received the Holy Spirit, which Jesus promised them in John 14-16. Luke writes:

[1]When the day of Pentecost arrived, they were all together in one place. [2]And suddenly there came from heaven a sound like a mighty rushing wind, and it filled the entire house where they were sitting. [3]And divided tongues as of fire appeared to them and rested on each of them. [4]And they were all filled with the Holy Spirit and began to speak in other tongues as the Spirit gave them utterance (Acts 2:1-4).

Luke uses quite intentional language of "a mighty rushing wind" and "tongues as of fire" to cause the reader to think about the presence of God. The Holy Spirit, the third person of the Trinity, the very presence of God, is no longer in a tabernacle or temple; rather, because of Christ, the presence of God is within his people. And through the work of the Holy Spirit, the nations are being reached with the gospel. God is building a new temple—the body of Christ—and He is doing it through His presence among His people.

ETERNITY AND THE PRESENCE OF GOD

In Revelation 21-22, John sees a vision of the new heaven and new earth, in which God's people will dwell with Him for eternity. At one point, he sees new Jerusalem coming out of the sky, but he describes it in very odd terms. Essentially, he describes a beautiful city that is as wide as it is long as it is deep, which is a cube. Now, I don't think John means the new heaven and new earth will be a cube; instead, John is forcing us to think about the presence of God throughout Scripture. The holy of holies was a cube, and it was the place where heaven and earth met. In the future, John says, the presence of God will no longer be veiled or restricted because of sin. Rather, God's presence will always be with his people. Heaven and earth will meet fully and wonderfully in eternity.

This is how John concludes:

²²And I saw no temple in the city, for its temple is the Lord God the Almighty and the Lamb. ²³And the city has no need of sun or moon to shine on it, for the glory of God gives it light, and its lamp is Lamb. ²⁴By its light the nations walk, and the kings of the earth will bring their glory into it, ²⁵and its gates will never be shut by day—and there will be no night there. ²⁶They will bring into it the glory and the honor of the nations. ²⁷But nothing unclean will ever enter it, nor anyone who does what is detestable or false, but only those who are written in the Lamb's book of life.

¹Then the angel showed me the river of the water of life, bright as crystal, flowing from the throne of God and of the Lamb ²through the middle of the street of the city; also, on either side of the river, the tree of life with its twelve kind of fruit, yielding its fruit each month. The leaves of the tree were for the healing of the nations. ³No longer will there be anything accursed, but the throne of God and of the Lamb will be in it, and his servants will worship him. ⁴They will see his face, and his name will be on their foreheads. And night will be no more. They will need no light of lamp or sun, for the Lord God will be their light, and they will reign forever and ever (Revelation 21:22-22:4).

Amen.

In your group, reflect on the following questions:

1. What stands out to you most about these passages from 2 Chronicles?

2. What is something new you learned from these chapters and their importance to the overall story of Scripture?

3. What themes or ideas above help you think well about these chapters?

Model the Word

1. Take time for each member to explain the importance of the temple/tabernacle and how it can help in reading and understanding the Old Testament.

2. How would you teach these passages from 2 Chronicles to someone else? What aspects or ideas would you emphasize? How could the theme of temple/tabernacle help teach these passages?

Share the Word

1. Think about reading these chapters from the perspective of an unbeliever. How could you use them to share the gospel or begin a gospel conversation? How can the idea of the temple/tabernacle be helpful to you as you share the gospel with others?

2. Why is it helpful to understand the role of temple/tabernacle throughout the Scripture? How can you use the idea of the presence of God as you share the gospel?

Pray the Word

1. As a group, spend time praying for each other to have a better understanding of God's Word.

2. Thank God for salvation, and that, as believers, we have the presence of God in us by the Holy Spirit.

3. Pray for opportunities to share the gospel with others. Pray that God will give you boldness to share with those in your family and at your job.

Daily Bible Reading

Day 1: Revelation 5-6
Day 2: Revelation 7-8

26. Kingdom of God

Know the Word
Read 2 Samuel 7:1-17

1. What do you see? (Observation)

2. What does it mean? (Interpretation)

3. What do you do? (Application)

4. How should you pray?

Last week we learned about the temple and tabernacle, the role they played in the Old Testament, the importance of the presence of God, and what value these themes have for us today. This week, we'll learn about the theme of the kingdom. Kingdom, or "the kingdom of God," is one of the most important themes in the biblical story. Kingdom is crucial because it is one of the themes we can use to help interpret the metanarrative of the Bible. What is metanarrative? A metanarrative is an overarching account or interpretation of a story. The Bible is one big story comprised of many smaller stories. One of the difficulties in reading the Bible is that it can be challenging to connect the smaller stories to the larger whole. How do the prophets connect to Jesus or Paul? In what ways does the life of David help us understand what goes on with the disciples? Without metanarrative, seeing the connections can be a struggle.

Themes, such as kingdom, help make sense of the larger story and provide a framework to build the story around. Another way to think about kingdom is like the lenses on glasses. Once you put the glasses on, they help you see more clearly. Lenses are a tool to help make sense of the world around you but are not the world itself. Biblical themes are the same way. Kingdom is a tool to help see and understand the Bible more clearly, but kingdom is not the biblical story itself. Nor is kingdom the only framework or lens you can use; it is just one of the more prominent ones. The theme of covenant, which we looked at a few weeks ago, is another one of the major themes theologians have used to help interpret the metanarrative of Scripture. Neither approach is wrong. Each emphasizes particular aspects, and both have tremendous value. Some approaches combine major themes like kingdom and covenant into an integrated whole, which is likely the most helpful strategy. Overarching themes like kingdom and covenant are not in competition; rather, they work together to allow readers to see the big picture and main ideas of the biblical story.

Many of the themes we've learned about to this point fit under the larger theme of kingdom. For example, the ideas of temple and tabernacle only make sense within the kingdom (we'll see why below). Law, although vital, can only be rightly understood in light of kingdom (and covenant). You may be thinking: "If this is so important, why don't we talk about it more?" There are many possible reasons, but here are a few: First, as westerners in the 21st century, we simply don't look at the world through the lens of kingdom. We have presidents and elected officials, who, technically, are supposed to be held responsible by the electing body for their actions. In a kingdom, the king answers to no one and can largely do as he pleases. The ideas of kings and kingdoms may appear silly and outdated to the modern mind. Second, and related to the first, as Christians, we are so far removed from the world and context of the Bible, it's easy for us to take the Bible out of context and overlay the political, socioeconomic, and cultural environment of the 21st century, which leads us to think about kingdom negatively. Third, we don't talk about the theme of kingdom enough. Kingdom is not an idea unique to the Old Testament. The New Testament authors were keenly aware of the importance of the kingdom of God and their place within it. Let's look at how this theme works in the Bible.

WHAT IS KINGDOM?

When you think of kingdom, maybe elaborate and beautiful castles come to mind, or possibly shiny armored knights on horses protecting the kingdom from intruders. You may think of a large number of peasants who are forced to do the will of an evil king. Whatever you think of when you think about kingdom is likely influenced by how Hollywood has portrayed them on screen, or how authors and artists have depicted them in children's books. Many things can be in a kingdom, but there are only a few elements necessary for kingdoms to exist.

First, there must be land or somewhere for the kingdom to be. Second, there must be a ruler or king. And third, there must be people who are under the king's rule and protection. Without land, a ruler, and people to rule, there can't be a kingdom. Now, that may seem painfully obvious, but it's crucial to be able to identify these three essential elements when thinking about the kingdom of God in Scripture. As you read through the Bible, the form of the kingdom changes, but there is always a place, a people, and a king.

Although a place, people, and a king are necessary for a kingdom, that doesn't mean those three things define the kingdom of God. The kingdom of God is God's sovereign reign and rule over all creation. In the New Testament, the kingdom of God is also referred to as the kingdom of heaven. Defining the kingdom in this way may seem simplistic at first. Using the three criteria for kingdom, we can say God is the king, humans are His people, and all of creation is the kingdom. In one sense, thinking about the kingdom of God this way is correct. We can say the kingdom of God is already here. Jesus Christ defeated sin and death, He rose from the dead, and He is seated at the right hand of the Father, ruling from where he is now. The spiritual battle is won. However, you can look around the world today at all of the sinfulness and brokenness, and find it hard to think God's kingdom is here in any real way. That's because, in another sense, the kingdom is not yet how it will be one day. There is still a battle of the flesh. We believe that Jesus Christ will return to defeat sin and death ultimately, to create the new heavens and new earth, and dwell with his people forever. Therefore, we can think about the kingdom of God using the terms already/not yet. This already/not yet terminology is helpful when thinking through many topics, particularly the kingdom of God. The kingdom of God is already present but is not yet how it will be one day.

It's at this point we need to think well about the theme of the kingdom of God, or we may get sidetracked and this theme can become unhelpful. At a certain point in Israel's history, they had a kingdom in the classical sense. There was a king (David), a people (Israel), and a place (the promised land). If we misinterpret the kingdom of God, we may be prone to think that particular form of the kingdom was the ultimate goal. It was not. The kingdom of Israel pointed to a greater reality of a coming kingdom: the kingdom of God. Remember, the form of the kingdom changes, but the criteria do not. The kingdom of God is his sovereign rule and reign over all creation. We can't confuse the kingdom of God with any kingdom of man or equate the kingdom of God with castles, buildings, temples, etc. Let's see how the kingdom is presented throughout the Scriptures. We'll look at different times in Scripture when God is with his people. We'll use the three criteria of a kingdom and examine in what ways these instances represent the kingdom of God, and whether or not they point to a greater reality (hint: they all point to a greater reality).

THE GARDEN OF EDEN

Test question: What is the first instance of the kingdom of God the Bible? If we use kingdom in the classical sense, we may be tempted to answer Israel under the rule of King David. Remember, we are talking about the kingdom of God. So, let's try again: When is the first time in the Bible we see God ruling and reigning over creation? Answer: creation (Genesis 1-2). At creation, God, the sovereign author of life, creates humans to worship and obey Him. The humans receive the blessing of dwelling in the presence of God and being in relationship with Him. God loves humans and desires good for them. Because He is the creator, He has the authority to give the people a command, and He expects them to follow that command. At the garden of Eden, we see God's goal and desire for humanity—to worship and obey Him in the place He has prepared for them.

Is the Garden of Eden a kingdom? Let's run through the criteria. Is there a king? Yes, God is the creating king, all-powerful, and worthy to be worshiped and obeyed. He protects and blesses His people on the basis of His mercy and grace and their obedience. Are there people who are subject to the king? Yes, Adam and Eve are created by the king and subject to His authority and love. Is there a place? Yes, the Garden of Eden is the place where God's people dwell in God's presence. We have a kingdom! The Garden of Eden, however, was not the ultimate goal. The garden pointed to a day when God's people would dwell in His presence under His rule and protection without the possibility of sin. The kingdom of God at creation didn't last too long before the serpent deceived man and woman, causing them to sin, which resulted in God casting them from the garden and His presence. The Garden of Eden was a prototype for a future kingdom.

ABRAHAM

In Genesis 12, God called Abraham out of a pagan nation to follow him. God promised Abraham that He would bless him and his family for generations to come. He promised to bless Abraham and make him into a great nation that would bless all the nations of the earth.

God also promised him a land in which his people would dwell. This was a promise to reverse the effects of the fall and make a new kingdom. In this promise God makes to Abraham, is there a king? Yes, God promises to be the king of this great nation. Is there a people? Yes, God promises to make a great nation come from Abraham. Is there a place? Yes, God promises a land for His people to dwell in His presence, under His sovereign rule.

MOSES

In Exodus 19-40, God met with Moses at Mount Sinai after saving His people from slavery in Egypt. In response to His saving work, God called Israel to covenant faithfulness. He gave them His law, which they were compelled to obey because of the great act of grace and mercy shown to them in the Exodus and Passover. God gave Israel instructions for the tabernacle, in which His presence would dwell among His people. The tabernacle was portable because the people of Israel were not yet in the land God promised Abraham. Israel set out from Sinai toward the land of Canaan. Is there a king? Yes, God saved His people from slavery and led them out by His mighty power. He then provided them the law, which Israel was to obey with covenant faithfulness. Is there a people? Yes, the nation of Israel was God's chosen people, set apart by the law and tabernacle. God dwelt with these particular people. Is there a place? Yes, but Israel wasn't there yet. God wanted them to journey to Canaan in worship and obedience so that they could one day be in the place He had for them. The kingdom at Mount Sinai pointed to a greater kingdom.

DAVID AND SOLOMON

Under the rule of King David, all the promises of God concerning the kingdom seem to be fulfilled. God's people are in God's presence under His rule. In 2 Samuel 7:1-17, David desires to build a temple for the presence of God to dwell among his people, but God tells David that his son, Solomon, will be the one to build the temple. In verses 12-16, God makes some incredible promises to David concerning the future of the kingdom of Israel. God tells David He will:

[12]*raise up your offspring after you, who shall come from your body, and I will establish his kingdom. [13]He shall build a house for my name and I will establish the throne of his kingdom forever. [14]I will be to him a father, and he shall be to me a son. When he commits iniquity, I will discipline him with the rod of men, with the stripes of the sons of men, [15]but my steadfast love will not depart from him, as I took it from Saul, whom I put away from before you. [16]And your house and your kingdom shall be made sure forever before me. Your throne shall be established forever"* (2 Samuel 7:12-16).

If you're familiar with the story of King Solomon, David's son, he does, in fact, build a house for God's name. Solomon built the temple where God's presence dwelt, but because of Israel's repeated sinfulness, the temple was eventually destroyed, as was the kingdom. If we stop at Solomon, it would seem as though the promise God made David was broken. However, we have to remember that the story of the kingdom of God isn't at all about temples and castles, kings and queens. The kingdom of Israel pointed to a greater reality: the kingdom of God. The offspring (Genesis 3:15 should be ringing loud and clear in your mind) from the line of David wasn't Solomon. Solomon wasn't the one to establish a forever throne. Solomon wasn't a son to God. The promises in 2 Samuel 7 point to a greater reality. They point to Jesus Christ. Is there a king? Yes, David and Solomon were kings of Israel, but they failed miserably in keeping God's commands, as did all the kings. Were there people? Yes, Israel was an imperfect people under the rule of imperfect kings. Was there a place? Yes, but Israel was eventually exiled from that place, and the temple was destroyed. The kingdom of Israel pointed toward the fulfillment of the kingdom of God.

JESUS

As Jesus began his earthly ministry, he said, "The time is fulfilled, and the kingdom of God is at hand; repent and believe in the gospel" (Mark 1:15). What does it mean that the kingdom of God was at hand? Jesus clearly thought the kingdom of God had not yet been a reality on earth to this point in history. That's because Jesus, the true king, came to defeat sin and death, and provide people a way to be in His presence for eternity, which was the only way for the kingdom of God to be realized. What's so interesting about Jesus is that He was not at all what Israel expected in their Messiah or their king. They wanted a warrior to come and overthrow the government, and reestablish the kingdom of Israel. But that isn't at all what King Jesus wanted to do. Jesus' kingdom was established on the principles of love, mercy, and forgiveness. Jesus' kingdom was for the salvation of the nations.

Throughout his ministry, Jesus provided examples of what the kingdom of God was like. Jesus compared the kingdom of God to a hidden treasure (Matt. 13:44), a pearl of great price (Matt. 13:45-46), household treasures (Matt. 13:52), leaven (Matt. 13:33), a mustard seed (Matt. 13:31-32), the sprouting seed (Mk. 4:26-29), and a fishing net (Matt. 13:47-50). The kingdom of God starts small and increases exponentially over time. God's sovereign rule over all creation starts with Jesus Christ. His perfect life, death at the cross for our sin, and resurrection from the dead provide the way for his people to be forgiven of their sin. In the kingdom of God, the king is a suffering servant who provides life for His people, and He calls them to follow Him in humility and love, inviting everyone to be part of the kingdom. Is there a king? Yes, King Jesus. Is there a people? Yes, the ones He died to save. Is there a place? Already there is a place where His people go to be in his presence when they die. But the place is not yet how it will be one day in the new heavens and new earth.

THE CHURCH

As Jesus was about to ascend into heaven after His resurrection, His disciples asked him:

[6]*"Lord, will you at this time restore the kingdom to Israel?"* [7]*He said to them, "It is not for you to know the times or seasons that the Father has fixed by his own authority.* [8]*But you will receive power when the Holy Spirit has come upon you, and you will be my witnesses in Jerusalem and in all Judea and Samaria, and to the end of the earth"* (Acts 1:6-8).

Even after Jesus' resurrection, the disciples misunderstood the kingdom of God. They wanted the physical kingdom to be restored, but the kingdom of God is much greater than an earthly kingdom. Upon receiving the Holy Spirit, the disciples understood that the kingdom of God was His sovereign rule over all creation. They understood that it was God's desire for people to be saved and come under His gracious rule as king of the universe. As the church continues to grow, God's sovereign rule is spreading across the earth. Is there a king? Yes, Jesus is ruling from where He is now. Is there a people? Yes, the church, and as it grows the kingdom spreads. Is there a place? The place is already/not yet. The church is already on earth and spreading, but is not yet in the new creation as it will be one day.

ETERNITY

The book of Revelation provides us with a glimpse of the future kingdom. In Revelation 21-22, John depicts what the future kingdom will look like. Stop and read Revelation 21-22 right now (no really, read it; it's incredible!). Is there a king? Yes, it's King Jesus, and He rules for eternity. Is there a people? Yes, the church, comprised of every tribe, tongue, and nation, is in the presence of God, unblemished for eternity. Is there a place? Yes, and the place is the new heaven and new earth where righteous dwells; the people of God in the presence of God for the glory of God for eternity. The kingdom of God will be fully realized in that day, and what a day that will be!

In your group, reflect on the following questions:

1. What stands out to you most about this passage from 2 Samuel 7?

2. What is something new you learned from this chapter and its importance to the overall story of Scripture?

3. What themes or ideas above help you think well about this chapter and the idea of the kingdom of God?

Model the Word

1. Take time for each member to explain the importance of the kingdom of God and how it can help in reading and understanding both Old and New Testaments.

2. How would you teach this passage from 2 Samuel 7 to someone else? What aspects or ideas would you emphasize? How could the theme of kingdom help in teaching this passage?

Share the Word

1. Think about reading these chapters from the perspective of an unbeliever. How could you use them to share the gospel or begin a gospel conversation? How can the idea of the kingdom be helpful to you as you share the gospel with others?

2. Why is it helpful to understand the role of the kingdom of God throughout the Scripture? How can you use the idea of the kingdom as you share the gospel?

Pray the Word

1. As a group, spend time praying for each other to have a better understanding of God's Word.

2. Thank God inviting you into His kingdom. Thank Him for being a king that is loving, merciful, and gracious.

3. Pray for opportunities to share the gospel with others. Pray that God will give you boldness to share with those in your family and at your job.

Daily Bible Reading

Day 1: Revelation 15-16
Day 2: Revelation 17-18
Day 3: Revelation 19-20
Day 4: Revelation 21-22
Day 5: Mark 1-2

27. Prophets

Know the Word
Read Isaiah 52:13-53:12

1. What do you see? (Observation)

2. What does it mean? (Interpretation)

3. What do you do? (Application)

4. How should you pray?

Last week we learned about the kingdom of God and its importance as a biblical theme. This week we'll learn about the Prophets, why they are important to the overall story of the Bible, how to read and interpret them, and what significance they have for us today. Prophets fit into biblical theology in at least two ways. First, the theme and role of prophet is one we can trace from Moses to Jesus. Second, the Prophets themselves pick up on several of the themes we've already studied, and they employ them in their messages to Israel. Let's see how all of this works.

What comes to mind when you see or hear the word "prophet"? Most people in our culture, and many cultures throughout history, associate prophets with fortune tellers, psychics, or predictors of the future. The Bible does not use "prophet" in these ways. This is important: if you think of prophets as people who only predict the future, you are bound to misread the prophetic books and misinterpret the text. Do the biblical prophets warn Israel concerning future events? Yes. Is that their only or even primary purpose? No.

PROPHETS IN THE BIBLE

What, then, is a prophet in the Bible? Most simply, a prophet represents God to the people. Prophets spoke on God's behalf to call Israel to covenant faithfulness. Think back to the sessions on the law and covenant. God's law to Israel at Mount Sinai was the code of the covenant. God promised His faithfulness and blessing to Israel if they were faithful to keep the law. As you read through the Old Testament, it doesn't take long to realize Israel wasn't good at keeping the law. They often went astray, disobeyed God, and even worshipped false gods. When Israel started to wander, God would send a prophet to warn Israel against His coming judgment, calling them back to covenant faithfulness. You can think of the Prophets as covenant watch-dogs. When Israel got out of line, prophets spoke up to get them back in line. The Prophets, however, were often not successful in their attempts. Most of them were actually on the fringe of Israel's society, and no one listened to their warnings of God's coming judgment. It was only once the judgments came true that people looked back to the Prophets to heed their warnings. Later prophets and scribes preserved the writings of some of the Prophets, which is why we have access to them today.

Typically, when we refer to the Prophets we are talking about the major prophets and minor prophets. The major prophets are Isaiah, Jeremiah, Ezekiel, and Daniel. The minor prophets are Hosea, Joel, Amos, Obadiah, Jonah, Micah, Nahum, Habakkuk, Zephaniah, Haggai, Zechariah, and Malachi. The minor prophets are referred to as "the twelve" in Hebrew literature. The distinctions major and minor do not mean some prophets are more important than others. The major prophets are simply longer than the minor. Jeremiah is the longest prophetic book, consisting of 52 chapters and 33,002 words (and is actually the longest book in the Bible by word count, not Psalms!), and Obadiah is the shortest prophetic book (1 chapter and 440 words). Despite varying length, the Prophets each provide tremendous value to the biblical story.

Although the 16 books that make up the major and minor prophets are the ones we typically think about when studying the Prophets, they aren't the only prophets in the Bible. You might be familiar with the Prophets Elijah and Elisha (1 and 2 Kings). Moses was also considered a prophet and was actually the prototype for the true and greater prophet coming after him (see Deuteronomy 18:15-22). There are many prophets in the Old Testament; however, there are some we have historical accounts about (Elijah and Elisha), and others from whom we have direct messages (the major and minor). The main focus of this lesson will be the major and minor prophets, since they comprise a major portion of the Old Testament, and are what we typically think of when we talk about the Prophets.

READING THE PROPHETS AS POETRY

Reading the Bible can be difficult. Reading the Prophets can be extremely difficult. If you've engaged the prophetic literature, you may have come away confused and frustrated. Why is that? Doesn't God want us to understand the Bible so we can apply it to our lives? Absolutely. Reading the Prophets isn't like reading historical narrative (Genesis, Exodus, the Gospels, Acts), nor is it like reading epistles (Romans, Ephesians, 1 Corinthians, etc.). Historical narrative and epistles are relatively straight-forward. Though they can be difficult to interpret at times, the language is discernable, as is the overall meaning.

Prophetic literature, on the other hand, is mostly poetic. Poetry makes up about one-third of the biblical text. The prophetic books are not the only poetic books. Psalms, Proverbs, Lamentations, Job, and Song of Songs all are primarily poetic as well, and poetry shows up in different places within books that are mostly historical narrative or epistles (think Exodus 15 or 1 Timothy 3:16). The Old Testament was written mostly in Hebrew, and Hebraic poetry operates by different rules than English poetry. Hebraic poetry uses simile, metaphor, indirect analogy, and personification (somewhat like English poetry). Hebraic poetry is also quite structured, using metrical patterns, parallelism, and things like alliteration, acrostics, and assonance. One of the major issues in reading biblical poetry is that when Hebrew is translated into English, many of these elements get lost and are not immediately obvious. Biblical poetry isn't going to sound or read like Dr. Seuss. Don't worry! You don't need to learn Hebrew to appreciate biblical poetry, it just takes a little more work to understand than narrative, and you are more than capable of doing it.

Here's an example of something you wouldn't immediately recognize because of translation loss: Psalm 119 isn't just a really long poem; it's structured according to the Hebrew alphabet. In your Bible, you will notice that Psalm 119 has 22 Hebrew headings every eight verses.

Those 22 headings are the letters of the Hebrew alphabet. Each of the eight verses under each heading start with the same letter. Therefore, Psalm 119:1-8 are under the heading Aleph (essentially the letter "A"). Each verse in that section begins with a word starting with the letter Aleph. The form follows through the whole chapter. This form is called an acrostic, and it helped ancient Israelites memorize the words of the Psalm. Moreover, each verse contains a special word that pertains to God's law, which is important because the entire Psalm is about the word of God. Reading Psalm 119 with these things in mind causes us to appreciate the text more.

Just as we wouldn't read English poetry 100% literally, we can't read Hebrew poetry 100% literally. For example, Hosea, speaking on behalf of and from the perspective of God, writes of sinful Israel, "So I am to them like a lion; like a leopard I will lurk beside the way. I will fall upon them like a bear robbed of her cubs; I will tear open their breast, and there I will devour them like a lion, as a wild beast would rip them open" (Hosea 13:7-8). Now, we must ask: is this passage meant to be taken absolutely literally? Is God actually a lion or leopard? Is He going to eat Israel? Of course not. The poetic language evokes in the reader a sense of horror concerning God's coming judgment toward Israel. The language describes the severity of God's judgment. We must be careful when reading and interpreting poetry.

PROPHECY: PAST OR PRESENT?

Not only do the Prophets use poetic language, but they also describe future judgment coming upon their listeners, which makes interpreting their message even more tricky. Misinterpreting the combination of poetry and the prophecy of future events is dangerous and can lead to incorrect conclusions about both the text and how it applies to the church today. Although the Prophets were not fortune tellers, they did describe to Israel what would happen to them if they did not repent and return to God. This is vital: the Prophets primarily announced Israel's immediate future. Therefore, the majority of what the Prophets announced happened pretty quickly after they proclaimed it. Only a small portion of their messages were messianic in nature, and even a smaller portion are about events that haven't happened yet..

Theologian Gordon D. Fee writes, "Consider in this connection the following statistics: Less than 2 percent of the Old Testament prophecy is messianic. Less than 5 percent specifically describes the new-covenant age. Less than 1 percent concerns events yet to come in our time. The Prophets did indeed announce the future. But it was usually the immediate future of Israel, Judah, and other nations surrounding them that they announced rather than our future. One of the keys to understanding the Prophets, therefore, is that for us to see their prophecies fulfilled, we must look back on times that for them were still future but for us are past."[1] Don't miss Fee's

---

[1] Gordon D. Fee and Douglas Stuart, *How to Read the Bible for All It's Worth* (Grand Rapids: Zondervan, 2003), 182.

point: when we read the Old Testament, we shouldn't try to use it as a guide for predicting our future; rather, we should seek to understand the immediate context of the text and discern how the prophecies were fulfilled in Israel's immediate future. Only then should we work to apply the text to our lives today.

You may not know the immediate context of each book of the Prophets, and that's okay. Getting a good study Bible will help tremendously with placing each prophet in his historical context. Knowing when the Prophets lived, where they prophesied, to whom they prophesied, and why (which world nations were coming against them as judgment), will help in reading and understanding each book. Also, at the end of this lesson, there is a brief (very brief) overview of all 16 prophetic books with contextual information. Don't rely on the information below alone; please consult a good study Bible.

ACCUSE, REPENT, AND HOPE

Though the details of each book vary, all the Prophets had the same basic three-point message. If you remember nothing else from this lesson, remember this three-point message. First, they accused Israel of breaking God's covenant and warned them of coming judgment because of their sin. Second, they called Israel to repentance. The Prophets always reminded Israel of God's grace and forgiveness, if only they would repent and quit chasing after the gods of the other nations and their sin. Third, they proclaimed a message of hope. The Prophets reminded Israel that despite their sin, God would one day save and redeem His people.

THE DAY OF THE LORD

The Day of the Lord is a significant theme within the Prophets and important for us to understand. Originally, the Day of the Lord was to Israel a coming day of hope when they would be reunited with God in His kingdom. However, upon the arrival of the Prophets, the Day of the Lord shifted from a day of hope to a day of judgment. Israel would never enter into rest with God in their sinful state, and the Prophets told Israel to either quit sinning or be judged. Therefore, the Day of the Lord was a future day of judgment for Israel. The immediate Day of the Lord for Israel was their exile from Jerusalem after Babylon took them over.

What's interesting is that the Prophets didn't lose sight of the Day of the Lord as future hope. In almost every prophetic message, there are promises of restoration for God's people. Though they promised Israel would be judged—and they were—the Prophets always end with a message of a future, eternal hope. There are traces of messianic promises, which were fulfilled in Jesus. And there are the promises that the ultimate Day of the Lord is yet to come, a day of joy and restoration. As New Testament followers of Jesus, we can hold on to the promises of a future Day of the Lord, when sin will be judged, and God's people will dwell in His presence forever. Remember the idea of already/not yet. The Day of the Lord has already come, but not yet as it will be one day. In this sense, there are several Days of the Lord. (See 2 Peter 3.)

HOW ARE THE PROPHETS HELPFUL TODAY?

"Wait," you may be thinking, "If the Prophets mainly spoke of Israel's immediate future, what good are they for the church today?" Remember, most of the prophetic announcements have already been fulfilled, but not all of them. There are portions of the prophetic literature that are messianic, meaning they found their fulfillment in Christ (like the reading for today), and there are portions of their messages that have yet to be fulfilled. Trying to discern what has yet to be fulfilled can be a daunting and dangerous task, so it helps to understand what exactly the Prophets were trying to accomplish in their messages to Israel. Also, the entirety of Scripture is beneficial for the Christian life. Just because the Prophets mainly spoke of Israel's immediate future doesn't mean there aren't lessons for us to learn. All Scripture is inspired by God and profitable for the Christian life (2 Tim. 3:16). Understanding what the Prophets were doing in their time will help us understand how we can apply the timeless truths of God's Word to our lives. Think back to lesson 3 on How to Study the Bible: for every text of Scripture, we must observe, interpret, and apply. Applying the truths from the Prophets will demand a little more work in observation and interpretation, but it is well worth the effort.

OBSERVE, INTERPRET, APPLY

As you read through the Prophets, ask these observation questions: 1. What is the prophet accusing Israel of doing and what is the impending judgment? 2. Where does he call Israel to repent? 3. Where is the message of hope? Identifying these three elements will allow you to make sense of the basic message of each book despite the often complicated and poetic language. Again, use a study Bible or the resource below to help provide historical context for each book

Because the Prophets all have the same basic message of an accusation of sin(s), call to repentance, and message of hope, interpreting and applying their messages is somewhat straightforward. God hated Israel's sin and unfaithfulness and did not allow it to go unpunished. These books should cause us to examine the sin in our lives. God hates our sin and so should we. God also called Israel to repentance because of His grace and mercy. As followers of Christ, we should daily confess our sin and repent. We've been shown infinitely more grace and mercy in Jesus Christ than we could ever hope or imagine. The Prophets should cause us to look to the work Jesus did on our behalf for our salvation and praise Him. Finally, the pPophets provided Israel messages of future, eternal hope. As Christians, we can read their messages of enteral hope and look forward to our future with God in the new heavens and new earth.

ISAIAH 52:13-52:12

Isaiah 52-53 isn't the only example of messianic prophecies, but it may be the clearest. Isaiah 1-39 paint a bleak image for Israel and results in the promises of future judgment and destruction of Jerusalem at the hands of Babylon because of Israel's sinfulness and inability to obey God. In Isaiah 40-66, we see a beautiful picture of hope. Where Israel was the unfaithful servant of God, through Isaiah, God promises a future servant who will be faithful. Throughout these chapters, Isaiah compares and contrasts sinful Israel and the faithful servant. However, because of God's love for his people, he promised that the faithful servant, who deserved no punishment, would,

[10]*make an offering for guilt, he shall see his offspring; he shall prolong his days; the will of the LORD shall prosper in his hand.* [11]*Out of the anguish of his soul he shall see and be satisfied; by his knowledge shall the righteous one, my servant, make many to be accounted righteous, and he shall bear their iniquities.* [12]*Therefore I will divide him a portion with the many, and he shall divide the spoil with the strong, because he poured out his soul to death and was numbered with the transgressors; yet he bore the sin of many, and makes intercession for the transgressors"* (Isaiah 53:10b-12).

The faithful servant provides a way for sinful people to be reunited to God. This language so clearly and wonderfully points to the person and work of Jesus Christ. Jesus Christ was and is the faithful servant of God who restores sinful people to a right relationship with Him through His perfect life, death on the cross, and resurrection from the dead. Ultimately, it is Jesus Christ who is the perfect prophet of God. Although the Prophets were men of God and used by God to proclaim His message, they were sinful. Jesus Christ didn't need to speak on behalf of God because He was God. He was and is the son of God who brought the word of God, the good news of salvation for the unrighteous, the perfect prophet. It's through Jesus Christ that the future Day of the Lord, the day of both judgment and hope, is possible.

CONCLUSION

There is so much more we could say about the Prophets. Hopefully, this session will help you think well about the Prophets, their books, and their purpose. What about today? Does the office of prophet still exist or was Jesus the last one? In Ephesians 4:11, Paul indicates that the role of prophet still exists. We must be careful, however, not to equate the New Testament role of prophet with that of the Old Testament. The New Testament role of prophet is not to speak a new word of God into the church or culture. We believe God has fully revealed Himself in the person and work of Jesus Christ, and, by the inspiration of the Holy Spirit, the Scriptures were written and completed. God does not use prophets to speak anything new that isn't in the Bible. However, there are those with the gift of prophetic ministry, those who speak God's

Word from the Bible into the church and the culture. God has gifted some to accuse the church and culture of grievous sin, call them to repentance, and help them look forward to the Day of the Lord. Pastors often perform such a prophetic ministry in the weekly preaching and teaching of God's Word.

Don't be discouraged as you read through the prophetic books. Rather, allow them to deepen your love for God, His grace and mercy, and the beautiful story of Scripture. Don't worry if you don't know all the details of each prophetic book right this moment! That knowledge will come with time and study. Remember their basic message: accusation of sin and warning of judgment, call to repentance, and message of future hope. As you study the Prophets, start with an easier book like Jonah. It is short and mostly narrative, so it's easy to understand. From there, try to read through the book of Amos. Don't get too distracted by the details or poetry on your first reading. Ask the questions: 1. Where are the accusations and impending judgment; 2. Where are the calls to repentance; 3. Where are the messages of future hope? Amos very clearly has each of those elements in his book, so try to identify them. As you read through it again, use your study Bible or resource below to get the historical context. If you use these strategies, you'll be well on your way to understanding and benefiting from the Prophets.

In your group, reflect on the following questions:

1. What stands out to you most about this passage from Isaiah 52-53?

2. What is something new you learned from these chapter and its importance to the overall story of Scripture?

3. What themes or ideas above help you think well about this chapter and the role of the Prophets?

Model the Word

1. Take time for each member to explain an important element of the Prophets and their writings, and how it can help in reading and understanding both Old and New Testaments.

2. How would you teach this passage to someone else? What aspects or ideas would you emphasize? How could the theme of the Prophets help in teaching this passage?

Share the Word

1. Think about reading these chapters from the perspective of an unbeliever. How could you use them to share the gospel or begin a gospel conversation? How can the idea of the Prophets be helpful to you as you share the gospel with others?

2. Why is it helpful to understand the role of the Prophets throughout the Scripture? How can you use this idea as you share the gospel?

Pray the Word

1. As a group, spend time praying for each other to have a better understanding of God's Word.

2. Thank God for sending Jesus Christ. Thank Him for being a king that is loving, merciful, and gracious.

3. Pray for opportunities to share the gospel with others. Pray that God will give you boldness to share with those in your family and at your job.

Daily Bible Reading

Day 1: Mark 3-4
Day 2: Mark 5-6
Day 3: Mark 7-8
Day 4: Mark 9-10
Day 5: Mark 11-12

OVERVIEW OF THE PROPHETS

To best understand the prophetic books, we have to know a little context. The prophecies in these books took place roughly between 760 BC – 450 BC. That's 310 years of history in which we have to figure out when, where, and to whom these men prophesied. Knowing a little world history will go a long way in making sense of each man's message. Below is a brief overview of Israel's history from about 930-450 BC. This section will help you understand which nations were world powers during particular periods and how that affected Israel. An important note: All of the dates listed below are approximate. It's difficult to know exactly when a lot of these events took place, but the date ranges are as accurate as possible.

King Saul, David, and Solomon reigned over Israel from the years 1050-930 BC. Sometime between 930-920 BC, Solomon died and was replaced by his son, Rehoboam. Because of his poor leadership and unfaithfulness to God, the ten northern tribes revolted against Rehoboam and split from the kingdom, forming two separate kingdoms. The northern kingdom was called Israel, and Samaria was its capital. The southern kingdom was called Judah, and Jerusalem remained its capital. Southern Judah was comprised of the tribes of Judah and Benjamin, and northern Israel was comprised of the other ten tribes. For almost 200 years, the kingdoms remained divided until Assyria invaded Northern Israel in 740 BC. 1 and 2 Kings record the histories of the two kingdoms and their kings, most of whom were evil in the sight of the Lord.

During the time of the Prophets, roughly 760-450 BC, there were three world powers God used to bring judgment upon sinful Israel—the nations of Assyria, Babylon, and Persia. If you can remember these three nations and the approximate time they ruled, reading the Prophets will become much easier. Starting in 740 BC, Assyria invaded northern Israel. By 722 BC, Assyria had destroyed Northern Israel and the ten tribes; those who remained were scattered among the nations. Around 700 BC, the Assyrians focused on conquering Southern Judah. Though they did destroy many cities and took about 200,000 captives, Assyria did not overtake Southern Judah. From the years 700-612 BC, Southern Judah managed to withhold an invasion from Assyria due to a few good kings and, ultimately, God's faithfulness.

By 620 BC, an emerging world empire, Babylon, threatened Assyrian rule. Babylon went to war with Assyria for about 12 years. In 612 BC, Babylon destroyed Assyria's capital city, Nineveh, which led to the fall of the Assyrian empire. In 605 BC, King Nebuchadnezzar of Babylon invaded Judah. By 598 BC, Babylon besieged Jerusalem. And in 597 BC, the first wave of Jews was sent into exile in Babylon. After a short rebellion in 589 BC, Nebuchadnezzar completely overthrew Jerusalem, destroyed the temple, and sent the second wave of Jews into exile in 587 BC. From 587-539 BC, the Jews remained in exile under Babylonian rule.

In 539 BC, the newest emerging world power, Persia, conquered Babylon. King Cyrus of Persia was far kinder than the Assyrian and Babylonian rulers and allowed the Jewish exiles to return to their homeland and worship their God. The Jewish return to Jerusalem was gradual and happened in four waves spread over about 92 years from 537-445 BC. From there, the Greeks fought the Persians from 499-449 BC and conquered them. Rome eventually conquered Greece, and that gets us to the time of Jesus, but, for the Prophets, the main nations we want to remember are Assyrian, Babylon, and Persia.

IMPORTANT DATE RANGES TO REMEMBER

Northern Israel – 930-722 BC
Southern Judah – 930-587 BC

Assyria – 740-612 BC
- Assyrian Invasion and Conquest of Northern Israel – 740-722 BC
- Assyrian Invasion of Southern Judah – 700-612 BC

Babylon – 612-539 BC
- Babylonian Conquest of Assyria – 612 BC
- Babylonian Invasion and Conquest of Southern Judah – 605-589 BC
- First Babylonian Exile of the Jews – 589 BC
- Second Babylonian Exile of Jews – 587-539 BC

Persia – 539-449 BC
- Jews Return from Exile – 537-445 BC

We covered a lot of dates and history in a short space! Use this as a reference as you're thinking about when and where the Prophets lived and spoke. Below is brief contextual information for each prophetic book. I've listed them chronologically instead of how they appear in our English Bible's to help you place them on the timeline of events we've looked at so far.

AMOS

- When: Roughly 760 BC

- Where: Amos was a shepherd and fig-tree farmer who lived in Southern Judah at the border between the two kingdoms. He traveled to Northern Israel to prophesy.

• Why: Amos went to Northern Israel to prophesy against the great evil of Jeroboam II (2 Kings 14:23-29). Jeroboam won new territory and generated massive wealth for Northern Israel, which caused him to have apathy for following God. He allowed idol worship and injustice toward the poor.

• What: This book is a collection of Amos's sermons, poems, and visions through the years of his ministry. Chapters 1-2 are a message to the nations and Israel (both kingdoms). Chapters 3-6 are a message of warning to Israel and its leaders. And 7-8 are visions of future judgment, destruction, and, finally, eternal restoration.

• Important Key: Social injustice is a major theme throughout all the Prophets, and can clearly be seen in Amos. Israel was to love God and neighbor; they did neither. Their injustice toward the needy and poor was an act of injustice toward God.

JONAH

• When: 786-746 BC (definite date of prophecy uncertain). Like Amos, he prophesied during the reign of Jeroboam II, and actually prophesied in Jeroboam's favor with the restoration of the border of Northern Israel; although, interestingly, through Amos God later reverses that same prophesy (Amos 6:13-14).

• Where: Jonah went to Nineveh, the capital city of Assyria to prophecy.

• Why: God sent Jonah to Nineveh to accuse them of evil and prophesy that the city would be overthrown.

• What: Of all the Prophets, Jonah says by far the least. He initially runs from his prophetic calling and even tries to kill himself, only to be rescued by God to complete the task at hand. We get one sentence of prophecy from Jonah to Nineveh, and it doesn't even come true. The people of Nineveh repent, and God spares them, which causes Jonah to be upset. This is the one prophetic book that isn't so much about what the prophet says but what the prophet does. This story is mostly narrative and describes the interaction between God, Jonah, and Nineveh. This little book ultimately shows Jonah's stubbornness and God's grace to the nations.

• Important Key: Jonah is unusual among the Prophets because it seems as though he isn't faithful toward God. In many ways, Jonah represents Israel. While they were supposed to be a light to the nations, they were unfaithful and actually hated the nations, just like Jonah.

HOSEA

• When: 758-722 BC, during the reign of Jeroboam II in Northern Israel. Hosea prophesied over a period of about 25 years.

• Where: Hosea lived and prophesied in Northern Israel.

• Why: The sin and corruption of Northern Israel continued to worsen under the rule of Jeroboam II. The people worshiped false gods and practiced mass injustice. Hosea warns the people of Israel against the impending judgment of God. However, through Hosea, God reminds Israel of His faithfulness despite their faithlessness.

• What: In chapters 1-3, God instructs Hosea to take Gomer as his wife. Gomer is unfaithful in their marriage and commits adultery repeatedly. God instructs Hosea to forgive and love Gomer despite her sin. Hosea and Gomer represent the relationship between God and Israel. Although Israel is unfaithful and whores after other gods, God is faithful to His covenant and promises to love and redeem Israel despite their sin. In chapters 4-11, Hosea accuses Israel and warns them against God's judgment, and in 12-14 he does the same. Each section ends, however, with hope of a glorious future with God because of His covenant love.

• Important Key: Hosea often refers to Northern Israel as "Ephraim" or "Jacob" throughout the book.

ISAIAH

• When: 740-687 BC, during the reigns of Kings Uzziah, Jotham, Ahaz, and Hezekiah (2 Kings 15:32-20:21).

• Where: Isaiah lived and prophesied in Southern Judah, specifically in Jerusalem.

• Why: God used Isaiah to accuse Southern Judah and its leaders of sin, idolatry, and unfaithfulness. Isaiah warned Southern Judah that if they continued in sin, God would use Assyria and then Babylon to enact judgment, and ultimately exile.

• What: Isaiah accused Israel of their sin and promised coming judgment. However, Isaiah also provided a message of hope. Through Isaiah, God promised a future Messiah who would be obedient to God's covenant and provide a way for Israel and the nations to live in God's presence for eternity. Chapters 1-39 are comprised mainly of accusation and judgment. And chapters 40-66 make up the messages of hope.

• Important Key: This is a complex book. Remember the rules for reading both prophetic literature and poetry. In chapters 40-66, notice the role of the promised "Servant" or "suffering Servant" who would save Israel. Much of the prophecy from this section is messianic and points directly to Jesus Christ.

MICAH

• When: 740-686 BC, during the reigns of King Jotham, Ahaz, and Hezekiah (he was a contemporary of Isaiah).

• Where: Micah lived and prophesied in Southern Judah.

• Why: God used Micah to accuse both Northern and Southern kingdoms of their sin and idolatry, and warn of God's coming judgment by way of Assyria and Babylon. He calls out the injustice of Israel's leaders and false prophets.

• What: Micah offers both messages of judgment and hope. Although Assyria and Babylon will destroy both Northern Israel and Southern Judah, God will one day save all the nations who will assemble on His "Holy Mountain" or "Zion." Micah ends with a message of hope for God's people. Although Israel (both kingdoms) are wicked and sinful, God will remain faithful to his covenant promises to Jacob and Abraham because of His steadfast love.

• Important Key: Micah refers to Northern Israel as Jacob (remember, the capital city is Samaria). In chapter 1, Micah refers to a lot of cities that may be unfamiliar. Each city is located within one of the two kingdoms and shows the breadth of how sinful Israel and Judah had become. It wasn't just the two capital cities that turned against God; it was everywhere and nearly everyone.

ZEPHANIAH

• When: 640-609 BC, during the reign of Josiah in Southern Judah (2 Kings 22:1-23:30).

• Where: Southern Judah in Jerusalem.

• Why: Zephaniah accused Southern Judah of sin and idolatry and warned of the impending judgment from Babylon. Although King Josiah made significant reforms in Jerusalem, the people were far too entrenched in the worship of other gods, which prompted God to enact judgment after his death.

• What: In this short book, Zephaniah warns of the coming judgment on Judah at the hands of Babylon. However, Zephaniah promises that Judah's enemies will eventually be destroyed. Ultimately, Israel and all the nations will be judged. In Zephaniah 3:9-20, God provides the wonderful promise of the salvation of both the nations and Israel because of His grace and mercy.

• Important Key: The "Day of the Lord" is an important theme in Zephaniah. Remember, the "Day of the Lord" signified a coming day of judgment on Israel. There are many "Days of the Lord" in the Bible. Each one represents an act of judgment and hope. In the final Day of the Lord, sin will be judged and punished forever, and God's people will be saved for eternity.

JEREMIAH

• When: 627-585 BC, during the reigns of Kings Josiah, Jehoiakim, and Zedekiah, until the Babylonian captivity of Jerusalem (2 Kings 22-25).

• Where: Jeremiah prophesied in Southern Judah, specifically in Jerusalem.

• Why: God used Jeremiah to warn Judah of the consequences of its sin, idolatry, and injustice. Jeremiah foretold that Babylon would come as God's servant of judgment and send the people into exile.

• What: Jeremiah prophesied for 20 years in Jerusalem. God called him to collect his sermons and poems into one work. He hired a scribe named Baruch to help him organize his work, and Baruch also included stories he gathered about Jeremiah and his life. The book has been specifically organized and arranged to present Jeremiah and a messenger of God's justice and grace. Some of the book is poetry, some is narrative, and some is commentary. The book ends with the temple being destroyed and the people being exiled to Babylon.

• Important Key: Jeremiah 31-33 are vitally important for understanding the hope within this often depressing story. It's in these chapters that God promises a new covenant. Remember the session we did on covenants. Just because the covenant is new doesn't mean it trumps or eradicates the promises from previous covenants. God promises that the Messiah or eternal king will come from the line of David to enact the new covenant, which will eternally restore God to his people.

NAHUM

• When: Before 612 BC, the year Nineveh fell (the capital of Assyria). Remember, Jonah prophesied to Nineveh between 786-746 BC and the entire city repented. However, between the time of Jonah and the time of Nahum, Nineveh returned to their sinfulness and worship of false gods.

• Where: Nineveh, the capital city of Assyria, was the target of the prophecy. By 722 BC, the Assyrians destroyed Northern Israel and sent them into exile. From 700-612 BC, Assyria made several attempts to invade and conquer Southern Judah. Judah longed for God to punish the Assyrians, and Nahum prophesied just that. In 612 Nineveh fell to the Babylonians.

• Why: Nineveh is destroyed because God promised to punish the nations who were against Israel, even though He used them for judgment. They served their purpose, and it was time for them to be punished for their sinfulness and wickedness.

• What: This short book is more than just a warning to Nineveh. The first chapter doesn't even mention Nineveh and contains many promises about a future day of hope and peace for Judah. In 1:15, Zephaniah promises one who will bring good news and peace, which is points to the Messiah.

• Important Key: This can be a difficult book to read. The language Nahum uses is graphic and violent. The language is meant to show God's wrath against sinfulness and His justice in enacting judgment on the nations.

HABAKKUK

• When: 612-599 BC, during the final decades of Southern Judah before the exile.

• Where: Habakkuk lived and prophesied in Southern Judah.

• Why: Unlike many of the other prophets, Habakkuk doesn't address the people of Judah or any of their kings. He doesn't accuse Judah at all. Rather, Habakkuk has a conversation with God. He makes a complaint to God about the injustice in the world and asks when God will make right what has gone wrong. He draws God's attention to all of the evil around him and wonders how God can be good in the midst of so much evil.

• What: In chapters 1-2, Habakkuk makes two complaints toward God, and God answers each. In the first, Habakkuk complains about the injustice and violence in Judah. He wonders when God will enact justice. God answers by saying He will use Babylon to judge Israel for its sin. Habakkuk responds in disbelief that a holy and just God would use a nation, Babylon, worse than Israel to enact judgment. God responds by showing Habakkuk a vision of the future when even Babylon will be destroyed. God tells Habakkuk that a time is coming when the righteous live by faith. God will not forget His promises to His people, and will redeem and restore them. Habakkuk responds in chapter 3 with a prayer of praise and rejoicing.

• Important Key: Habakkuk learns that God will always enact justice on sinful people. Although He may use a particular nation, like Babylon, to enact justice on Israel, He does not allow the sin of Babylon to go unpunished. Everyone is accountable for their sin, and everyone will be judged. God is not idly watching the sin of the world; He is providentially moving all of history toward the restoration of all things. This is a tremendous apologetic book for God's sovereignty.

DANIEL

• When: 606-530 BC. Daniel was among the first wave of exiles from Jerusalem after Nebuchadnezzar attacked Jerusalem while Jehoiakim was king (2 Kings 23:36-24:7). Daniel lived through the reigns of Kings Nebuchadnezzar, Belshazzar, and Darius of Babylon, and into the reign of King Cyrus of Persia after they defeated Babylon in 539 BC.

• Where: The majority of Daniel's life and prophecy took place in Babylon, in the land of Shinar.

• Why: This book serves at least two purposes. First, Daniel contains stories about Daniel and his friend and records their faithfulness to God despite being in exile in a foreign land. Second, this book also contains the prophecies of Daniel about events in the future and provided a future hope for Israel while they were in exile, and it provides future hope for believers today as well.

• What: The book is broken up into two parts. Chapters 1-6 are about the life of Daniel and his friends while in exile, and 7-12 are the prophecies of Daniel. The prophecies in 7-12 are difficult to interpret and must be done so with great caution and care.

• Important Key: The book of Daniel was originally written in both Hebrew and Aramaic. Chapter 1 is in Hebrew and serves as an introduction to the book. Chapters 2-7 are in Aramaic and form a cohesive section. And in chapters 8-12, the book returns to Hebrew. Ultimately, the book shows that God will overthrow all the kingdoms of this world, and the Son of Man will come to save the nations and establish His kingdom forever. Jesus most frequently referred to Himself as the Son of Man, and He intentionally does so to remind His hearers of the promises in Daniel 7.

EZEKIEL

• When: 593-571 BC, during the Babylonian exile. His first vision came about five years after the first wave of exiles left Jerusalem, which Ezekiel was part of.

• Where: Ezekiel said he was by the Chebar canal in the land of the Chaldeans (biblical authors often refer to the Babylonians as Chaldeans).

• Why: Although the temple had been captured and robbed upon the first Babylonian invasion, it still stood and was an emblem of hope for the exiled Jews. They longed for a day when God would save them and allow them to return to their land and the temple. However, Ezekiel accuses the Jews of sinfulness and idolatry and warns them that God's glory will leave the temple, and it will be destroyed, which it was (2 Kings 25). This was not just bad news for the Jews; it meant their land and their temple were gone. God had abandoned them.

• What: Ezekiel, however, offered Israel a message of hope. Through Ezekiel, God promised to restore His people. He promised to put within His people a new heart, one that could faithfully worship and obey Him. And although God's glory left the temple, He provided a vision of the new temple in Ezekiel 40-48.

• Important Key: Chapters 40-48 should be read with the end in mind. Ezekiel pulls imagery from Genesis 1-2, the Torah, and other prophets to paint the picture of the future temple. In Revelation, John borrows language and imagery from Ezekiel. Remember, as a prophet, Ezekiel uses imagery and metaphor to make a bigger point. Through Christ, the Father is building a new temple, the church. And the presence of God no longer rests in a building but in a people, the church. We shouldn't look for a physical temple in the future. The New Testament authors help us interpret passages like these from Ezekiel.

OBADIAH

• When: Possibly around 586 BC (just after the fall of Jerusalem).

• Where: Obadiah was likely already in exile or just about to go into Babylonian exile.

• Why: Obadiah prophesied against Edom because of their sinfulness toward Southern Judah. Who is Edom? Think back to Genesis. Abraham and Sarah had Isaac who married Rebekah. Isaac and Rebekah had two sons, Jacob and Esau. Their relationship was contentious because Jacob stole Esau's birthright and blessing. God promised that two nations would come from Jacob and Esau. Israel came from Jacob, and Edom came from Esau. Throughout the histories of Israel and Edom, there was conflict. When Babylon invaded Jerusalem and sent the Jews into exile, Edom plundered several cities in Southern Judah, abused the exiles, and even killed some (Ezekiel 35, Amos 1).

• What: This short book is only 21 verses. In 1-9, Obadiah declares that Edom will be humbled; in 10-14, he recounts Edom's violence against Jacob (Israel/Judah); in 15-18 he promises that the Day of the Lord is near; and in 19-21 Obadiah provides future hope for Israel, declaring that God will rule.

• Important Key: God promised Abraham that He would bless those who blessed his family and curse those who cursed them. We see here that even Edom, descendants of Abraham, were cursed for their sin.

HAGGAI

• When: 520 BC, during the reign of King Darius of Persia, after King Cyrus of Persia allowed the Jews to return to Jerusalem to rebuild the temple in 539 BC.

• Where: Haggai lived and prophesied in Jerusalem.

• Why: Haggai challenges the Jews not to be discouraged by the new temple, but to remember the promises of the earlier prophets about the coming kingdom of God. He offers Israel future hope, even after the return from exile.

• What: When the Jews returned to Jerusalem, they began rebuilding their own homes, but Haggai rebuked them because they were not concerned about rebuilding the temple. He told them they were no better than the generation that was exiled from the land. They respond by rebuilding the temple, but they were quite sad when they realized it was nothing like Solomon's temple. Haggai challenges them to remember the promises of the Prophets and the future glory of God's temple.

ZECHARIAH

• When: 520-518 BC, during the reign of King Darius of Persia (a contemporary of Haggai).

• Where: Jerusalem after the return from exile.

• Why: The prophet Jeremiah said the exile would last 70 years, but that at the end of the 70 years God would restore His presence to a new temple under the rule of the Messiah. During the time of Zechariah, the 70 years were almost up, and there was no sign of the Messiah or new Jerusalem. Zechariah offers an explanation as to why the promises of Jeremiah didn't seem as if they were going to be true.

• What: This is one of the more complex prophetic books, and it is filled with some strange visions Zechariah has while he is sleeping. 1:1-6 is an introduction to the whole book. In 1:7-6:15, Zechariah has nine visions that are organized according to Hebrew symmetrical form. Essentially, visions 1 and 8 correspond, 2 and 7 correspond, 3 and 6 correspond, and 4 and 5 correspond. They are completed by a ninth vision that is the symbol of the future Messiah, who will be both king and priest over His people, the same Messiah promised by Jeremiah. However, Zechariah told Israel the Messiah would only come if the current generation was faithful to God. Like all the Prophets before him, Zechariah calls Israel to covenant faithfulness with God. And, like the previous generations, they fail. The latter half of the book is a collection of poems about the coming messianic kingdom. It is meant to cause Israel to continue to look forward to God's promises and hope for the coming Messiah.

• Important Key: Read this book slowly. It can be easy to get lost in each particular vision. Remember the symmetry of the visions and how they are all building up toward the coming Messiah.

JOEL

• When: Date is unknown. Most likely it is some time after the exiles returned from Babylon. Joel is familiar with the Prophets and quotes Isaiah, Amos, Nahum, Zephaniah, Ezekiel, Obadiah, and possibly Malachi, which puts the date of his prophetic ministry after the year 500 BC.

• Where: Joel lived and prophesied in Jerusalem.

• Why: Joel doesn't accuse Israel of any particular sin, rather he calls Israel to repentance and looks forward to the future Day of the Lord and the hope of the Messiah.

• What: In the first chapter of Joel, he calls Israel to repentance. Chapters 2-3 are beautiful depictions of the glorious future of Judah (Israel) and God's people. The book of Joel is meant to help Israel think about their past and their future so that they will live in covenant faithfulness to God in expectation of the Messiah. Joel, along with Malachi, is one of the last books of the Prophets until God ceases to speak until the arrival of John the Baptist and Jesus. Peter quotes Joel in Acts to explain the outpouring of the Holy Spirit at Pentecost. Joel still provides future hope for believers today as we look toward the glorious future we have with God.

MALACHI

- When: 475-450 BC, about 100 years after the Jews returned from exile.

- Where: Malachi lived and prophesied in Jerusalem.

- Why: The new generation living in Jerusalem proved to be no better than the ones before them. There was mass injustice, the priests gave polluted offerings, and they robbed God by withholding tithes and contributions.

- What: Six times in the book, God makes a claim about Israel's sin, they disagree, and God ends with a counterclaim. In the last chapter, Malachi ends with a promise about the coming Day of the Lord. Interestingly, Malachi is the last prophet to give a word to Israel from God. All they are left with is all the promises of the Prophets about the coming Messiah and future kingdom.

- Important Key: It's helpful to remember the importance of the Day of the Lord. It's both an act of judgment and future hope. When Jesus Christ arrives on the scene, his life, ministry, death, and resurrection is both an act of judgment against Israel and future hope for Israel and the nations.

28. Exile and Restoration

Know the Word
Read 2 Kings 17:6-23; 2 Chronicles 36:17-22

1. What do you see? (Observation)

2. What does it mean? (Interpretation)

3. What do you do? (Application)

4. How should you pray?

Last week we looked at the Prophets, the role they serve in the biblical story, and how to read and interpret them faithfully. This week we will learn about the themes of exile and restoration. These themes may not be immediately obvious, but both can be traced from Genesis 1-3 to the present day. Exile and restoration are most obviously tied to the people of Israel, their banishment from the promised land, and eventual return. The Prophets all preached either pre-exile (warning of the impending judgment), during the exile (explaining why Israel was in exile and providing hope), or post-exile (commanding Israel to be faithful and to look to the future kingdom). Starting in 2 Kings 17 and 2 Chronicles 28, the biblical authors recount the beginning of the exile through the eventual return at the command of the king of Persia. The books Ezra and Nehemiah tell the story of Israel's return to Jerusalem, as they settled in the land, rebuilt the temple, and waited for the Messiah. This lesson will not provide dates and historical information about the exile; rather, the aim is to learn about exile and restoration as themes and how they are treated throughout the Bible. At the end of Lesson 27, there is a brief historical overview of Northern Israel and Southern Judah, when they went into exile respectively, which world powers were in control during what times, and when and where the Prophets preached. I recommend you glance at the historical overview and the date ranges provided if you need some context for this lesson.

EXILE AND RESTORATION

Exile is the state of being barred from one's native country, usually for political, military, or punitive reasons. Sometimes, exile can be forced by one's native country (the government can kick you out), or it can be forced by another country (an invasion during war). Exile can even be inflicted by one's family or oneself (someone converts their religion and has to leave because of the risk of injury or death at the hands of one's family or society). Those in exile are called refugees. If you're a natural-born American citizen, the chances are that you've never been in any form of exile. Therefore, this can be a difficult theme to grasp.

Imagine, however, the police show up at your door tomorrow and take you to jail. They say you've been accused of treason and you can either go to prison for life or leave the country for life. Either way, you will never be able to contact your family or friends. You don't want to go to prison, so you choose to go to another country. Here's the kicker: you don't get to pick what country you go to, so the government sends you to a country that doesn't speak English, has a vastly different culture, isn't Christian, and has limited access to technology. No one there cares that you're American, and you're on your own with some others who were also accused of treason and sent with you. Several weeks later, after the initial shock of such jarring events, you're sitting alone in a small room at night. Imagine the loneliness. Imagine being unable to talk with your family. Think about never being able to go to church and worship with the friends you once knew. Everything is gone, and everything is changed. That would be immensely defeating.

After several years in exile, the government in your home country has new officials who allow all the exiles to be pardoned and come back home. As you get off the plane, your family and friends are standing there waiting for you. Tears flow as you see your spouse, your kids, your parents. You embrace one another tightly with no intention of letting go. You stop at your favorite restaurant and have a feast. Eventually, you get home and walk through your front door. You're home. As you sit down in your favorite chair, everything is back to normal. The sense of home and peace is restored to what it once was. Imagine the relief and joy you would feel being home, being restored.

Such an example may seem extreme; however, the exile of Israel from the promised land was much worse. Israel's entire history was aimed at dwelling in God's presence in the place He had for them. God's presence dwelt in the temple among His people, providing security for Israel. However, Israel's sin was so grievous that God had to drive them from the land into exile. If Israel wasn't holy, if they wouldn't worship and obey God, they couldn't dwell in His presence in the promised land. The pattern of exile isn't unique to Israel. This pattern is actually a theme, and understanding this theme will help you greatly as you read the Bible.

EXILE IN EDEN

God created Adam and Eve to dwell in His presence in a place He prepared for them. That place was the Garden of Eden. Their task was to worship and obey God, be fruitful and multiply, and spread His glory across the whole earth. But Adam and Eve chose to disobey God, and sin entered into the world. Sinful humans couldn't be in the presence of God, so He graciously kicked them out of the garden and out of His presence so they wouldn't die. God sent Adam and Eve into a form of exile. The wilderness was nothing like the garden. Adam's labor was hard, and Eve's childbirth was painful. Death was abundant, and sin rampant. Imagine how badly they wanted to get back to the garden, back to God's presence. They once were at home in a glorious situation, but, because of their sin, they found themselves in exile, longing to be restored to their former state. They knew the wilderness wasn't home. God promised in Genesis 3:15 that He would send an offspring from Eve to fix what they had done wrong. Someone would come who could take humanity from exile to restoration. The whole story of Scripture asks this question: How will humanity get from exile to restoration? The story in Genesis sets a pattern of exile that is important for us to identify as we move along.

EXILE IN DANIEL

As promised by the Prophets, Babylon invaded and destroyed Jerusalem. Daniel was among the first wave of Jewish exiles to Babylon. The story of Daniel is fascinating. Not only does Daniel provide us an example of what life in the exile was like, but he is also a model of how God's people are to act as exiles in a foreign land. Nebuchadnezzar's armies took Daniel away from Jerusalem, away from his family and friends, away from the temple, and away from his home. Babylon was drastically different than Jerusalem, and Jews were a vast minority within Babylon. Some of the Jews revolted against Babylon, but that didn't go well for them. Many others adopted the culture, practices, and, most unfortunately, the gods of Babylon. These weren't the only two options though. Daniel provides a third way.

Daniel was in Babylon without being of Babylon. He learned the culture, worked, and participated in society, which is precisely what the prophet Jeremiah told all of the Jews to do. In a message to the exiles, Jeremiah writes:

⁴Thus says the LORD of hosts, the God of Israel, to all the exiles whom I have sent into exile in Jerusalem to Babylon: ⁵Build houses and live in them; plant gardens and eat their produce. ⁶Take wives and have sons and daughters; take wives for your sons, and give your daughter in marriage, that they may bear sons and daughters; multiply there, and do not decrease. ⁷But seek the welfare of the city where I have sent you into exile, and pray to the LORD on its behalf, for in its welfare you will find your welfare. ⁸For thus says the LORD of hosts, the God of Israel: Do not let your prophets and your diviners who are among you deceive you, and do not listen to the dreams they dream, ⁹for it is a lie that they are prophesying to you in my name; I did not send them, declares the LORD. ¹⁰For thus says the LORD: when seventy years are completed for Babylon, I will visit you, and I will fulfill to you my promise and bring you back to this place. ¹¹For I know the plans I have for you, declares the LORD, plans for your welfare and not for evil, to give you a future and a hope. ¹²Then you will call upon me and come and pray to me, and I will hear you. ¹³You will seek me and find me, when you seek me with all your heart. ¹⁴I will be found by you declares the LORD, and I will restore your fortunes and gather you from all the nations and all the places where I have driven you, declares the LORD, and I will bring you back to the place from which I sent you into exile (Jeremiah 29:4-14).

What a message! God wanted the Jews to live in the society and flourish there because the welfare of Babylon meant the welfare of the Jews. On the other hand, God instructed the Jews not to succumb to or worship the false gods of Babylon. They could live in Babylon and prosper, but they couldn't be of Babylon and forget God. Though many of the Jews revolted or adopted all of Babylonian culture, some, like Daniel, adopted the third way, the way Jeremiah instructed, the way of the exile. As with every prophetic message, Jeremiah provided future hope for the Jewish people. God promised to restore Israel, and it was that promise that was supposed to motivate them to live faithfully to God, even as exiles.

EXILE IN EZRA AND NEHEMIAH

Wait a minute! Ezra and Nehemiah recount the return of the Jews from exile to Jerusalem, right? Well, yes, but we need to see the bigger picture of what's going on. When Persia defeated Babylon, King Cyrus allowed all of the Jews to return to Jerusalem to worship God and rebuild the temple. Remember, Jerusalem was destroyed, so rebuilding the whole city and temple was a monumental task. The new temple was nothing in comparison to Solomon's temple. The younger Jews rejoiced at the completion of the temple, but the elders and priests who remembered Solomon's temple wept bitterly (Ezra 3:10-13). Moreover, just because the Jews had returned to Jerusalem, it was still under Persian rule, and it remained under the rule of foreign leaders for centuries to come.

Just because they were back in the land, they weren't home. Israel had not been restored. We know they weren't restored because God sent prophets like Haggai, Zechariah, and Malachi to preach messages of warning and future hope of the coming kingdom and Messiah, even after the Jews returned to Jerusalem. In the Hebrew ordering of the Old Testament, 1-2 Chronicles are the last two books listed. 1-2 Chronicles are a summary of Israel's history. 1 Chronicles starts with a genealogy from Adam to Abraham. Interestingly, 2 Chronicles doesn't record the Jewish return from exile and the rebuilding of Jerusalem. This is how 2 Chronicles ends:

[22]*Now in the first year of Cyrus king of Persia, that the word of the LORD by the mouth of Jeremiah might be fulfilled, the LORD stirred up the spirit of Cyrus king of Persia, so that he made a proclamation throughout all his kingdom and also put it in writing:* [23]*"Thus says Cyrus king of Persia, 'The LORD, the God of heaven, has given me all the kingdoms of the earth, and he has charged me to build him a house at Jerusalem, which is in Judah. Whoever is among you of all his people, may the LORD his God be with him. Let him go up'"*
(2 Chronicles 36:22-23).

Why is that how the Hebrew scriptures end? Did the author of Chronicles not know about the rebuilding of Jerusalem? The author absolutely knew about it, as did the rest of the Jewish people! The Jews strategically end their scriptures this way because it provides hope. The Jewish return from exile was not at all what they were expecting. If anything, the books of Ezra, Nehemiah were a bit depressing. Just because they were in Jerusalem didn't mean they were home. Just because they returned from exile didn't mean they were restored. The Jews were and are still hoping for the coming kingdom and the Messiah. Even in Jerusalem, they were in exile.

EXILE IN THE GOSPELS

After Malachi's ministry, God didn't speak to His people through a prophet for over four hundred years. God's people remained in exile and found themselves under the rule of another suppressive empire—Rome. God used John the Baptist to call the Jews to repent and be baptized because the kingdom of God was near. Rather than sending yet another prophet to promise future hope of restoration, God the Father sent the one who was the very means to make restoration possible—Jesus Christ. To restore His people, the Son of God went into exile. Christ left His position with the Father, took on flesh, and entered a sinful world. He didn't go into exile because of any sin of His own but because of the sin of people He loved and desired to be in relationship with. Whereas Adam was forced into exile because of his sin, Christ willingly went into exile to fix humanity's sinful condition. Though Israel continued to sin in exile, Christ was faithful through exile. And although Adam and Israel couldn't find restoration because of sin; the sinless one, Jesus Christ, made a way for people to be restored to a right relationship with God.

Jesus had particular interest in those without a home. He cared for the orphan, the widow, and the sick. He was keenly aware of the poor and the outcast. Jesus preached about the future kingdom of God. In God's kingdom, there is no exile; there is only restoration. Jesus, like the Prophets before Him, promised future hope. What is so amazing about Jesus, however, is that He provided exiles a way to be restored to the presence of God. Jesus said He was the way. Only through faith in Jesus can exiles be restored. Jesus said, "I am the way, and the truth, and the life; no one comes to the Father but through me" (John 14:6). Jesus was and is the way of the exile.

EXILE IN THE CHURCH

After His death and resurrection, Jesus tasked His followers to go and make disciples. They believed He was the Messiah, which meant they believed He would provide restoration for Israel. They didn't want to wait; they wanted the kingdom to be restored quickly. Luke writes of the disciples, "So when they had come together, they were asking Him, saying, 'Lord, is it at this time You are restoring the kingdom to Israel?" (Acts 1:6). The disciples didn't yet have the Spirit, so they didn't understand what God was about to do with them. Not only was God at work to restore Israel but also every tribe, tongue, and nation, and He was going to use them to start it.

Once the disciples received the Spirit, their task became apparent. They preached the gospel and started the church. The church spread and is continuing to spread today. Interestingly, the disciples and the early church considered themselves as exiles. Their citizenship was not on earth but in heaven. Paul writes:

¹⁸For many walk, of whom I often told you, and now tell you even weeping, that they are enemies of the cross of Christ, ¹⁹whose end is destruction, whose god is their appetites, and whose glory is in their shame, who set their minds on earthly things. ²⁰For our citizenship is in heaven, from which also we eagerly wait for a Savior, the Lord Jesus Christ; ²¹who will transform the body of our humble state into conformity with the body of His glory, by the exertion of the power that He has even to subject all things to Himself" (Philippians 3:18-21).

Early Christians considered themselves sojourners—those on earth for a temporary time until God made the new heaven and new earth, the ultimate restoration.

Today the church still awaits its final restoration to God. You and I are in exile. The good news is that we know the way to restoration and His name is Jesus Christ. As a follower of Jesus, you know this isn't your home. We remain in a world filled with sin and death. Our task is to live as faithful exiles. Part of being a faithful exile is inviting others to walk the path that leads to restoration. The church isn't to be secluded from the world awaiting restoration; rather, the church is to be on mission in the world to share the gospel and make disciples. Just like Jeremiah commanded Israel to live in Babylon without being of Babylon, Jesus commands us to live in this world without being of this world, living and sharing the hope of restoration.

In your group, reflect on the following questions:

1. What stands out to you most about this passage from 2 Kings 17 and 2 Chronicles 36?

2. What is something new you learned from these chapters and their importance to the overall story of Scripture?

3. What themes or ideas above help you think well about this chapter and the idea of the kingdom of God?

Model the Word

1. Take time for each member to explain the importance of the exile and restoration and how these two themes can help in reading and understanding both Old and New Testaments.

2. How would you teach these passages to someone else? What aspects or ideas would you emphasize? How could the themes of exile and restoration help in teaching this passage?

Share the Word

1. Think about reading these chapters from the perspective of an unbeliever. How could you use them to share the gospel or begin a gospel conversation? How can the ideas of exile and restoration be helpful to you as you share the gospel with others?

2. Why is it helpful to understand exile and restoration throughout the Scripture? How can you use the ideas of exile and restoration as you share the gospel?

Pray the Word

1. As a group, spend time praying for each other to have a better understanding of God's Word.

2. Thank God for providing a way from exile to restoration. Pray for wisdom as you figure out how to live in this world without being of it.

3. Pray for opportunities to share the gospel with others. Pray that God will give you boldness to share with those in your family and at your job.

Daily Bible Reading

Day 1: Mark 13-14
Day 2: Mark 15-16
Day 3: Psalm 1 and Proverbs 1
Day 4: Psalm 2 and Proverbs 2
Day 5: Psalm 3 and Proverbs 3

29. The King Comes

Know the Word

Read John 1:1-18

1. What do you see? (Observation)

2. What does it mean? (Interpretation)

3. What do you do? (Application)

4. How should you pray?

Last week we learned about the themes of exile and restoration and concluded our study of the major themes in the Old Testament. This week we'll get into the New Testament and look at material that is probably more familiar—the gospels of Jesus Christ. While you may know the story of Jesus better than that of Isaiah or Haggai, you may not know exactly how the gospels relate and connect to the Prophets or any other parts of the Old Testament. To rightly understand the story of Jesus Christ, we need to know how His story completes and fulfills all the stories that came before him.

Think about this: after Jesus' resurrection, two of his disciples were walking on the road to Emmaus, discussing the death of Jesus and the empty tomb. Jesus veiled His identity and appeared to them. He asked what they were talking about, and they explained to Him the recent events concerning Jesus of Nazareth. It was clear they didn't understand the meaning or significance of the events. Luke gives Jesus' response, "And he said to them, 'O foolish ones, and slow of heart to believe all that the prophets have spoken! Was it not necessary that the Christ should suffer these things and enter into his glory?' And beginning with Moses and the Prophets, he interpreted to them in all the Scriptures the things concerning himself" (Luke 24:26-27). What Scriptures were Jesus referring to? There was no New Testament yet; all Jesus had was the Old Testament, which is precisely the point.

Jesus believed that everything Moses wrote, the Prophets wrote, and the other Old Testament authors wrote was about Him! He was telling the disciples that if they rightly read and understood the Old Testament, they would have known and understood the life and ministry of Jesus Christ. The Old Testament pointed toward the coming Messiah, Jesus Christ. Not only did the Old Testament point toward Jesus, but Paul also says that all of God's promises find their "yes" in Jesus (2 Cor. 1:20). "Wait," you may be thinking, "all of God's promises?" Yes, all of his promises. While we don't have space to examine every promise, we'll look at some of them, and hopefully it will start to make sense as to how and why Jesus Christ is the key to rightly reading, understanding, and interpreting the entirety of Scripture.

So how exactly were Moses and the Prophets pointing toward Jesus Christ? And how does Jesus Christ fulfill the promises of God? Today we'll see how the story of Jesus relates and connects to so many of the themes we've looked at so far. This lesson will only begin to scratch the surface of the depths of Christ, but it should be a helpful starting point for more study.

JOHN 1:1-18

If you think the beginning of John's gospel sounds a lot like the beginning of Genesis, you've made the right connection! John intentionally causes his readers to think back to Genesis 1-2, and he begins by interpreting the Old Testament through the lens of Jesus Christ. Christ was present and active in the beginning. Remember, one of the more helpful themes from the creation account is the presence of God. God's presence made the garden of Eden such a wonderful place for Adam and Eve. However, their sin forced God to drive them out of His presence into a world of sin and death. The biblical story is all about God's saving work to provide humanity a way back into His presence. In the Old Testament, humans could never be directly in God's presence because of their sin. If they got too close to Him, they would die. His presence was always veiled, whether in the temple or tabernacle. Though the presence of God could lead to death, it provided Israel safety and hope, which is why the tabernacle and temple were so important.

John knew how important the tabernacle and temple were in Israel's history, and he also knew that Jesus Christ was God, so he writes, "And the Word became flesh and dwelt among us, and we have seen his glory, glory as of the only Son from the Father, full of grace and truth" (John 1:14). The importance of John's statement isn't immediately clear because of the English translation from Greek. What's translated as *dwelt* is the Greek word *eskēnōsen* (don't worry about pronouncing that), which can also be translated "to dwell in a tent, encamp, or tabernacle." Therefore, it would be appropriate to translate John 1:14 as, "And the Word became flesh and tabernacled among us." John wants his readers to understand this: the presence of God that was once in Eden, the tabernacle, and the temple is now in the person of Jesus Christ. The safety, security, and salvation of God's presence is no longer in a building; it's in a person. It's through Jesus Christ that humans can see God's glory and grace, and it's through Jesus Christ that they can experience salvation and be restored to God's presence.

Early Jews reading John's gospel would have immediately recognized the claims John was making, and they would have been quite offended, perplexed, or intrigued. Throughout John's gospel, he interprets the Old Testament through the lens of Jesus Christ and shows how Moses and the Prophets pointed to Jesus. Several times in this text, John calls Jesus the light, which is another reference to the presence of God being in the person of Jesus Christ. Each year Israel celebrated the Festival of Tabernacles (Lev. 23:39-43). During the Festival of Tabernacles, there was a ceremony called the Illumination of the Temple, which involved the lighting of four tall and large candles that were placed on the temple grounds. The candles burned through the night, and, because the temple was on a hill, they could be seen throughout Jerusalem. Seeing the light shining in the darkness caused Jews to remember when the presence of God led Israel through the wilderness after leaving Egypt in the form of a cloud by day and fire by night, and it prompted them to look forward to the future hope of the Messiah who would restore God's people to His presence. John says that the presence of God is in Jesus Christ, and He is the light shining into a dark world.

In verse 7, John calls Jesus the true light. He doesn't mean that the former light was false. God's glory was really in the temple and tabernacle, but it wasn't supposed to stay there permanently. God's desire was for His people to be in His presence without a veil like Adam and Eve were in Eden. The tabernacle and temple pointed toward a greater reality. Jesus, then, was and is the true and better temple. It doesn't mean the old temple was false. It means the temple was never the final plan; it was imperfect. This idea of Jesus being the true and better can be applied to many of the themes and characters we've looked at to this point. If you can remember this formula of Jesus as the true and better thing, the gospels will begin to make a lot of sense in regard to biblical theology. Also, it's crucial to realize that Jesus is both doing perfectly what the former things (Adam, the temple, Israel) couldn't do perfectly, and He's reversing the effects of sin brought about because of Adam (examples below).

THE TRUE AND BETTER

Jesus Christ is the true and better Adam. Whereas the first Adam disobeyed God while in His presence and was cast into the wilderness, the second Adam (Christ) willingly went into the wilderness and remained faithful to the Father. Where the first Adam brought sin and death into the world because of disobedience, the second Adam brought life and salvation because of His obedience (Rom. 5:12-21). Luke shapes his gospel in such a way as to display Christ as the new and better Adam. In chapter 3:23-38, Luke gives the genealogy of Jesus and traces Him back to Adam. At the beginning of chapter 4, Luke recounts the temptation of Jesus. He very much wants us to think about Adam's failure in the garden and see that Jesus Christ is the faithful Adam who will not be tempted by Satan.

Christ is the true and better Moses. Whereas the first Moses couldn't enter into the promised land because of his sin, the second Moses leads His people into God's presence because of His righteousness. In Matthew's gospel, he draws pointed parallels between Moses and Jesus. Remember, in Deuteronomy 18:15-22, God promised that a prophet like Moses would come and lead Israel. Matthew believes the true and better Moses is Jesus Christ. In chapters 2-5, Matthew records the following four events: 1) Jesus's family flees to Egypt, and they return from Egypt to Nazareth to fulfill prophecy (Moses came out of Egypt with Israel); 2) Jesus is baptized in the Jordan River (Moses crossed the Red Sea [remember the significance of going into the waters of death from Lesson 22]); 3) Jesus goes into the wilderness for 40 days and nights, is tempted by Satan, and remains faithful (Moses and Israel wandered in the desert for 40 years and were unfaithful, which meant Moses couldn't enter the promised land [Ex. 20:10-13; Deut. 34:1-8]); 4) Jesus goes up on a mountain to deliver God's law (Moses went up on a mountain to receive God's law). Matthew paints the picture of the true and better Moses. The second Moses was able to free God's people from spiritual slavery, forgive sin, and initiate a new covenant. There are even five distinct sections in Matthew where Jesus teaches (chapters 5-7, 10, 13, 18, and 23-25). This is likely meant to reflect the five books of Moses in the Torah, which, if you remember from lesson 23, means "teaching," showing Jesus is the true and better teacher.

Christ is also the true and better David. Whereas the first David was a king who fell to his sinful desires, the second David is a king who rules in faithfulness, holiness, and justice. David was Israel's greatest king and a man after God's own heart, but David was also sinful and committed both adultery and murder. Jesus Christ is the king who defeated sin and death and rules from the right hand of the Father, and He is the king to whom every knee will bow and every tongue confess that He is Lord. Remember God's promise to David from 2 Samuel 7:1-17. God told David that a king would come from his line who would establish God's kingdom and rule on the throne forever. Only a true and better David could do such a work.

These are just a few examples of Jesus being true and better. However, Jesus is the true and better Abraham, the true and better Isaac, the true and better Joseph, the true and better Aaron, the true and better Solomon, and the true and better prophet. Jesus is also the true and better temple and the true and better Passover lamb. As a whole, Jesus is the true and better Israel. Whereas Israel was to be faithful to God's covenant but failed time and time again, the true and better Israel, Jesus Christ, was faithful. Where everyone and everything in the Old Testament fell short because of sin, Jesus prevailed because He is the true and better. Prophet, Priest, and King

John also wrote the book of Revelation, and in it he calls Jesus, "the faithful witness, the firstborn of the dead, and the ruler of the kings on earth" (Rev. 1:5). As a faithful witness, Jesus is a faithful prophet. As the firstborn of the dead, Jesus is the great high priest. And as ruler of the kings of the earth, Jesus is the ultimate king. Traditionally, the three roles of prophet, priest, and king are called the three-fold offices of Christ. It's His work in each of these roles that frees us from the bondage of sin. Therefore, in combination with the true/better idea, we can say Jesus is the true and better prophet, priest, and king.

Prophets represented God before the people. The Old Testament prophets often started their messages by saying, "Thus says the Lord." Jesus Christ not only brought the word of God but also was the Word of God. It was his words and life, death, and resurrection that brought and provided the good news of salvation. Jesus Christ also fulfilled the role of priest. Priests represented the people before God. The High Priest would enter into the holy of holies once a year and offer a sacrifice for sin on behalf of the people. Jesus Christ not only offered a sacrifice, but He was the sacrifice. Because he was sinless, he was the perfect, once-for-all sacrifice for sin (see Heb. 7-10). After His death and resurrection, Jesus Christ returned to be with the Father and sat down on his throne as king. In Revelation, John provides a sneak peek of what the throne room of heaven is like (Rev. 4-5). As king, Jesus rules with perfect equity and justice, and He will rule forever. The framework of the three-fold offices of Christ helps us better understand Jesus's life and ministry in the gospels.

THE KINGDOM OF GOD

In lesson 25, we looked at the importance of kingdom, and specifically the kingdom of God (refer to the lesson if you need a refresher). When Jesus began His earthly ministry, he said, "The time is fulfilled, and the kingdom of God is at hand; repent and believe in the gospel" (Mk. 1:15). The Jewish people had been waiting a long time on the Messiah to come and establish God's kingdom. When Jesus Christ arrived, He was not at all the king they expected. They wanted a strong military leader to come and overthrow the government, but that's not how Jesus established His kingdom. Jesus proved himself to be king by humility and sacrificial love. He didn't count equality with the Father a thing to be grasped; rather, He humbled himself and took on the form of a servant. King Jesus showed that His kingdom would be vastly different than the kingdoms of the earth. Unlike any king before, King Jesus went to the cross and died the death you and I deserve. Incredibly, He has invited us into His kingdom. We are under His rule and sovereign reign. Remember, there is an already/not yet aspect to God's kingdom. King Jesus is already ruling, and His kingdom is already here, but not yet as it will be one day. As the church, we are to participate in the mission Jesus Christ has called us into. We wait and long for the day that King Jesus returns. Until then, let's be found faithful to invite others into the kingdom of our gracious and loving God.

CONCLUSION

There is so much more we could say about Jesus's life and ministry. The key concept for you to understand is Jesus as the true and better. All God's promises are a yes in Jesus Christ. He is the faithful prophet, priest, and king. Hopefully, this lesson provided a glimpse into how important it is to read and understand the Old Testament. Without understanding the important themes and ideas from the Old Testament, it's difficult to make much sense of Jesus Christ. He is the key to connecting the Old and New Testaments and making sense of the Christian faith. We don't study biblical theology for the sake of knowledge. We study biblical theology for the sake of knowing and loving Christ and living to glorify Him. May this help toward that end.

In your group, reflect on the following questions:

1. What stands out to you most about this passage from John 1:1-18?

2. What is something new you learned from this chapter and its importance to the overall story of Scripture

3. What themes or ideas above help you think well about this chapter and the life and ministry of Jesus?

Model the Word

1. Take time for each member to explain an important aspect of Jesus's life and ministry.

2. How would you teach these passages to someone else? What aspects or ideas would you emphasize?

Share the Word

1. Think about reading these chapters from the perspective of an unbeliever. How could you use them to share the gospel or begin a gospel conversation? How can connecting Jesus's life and ministry to other themes we've studied help?

2. Why is it helpful to understand the three offices of Christ (Prophet, Priest, King)? How can you use these ideas as you share the gospel?

Pray the Word

1. As a group, spend time praying for each other to have a better understanding of God's Word.

2. Thank the Father for sending the Son so that we may have life. Praise God for the gospel.

3. Pray for opportunities to share the gospel with others. Pray that God will give you boldness to share with those in your family and at your job.

Daily Bible Reading

Day 1: Psalm 4 and Proverbs 4

Day 2: Psalm 5 and Proverbs 5

Day 3: Psalm 6 and Proverbs 6

Day 4: Psalm 7 and Proverbs 7

Day 5: Psalm 8 and Proverbs 8

30. The King Establishes His Church

Know the Word
Read Acts 2:1-47

1. What do you see? (Observation)

2. What does it mean? (Interpretation)

3. What do you do? (Application)

4. How should you pray?

Last week we looked at the life and ministry of Jesus Christ and how He not only relates to the rest of Scripture but also holds it all together. Christ is the key to connecting the Old Testament to the New, and it's only through Jesus Christ that the whole Bible makes sense. The gospels record the arrival of King Jesus and His saving life, death, and resurrection. In the book of Acts, we see the establishment of King Jesus's church and their response to His mission. Much of the New Testament is dedicated to the story of the church and instructions for the church. Today, we'll learn about the church as a theme in Scripture and how it relates to the overall story of the Bible. Some of the material below may seem a bit repetitive or familiar. If so, that's a good thing! Understanding the themes of the Old Testament help make sense of the New Testament because the New Testament authors pull from the themes and material of the Old Testament and interpret them through Christ. While there are certainly new ideas introduced in the New Testament, much of what we'll study today and the next couple of weeks builds upon previous themes, like the presence of God, the temple, etc. If you're able to connect the dots between the Old and New Testaments and easily identify how they relate, that means you're learning, and that's the goal!

THE CHURCH

In the broadest sense, the church is all believers of all time, past and present. This is called the universal church. In a narrower sense, a church is a group of Christians who meet to worship, study God's Word, and practice the ordinances together consistently. This is called a local church. The universal church has been and is comprised of many local churches. For this lesson, we'll focus on the universal church. We want to understand how the biblical authors think about the church and which themes, if any, help us think well about the church today.

METAPHORS FOR THE CHURCH

The biblical authors use many different metaphors to explain the church and its purpose. These metaphors were not haphazardly chosen. Instead, the authors use metaphors that are meant to cause their readers to think about the various parts of the story we've learned about so far. For example, Jesus says, "I am the vine; you are the branches" (Jn. 15:5). The church, then, can be compared to branches on a vine. But why? That seems like a weird metaphor. Remember the part of last week's lesson about Jesus being true and better. In John 15, Jesus claims to be the true and better vine. In Psalm 80 and Isaiah 5, Israel is compared to a vine, and God is compared to a vinedresser. Where Israel failed to be a faithful vine, Jesus proved to be the faithful vine. He is both the true and better vine and the true and better Israel. The church, then, is compared to branches stemming from the true vine, Jesus Christ. The metaphor makes sense in light of prior biblical themes, and it emphasizes how connected the church is and should be to Jesus Christ. The church's very life depends on being connected to Jesus.

The church is also called the family of God. Jesus says that those who follow Him are His brothers and sisters (Matt. 12:46-50). The church has been adopted into God's family (Eph. 1:5; Gal. 4:5) and are His children (Rom 8:12-17), which means Christians are spiritually brothers and sisters. The church not only is like a family but also is a family. The idea of family in the Old Testament is quite important. In Genesis, God uses Abraham and Sarah to start a family. Through that family came a nation, and through that nation all the families of the earth were supposed to be blessed. Israel failed to be a blessing to the nations, but the Messiah came from the family of Abraham to make a way for both Israel and the nations. Because of Jesus Christ, the church is the family of God through whom the nations are currently being blessed.

THE CHURCH AS THE PRESENCE OF GOD

There are some other important metaphors for the church used in the New Testament, like the bride of Christ and the body of Christ. One of the most helpful metaphors for biblical theology is the church as a spiritual temple or the house of God (1 Pet. 2:4-5; Heb. 3:1-6). Think back to the lesson on the temple/tabernacle. Why were the temple and tabernacle so important? They were where the presence of God dwelt among His people. God's presence is a theme that starts in Genesis 1-2 and runs right through the Bible until the final chapters of Revelation. As the house of God or the new temple, the church is where God's presence dwells not only among His people but also within His people. In Acts 2, the Holy Spirit indwells the Apostles and, eventually, the church. The Holy Spirit, because He is God, is the presence of God in believers. When the Son of God took on human flesh, the presence of God was in the person of Jesus Christ. Jesus Christ is the true and better tabernacle and the true and better temple. What is true of Christ is also true of the church He saved. The church is the temple or house where the presence of God dwells.

THE CHURCH FULFILLS ISRAEL'S PURPOSE

Why is it helpful to think about the church as the temple of God's presence? In Israel, the temple was where God's presence dwelt. His presence meant both physical and spiritual safety for Israel. God's salvation, however, wasn't meant for Israel alone. Since the beginning, God desired the nations to know and worship him. God wanted Israel to be a light to the nations; their covenant faithfulness to God was supposed to attract others to follow the LORD. God wanted the nations to come to the temple and offer sacrifices and worship. The temple was a light in the darkness, calling the nations to come and worship Yahweh. In this sense, Israel was supposed to draw the nations to God. Isaiah writes:

6And the foreigners who join themselves to the LORD, to minister to him, to love the name of the LORD, and to be his servants, everyone who keeps the Sabbath and does not profane it, and holds fast my covenant—7these I will bring to my holy mountain, and make them joyful in my house of prayer; their burnt offerings and their sacrifices will be accepted on my altar; for my house shall be called a house of prayer for all people (Isaiah 56:6-7).

Israel, however, failed time and time again at keeping covenant faithfulness to God. Israel was also supposed to take the knowledge of Yahweh to the nations. Isaiah writes:

[18]For I know their works and their thoughts, and the time is coming to gather all nations and tongues. And they shall come and shall see my glory, [19]and I will set a sign among them. And from them I will send survivors to the nations, to Tarshish, Pul, and Lud, who draw the bow, to Tubal and Javan, to the coastlands far away, that have not heard my fame or seen my glory. And they shall declare my glory among the nations (Isaiah 66:18-19).

Just as Israel failed to draw the nations into Yahweh, they also failed to take the salvation of God to the nations. Think of the prophet Jonah. God gave him the special task to call Nineveh to turn from its sin and confess Yahweh as the true God, or else God would destroy the city and its people. Rather than being excited to proclaim the salvation of the God of Israel, Jonah ran from his divinely appointed task. Even after he eventually preached the good news to Nineveh, he was upset that God was gracious and merciful toward a foreign nation of pagans! The story shows Jonah's hard heart toward the nations, but it is also representative of Israel's hard heart toward the nations. Just as Jonah was unwilling to take the good news of Yahweh to the nations because of his sin, Israel was unwilling to take the good news to the nations because of its sin. Israel, therefore, failed to bring the nations to God and failed to take God to the nations.

As the true and better Israel, Jesus Christ was faithful where Israel was faithless. Through his perfect birth, life, death, burial, and resurrection, Jesus provided a way for sinners to know God and worship Him. Because of Christ, the church now can fulfill the two roles Israel could not. First, the church is the light shining in the darkness, calling all people to come and worship the true God. Second, the church is sent on God's mission to take the gospel to the nations, so that they may worship Him where they are. Here's the neat thing: in the Old Testament, the presence of God was in the temple, and the temple was stationary. It was in Jerusalem, and it couldn't move. Therefore, if the nations wanted to make sacrifices and worship God, they needed to go to Jerusalem. Today, however, the presence of God is in believers who comprise the church. The church is incredibly mobile. The church is where believers gather together, and that can be anywhere. The nations don't need to travel to Jerusalem to worship God; they simply need to meet where they are. The presence of God is in the church, and the church is all over the world. As the church continues to be faithful on God's mission, the nations will continually be drawn into the church and God's kingdom. Because of Christ, the church can draw the nations to God by taking the gospel to the nations.

THE CHURCH AND BAPTISM AND THE LORD'S SUPPER

You may have never thought about baptism and the Lord's Supper, known as the ordinances, being the continuation of themes within biblical theology. Baptism, for example, has a spiritual meaning that is closely tied with themes and ideas in the Old Testament. Think about the Exodus. Remember when God brought Moses and Israel through the Red Sea. Chaotic waters, or the sea, in the Old Testament represented death. What should have been death for Israel led to life because of God's grace and mercy. Once God allowed Israel to pass through the waters, He caused the waters to crash in on Pharaoh and his armies and cause them death as an act of judgment. When Jesus is baptized (Matthew 3:13-17), He portrays what His life and ministry will look like. Jesus passes through the waters of death, but, because He is God, He comes out of them alive. After His crucifixion, Jesus physically died, but, because He is God, He resurrected from death and is alive. When a new follower of Jesus is baptized, that individual publicly confesses that they have spiritually died and been buried with Christ and have been raised with Him to walk in the newness of life. Paul writes:

3Do you not know that all of us who have been baptized into Christ Jesus were baptized into his death? 4We were buried therefore with him by baptism into death, in order that, just as Christ was raised from the dead by the glory of the Father, we too might walk in the newness of life" (Romans 6:3-4).

Baptism points toward the future reality of the church as well. Until Jesus Christ returns, every believer will pass through the waters of physical death. Because of the work of Christ, however, every believer will one day be raised from the dead and spend eternity with God (1 Cor. 15). The act of baptism pulls from several Old Testament themes.

The Lord's Supper is closely tied to the Passover, another event from the Exodus. Prior to the Exodus, God brought the final plague upon Egypt, the death of the firstborn son. Only the homes that had the blood of the lamb on the doorpost would be spared from death. The homes in Israel were spared by God's grace and mercy, while the homes in Egypt were not. After Israel left Egypt, they celebrated the Passover each year in remembrance of God's salvation. Jesus was crucified during the time of the Passover celebration. Prior to His death, He was with His disciples and reinterpreted for them the meaning of the Passover (Matt. 26:26-29). Jesus told them that His body was going to be broken and His blood shed for the sins of humanity. Jesus Christ was the once-for-all sacrifice for sin. The church celebrates the Lord's Supper both looking backward and forward. We remember Christ's body that was broken and blood that was shed on our behalf for our sins. We also look forward to when Jesus will return to save us from the flesh. The Lord's Supper entails many themes and ideas found in the Old Testament.

CONCLUSION

The church is comprised of all the followers of Jesus throughout history. The New Testament authors use many different metaphors to describe the church. Many of those metaphors derive from Old Testament themes and ideas. One such metaphor is the church as the spiritual temple or house of God. The church is the spiritual temple that is able to both draw the nations to God and take the gospel to the nations because of the work of Jesus Christ. Where Israel was faithless, Jesus was faithful. Because of the completed work of Christ, God's family and God's kingdom is spreading across the world. As the church practices baptism and the Lord's Supper, it is helpful to know how and why the ordinances pull from biblical themes and ideas. Today, the church is to be faithful to the task Christ has given. It should be our goal to take the gospel to those who have never heard it and draw them to Christ.

In your group, reflect on the following questions:

1. What stands out to you most about this passage from Acts be his servants 2:1-47?

2. What is something new you learned from this chapter and its importance to the overall story of Scripture?

3. What themes or ideas above help you think well about this chapter and the church?

Model the Word

1. Take time for each member to explain an important aspect of the church as it relates to biblical theology.

2. How would you teach this passage to someone else? What aspects or ideas would you emphasize?

Share the Word

1. Think about reading this chapter from the perspective of an unbeliever. How could you use it to share the gospel or begin a gospel conversation?

2. Why is it helpful to understand the importance of the church and how it relates to the Old Testament? How can you use these ideas as you share the gospel?

Pray the Word

1. As a group, spend time praying for each other to have a better understanding of God's Word.

2. Thank God for the church, the body of Christ. Pray for one another to love the church.

3. Pray for opportunities to share the gospel with others. Pray that God will give you boldness to share with those in your family and at your job.

Daily Bible Reading

Day 1: Psalm 14 and Proverbs 14
Day 2: Psalm 15 and Proverbs 15
Day 3: Psalm 16 and Proverbs 16
Day 4: Psalm 17 and Proverbs 17
Day 5: Psalm 18 and Proverbs 18

31. The King Nurtures His Church

Know the Word

Read Philippians 1:1-4:23

1. What do you see? (Observation)

2. What does it mean? (Interpretation)

3. What do you do? (Application)

4. How should you pray?

During the past two weeks, we've learned about some themes from the Gospels and Acts. The Gospels concern the life and ministry of Jesus Christ, and Acts focuses on the work of the Holy Spirit through the newly formed church. What about the rest of the New Testament? The Gospels and Acts are only five of 27 New Testament books (albeit five sizable and important books). 21 of the 22 remaining books are called Epistles. Epistle means letter, and that's exactly what these 21 books are. Some are letters directed to an individual (1 and 2 Timothy, Titus, Philemon). Others are written to a church or groups of churches in an area (Galatians, Ephesians, 1 and 2 Peter). Some are quite long, like Romans or Corinthians, while others are quite short, like Philemon, Jude, or 1 and 2 John. The Epistles may be some of your favorite books to read, and they are certainly some of the most often taught and preached books. Why is that so?

First, they are much shorter than a lot of the other books in the Bible. Preaching or reading through Isaiah would take considerably more time than Philippians. Second, the Epistles are some of the clearest writings in the Bible. Reading the Epistles is certainly easier than reading the prophetic books because the authors use plain language instead of poetry. Third, the Epistles tell us what to do or how to live the Christian life. Reading narrative can be entertaining and informative, but it's often difficult to know how to apply stories from Scripture to the Christian life. The Epistles, on the other hand, give direct instructions, which makes application a bit easier.

Although the Epistles are short, clear, and tell us what to do, they are not necessarily simple. We can't confuse clarity with simplicity. These are some of the most theologically rich books of the Bible. Read Romans 1-9, Ephesians 1-3, Philippians 1-2:11, or the entire book of Hebrews. These letters aren't simple. In them, the authors provide great insight into the depths of who God is and what He has done. Think about what Peter says of Paul's writing: "And count the patience of our Lord as salvation, just as our beloved brother Paul also wrote to you according to the wisdom given him, as he does in all his letters when he speaks in them of these matters. There are some things in them that are hard to understand, which the ignorant and unstable twist to their own destruction, as they do the other Scriptures" (2 Pet. 3:15-16). Even Peter thought Paul's writings could be confusing! That doesn't mean, however, that you can't understand or apply them to your life. Though the letters aren't necessarily simple, they are incredibly clear. In this lesson, you'll learn more about the Epistles, how to read them, and how they connect to the rest of Scripture.

CONTEXT

As with any books in the Bible, context is vital for properly reading, interpreting, and applying the Epistles. Ask the questions who, what, when, where, and why? Typically, those questions can be answered by simply reading the letter. Letters during the time of the New Testament had a particular form, much like letters or emails do today. The general form had six parts: 1) The name of the writer, 2) name of the recipient, 3) greeting, 4) prayer wish or thanksgiving, 5) body, 6) final greeting and farewell.[1] The Epistles follow this form generally; although, there are letters that deviate from it slightly. Because Epistles are structured this way, knowing the context is fairly easy because the authors provide much of it for us. It's important to remember that each letter was written for a specific purpose. If you don't understand why the letter was written, you are bound to misunderstand how it applies to you today. The letter had meaning then, and the letter has meaning now. We must understand the difference to read the Epistles properly.

THEN AND NOW

Epistles had meaning then, when they were written, and they have meaning now. The New Testament authors wrote these letters for specific purposes. Think about this: You wouldn't write a letter today if you didn't have a reason for writing it, right? You wouldn't write a thank you letter to someone who didn't do something for you or get you something. And you wouldn't send a Christmas card in June (if you do, shame on you!). We write letters because there is a reason for doing so. The New Testament authors were no different. Some letters were written to address problems in the church or bad theology (1 Corinthians and Galatians). Some were written to encourage an individual and to provide instruction (Timothy and Titus). Each letter had a specific purpose. The instructions that come from the Epistles are in response to the purpose for which they were written. For example, Paul wrote the letter to the Galatians because they started believing a false gospel. Some people were teaching that Gentiles needed to be circumcised in order to be saved, and the Christians in Galatia believed them. Paul rebuked the church and reminded them that salvation was through faith alone. The entire letter, then, addressed that issue. Therefore, the instructions Paul gave were in relation to the problem of false teaching. To read and interpret the Epistles properly, we must figure out why the letter was written and what it meant for the church then.

Why is it so important to understand what it meant then? Because, if we don't get the context, we are bound to misinterpret what the letter means now. Take the example from Galatians. My guess is that you nor anyone else in the church today struggles with believing circumcision is necessary to be saved. We believe, however, the truth of God's Word is applicable for everyone, everywhere, during any time. So how is Galatians applicable for us today? While you may not struggle with whether or not circumcision is necessary for salvation, you may struggle at times whether or not regularly attending church or reading your Bible every day is necessary for salvation. Maybe you question whether or not the sin in your life keeps God from loving you. Paul is clear in his letter to the Galatians: you are justified by faith alone! The necessary

---

[1] Gordon D. Fee and Douglas Stuart, *How to Read the Bible for All Its Worth* (Grand Rapids: Zondervan, 2003), 56-57.

condition for salvation is faith, not faith plus something else. That's good news for us today! In this way, we can say Galatians meant something to the church then and means something to the church now. Although the letter's purpose was for an issue in a specific period in time, the truths of the letter are timeless.

The truths of the letters are also contextual at times. 1 Corinthians 11:14-15 says, "[14]Does not nature itself teach you that if a man wears long hair it is a disgrace for him, [15]but if a woman has long hair, it is for her glory? For her hair is given to her for a covering." Is this a contextual truth or timeless truth? Is it always wrong for men to have long hair or women to have short hair? From the evidence of Scripture, it must be a contextual truth. In the Old Testament, Samson had long hair as part of his Nazirite vow. God told his mother not to cut his hair. God said to Moses of those who take the Nazarite vow, "All the days of his vow of separation, no razor shall touch his head. Until the time is completed for which he separates himself to the LORD, he shall be holy. He shall let the locks of hair of his head grow long" (Num. 6:5; see Num. 6 for more on the Nazarite vow). If Paul's instruction in 1 Corinthians 11:14-15 is a timeless truth, then we have to admit Scripture is contradictory, or God changed his mind about hair. Neither of those are true, so Paul's command must be a contextual truth. In Corinth, the cultural norm was for men to have short hair and women to have long hair. Women would wear a head covering in public, which would hide their hair. When women showed their hair in public, it was often a sign that they were prostitutes. When men had long hair, it was often a sign that they practiced paganism or were homosexual. Paul, then, instructs the church in light of contextual realities. Today, it is normal for men to have long hair and women to have short hair. It's also normal for women to go in public without a head covering. Paul's instruction in 1 Corinthians 11 is a contextual truth. To faithfully read, interpret, and apply the Epistles, we must know the context and discern which truths are contextual and which are timeless. The Epistles had meaning then, and they have meaning now.

INDICATIVES AND IMPERATIVES

One of the reasons we love the Epistles so much is because they tell us what to do or how to live the Christian life. The biblical authors give us commands, which are also called imperatives. Paul says, "Children, obey your parents in the Lord, for this is right" (Eph. 6:1). James says, "My brothers, show no partiality as you hold the faith in our Lord Jesus Christ, the Lord of glory" (Jm. 2:1). Paul and James give the church imperative commands for how to live the Christian life. Imperatives in the Epistles are typically straightforward and easy to understand (although they aren't always easy to obey!). These commands are not arbitrary, however. Imperative commands always follow indicative truths. An indicative signifies a truth that has already taken place. The Epistles are comprised of indicatives and imperatives. The authors always provide some amount of indicative truth about the good news of Jesus Christ. Sometimes the indicatives make up the majority of the letter. Romans, for example, is mostly indicative truths.

Chapters 1-11 are about who God is and what he has done. Chapters 12-16 are imperative commands. Other letters, like James, are mainly comprised of imperatives.

Identifying indicatives and imperatives in the Epistles is important for a couple of reasons. First, it helps to make sense of the main ideas in each letter. If you can find when and where each author gives truths and commands, it will greatly help make sense of their purpose for writing the letter, specific contextual issues, and their overall argument. Second, it helps us understand that the biblical authors never give imperative commands without first providing indicative truth. Obedience to commands is pointless if we don't have a right understanding of who God is and what He has done. In Ephesians 1-3, Paul provides an in-depth and robust theology of God's work in salvation. In chapters 4-6, he gives imperative commands in response to the indicative truths. Chapters 4-6 are simply a response to the beauty of 1-3. The church should live rightly before God because of His grace and mercy through Christ Jesus. The biblical authors never want their readers to follow commands for the sake of following commands—that's legalism! They make much of the gospel and much of Christ, and, only then, draw application for their readers. It can be easy to focus on the imperatives and not the indicatives. The imperatives are understandable and straightforward, and, honestly, the indicatives can be the most confusing parts. But the indicatives, or the truths of the gospel, are the best part of the Epistles! We can only live rightly before God if we first think rightly about God. The Epistles help us do both.

THEMES IN THE EPISTLES

The authors of the Epistles were keenly aware of the Hebrew Scriptures, the themes within them, and how Jesus Christ was the fulfillment of God's many promises. Paul writes of Jesus Christ, "For all the promises of God find their Yes in him. That is why it is through him that we utter our Amen to God for his glory" (2 Cor. 1:20). They utilize Old Testament themes like the presence of God, the kingdom of God, covenants, and others. They also introduce new themes that apply to God's newly formed church. In Romans and Galatians, Paul makes a big deal about the themes of justification and righteousness. Justification is God's act of making or declaring someone to be righteous, which means to be in right standing with God. Paul says the only way people can experience justification is through faith alone. That's huge! The theme of justification by faith alone is one that has been vital to Christians throughout history. It was one of the issues that sparked the Protestant Reformation!

Resurrection from the dead is another theme that is crucial for the New Testament authors. Paul says without the resurrection, Christians are hopeless: "But if there is no resurrection of the dead, then not even Christ has been raised. And if Christ has not been raised, then our preaching is in vain and your faith is in vain" (1 Cor. 15:13-14). The church, then, needs to think well about resurrection and how it connects to Christ, baptism, and the end times. Justification by faith and resurrection are just two of many themes in the Epistles. Because there are so many Epistles, there isn't time or space to handle all the themes. Below is a brief synopsis of the important themes within each Epistle. All possible themes are not listed for each book.

Romans
- The Gospel (Paul's most complete explanation of the gospel)
- The Righteousness of God
- Justification by Faith
- Christian Ethics

1-2 Corinthians
- The Resurrection
- The New Covenant and Old Covenant
- The Ordinances (Baptism and Lord's Supper)

Galatians
- Justification by Faith
- Atonement
- Transformation of the Believer
- Identity of Jesus

Ephesians
- The Lordship of Christ
- Salvation
- Predestination and Election
- The Church
- Christian Ethics
- Spiritual Warfare

Philippians
- The Gospel and its Implications
- The Person and Work of Christ
- Christian Unity
- Joy in Christ
- Christian Suffering

Colossians
- The Supremacy of Christ
- The Work of Christ in Salvation
- Christian Ethics

1-2 Thessalonians
- The Second Coming of Christ
- The Antichrist
- Eternal State of Believers and Unbelievers
- Christian Work Ethic
- Election and Perseverance

1-2 Timothy
- Qualifications for Church Leaders
- Preservation of Believers
- Salvation
- Trustworthy Sayings
- Discipleship

Titus
- Qualifications for Church Leaders
- Sound Doctrine
- Christian Ethics

Philemon
- Mutual Love and Brotherhood in the Body of Christ
- Christian Approach to Slavery and Other Social Issues

Hebrews
- The God who Speaks in Scripture
- The Person and Work of Jesus Christ
- Jesus the High Priest
- Perseverance of Believers
- Discipleship

James
- Relationship Between Faith and Works
- Wisdom
- Ethics
- Christology
- Eschatology

1-2 Peter
- Christian Ethics
- Suffering and Persecution
- Proper Teaching and Heresy

1-3 John
- Christian Ethics
- Christian Doctrine
- Discipleship
- Salvation
- Love

Jude
- False Teaching
- Contending for the Faith

CONCLUSION

The Epistles are immensely helpful books for thinking rightly about who God is, what He has done, and how to live rightly in response. It's important to remember that each letter was written by a specific person, to a specific person or persons, and for a specific reason. Though we derive much of our Christian theology from the Epistles, none of the Epistles are a complete overview of any one person's theology. For example, if you just read Romans and Galatians, you might think that justification is the only way Paul talks about salvation. He uses "justify" fifteen times in Romans and eight times in Galatians. However, across his other eleven letters, he only uses it twice (once in Corinthians and once in Titus).[2] Context dictates the content of these letters, which means context must dictate how we read, interpret, and apply the epistles. As you continue to read the Epistles, look for the themes listed above. It's also a good practice to read the entire letter in one sitting. The authors make sustained arguments, and you're more likely to misinterpret their argument if you only read small sections. Get a big-picture view of what the author is saying, then take time to study smaller sections. A good study Bible will help provide context and background information for each book, which will help make sense of odd or difficult passages.

---

[2] *Ibd.*, 58-59.

In your group, reflect on the following questions:

1. What stands out to you most about Philippians?

2. What is something new you learned from this book and the importance of the Epistles?

3. What themes or ideas above help you think well about this book?

Model the Word

1. Take time for each member to explain an important aspect of the Epistles and how to read them well.

2. How would you teach the importance of the Epistles to someone else? What aspects or ideas would you emphasize?

Share the Word

1. Think about reading this book from the perspective of an unbeliever. How could you use it to share the gospel or begin a gospel conversation?

2. Why is it helpful to understand the importance of the Epistles in relation to the whole Bible? How can you use these ideas as you share the gospel?

Pray the Word

1. As a group, spend time praying for each other to have a better understanding of God's Word.

2. Pray for opportunities to share the gospel with others. Pray that God will give you boldness to share with those in your family and at your job.

Daily Bible Reading

Day 1: Psalm 19 and Proverbs 19
Day 2: Psalm 20 and Proverbs 20
Day 3: Psalm 21 and Proverbs 21
Day 4: Psalm 22 and Proverbs 22
Day 5: Psalm 23 and Proverbs 23

32. The King Returns

Know the Word
Read Revelation 21-22

1. What do you see? (Observation)

2. What does it mean? (Interpretation)

3. What do you do? (Application)

4. How should you pray?

Over the past twelve weeks, we've studied a brief biblical-theological overview of the Bible. This week we'll conclude this portion on biblical theology by learning about the return of Jesus Christ, the end times, and the book of Revelation. Everyone wants to know what the end times will entail. Oddly, the Bible doesn't provide a ton of information about the particular details surrounding the return of Christ and the end times. Many theologians, pastors, and Christians throughout church history have debated and speculated about when Jesus Christ will return and what will happen when He does. While those discussions can be helpful, the focus for today is to look at the return of Jesus Christ from the perspective of biblical theology. The Bible provides a beautiful picture of the return of Christ and what the church can look forward to in eternity.

WAITING FOR THE KING

While the Bible isn't clear about when Jesus Christ will return, it is quite clear that He will (Heb. 9:28; Lk. 21:5-28; Rev. 1:7; 1 Thess. 4:16-17). But the question we all want the answer to is, "when?" It's been roughly 2,000 years since Jesus ascended into heaven; when is He coming back? Anyone can look at the world and see it is broken and sinful. This world is not as it should be. God certainly has the power to fix and restore it, and He promised he would; so, why hasn't He yet? What is He waiting on? Have you ever asked any of these questions? If so, you're not alone. All Christians want to know when Jesus Christ is coming to restore His kingdom. Before Jesus' ascension into heaven, the disciples asked about this very thing: "So when they had come together, they asked him, 'Lord, will you at this time restore the kingdom to Israel?'" (Acts 1:6). Jesus had not even left yet, and they wanted to know when He was going to fix and restore the world. Rather than giving them an exact time and date of His return, Jesus told them, "It is not for you to know times or seasons that the Father has fixed by his own authority. But you will receive power when the Holy Spirit has come upon you, and you will be my witnesses in Jerusalem and in all Judea and Samaria, and to the end of the earth" (Acts 1:7). Jesus didn't tell them what they wanted to hear, but He did tell them what they needed to hear. He told them to wait on the Holy Spirit. Once the disciples received the Spirit, they would understand Jesus' mission and their part in it.

Although the disciples in the context of Acts 1 and 2 were waiting for a particular purpose (the coming of the Spirit), they still longed for and awaited the return of Christ throughout their ministries and lives. Paul writes, "But our citizenship is in heaven, and from it we await a Savior, the Lord Jesus Christ" (Eph. 3:20). Peter tells the church, "But according to his promise we are waiting for new heavens and a new earth in which righteousness dwells" (2 Pet. 3:13). And Jude says, "keep yourselves in the love of God, waiting for the mercy of our Lord Jesus Christ that leads to eternal life" (Jude 1:21). Waiting is part of the Christian life, but waiting isn't new for God's people. Think about how long Israel waited for the Messiah, who was promised in Genesis 3:15. As we saw throughout the Old Testament, waiting can be difficult. Israel often failed as they waited for the promises and plans of God to unfold. What happened right after the Exodus? Israel complained and wished they were back in Egypt. What happened when Moses went to receive God's law on Mount Sinai? It took hardly no time before the people worshiped an idol. Each time God showed Israel grace and mercy, it wasn't long before they turned back to their sinful ways. Israel lost sight of their purpose in waiting. Israel was supposed to be a light to the nations, drawing those far from God close to Him. But Israel lost sight of the mission.

Today, the church faces the same struggle. It's difficult to wait well. Some Christians may be like Israel, constantly losing sight of God's plan and purpose, and they frequently give in to temptation and fall into sin. Others may be like the disciples were before Jesus ascended into heaven. All they do is question and try to figure out when the end will come, without doing any of the work Christ commanded. We want to be like the disciples after they received the Holy Spirit. They worked for the King while they waited on the King.

WORKING FOR THE KING

You can probably guess by now what the work is for those who are waiting on the King. That's right: making disciples! Jesus said to his disciples, "Go therefore and make disciples of all nations, baptizing them in the name of the Father and of the Son and of the Holy Spirit, teaching them to observe all that I have commanded you. And behold, I am with you always, to the end of the age" (Matthew 28:18-20). The last command Jesus gave His followers was for them to make disciples. You've spent the last 30 weeks learning about what a disciple is, does, looks like, lives like, and knows. All the information you've received isn't meant to be stored away in the depths of your brain; it's meant to be shared with and taught to others.

Next week, we'll learn more about the process of making disciples, and you will be challenged to go and do the work of discipleship. The thought of making disciples on your own may scare you. You might get asked questions you don't know the answers to, or maybe you feel unequipped to lead someone else spiritually. Guess what? You're human; there are always going to be answers you don't know, and there will always be times when you don't feel like you have all the tools you need. The work of discipleship isn't for those who have it all together or know the most information. Discipleship is for anyone who is a follower of Jesus Christ.

Consider the parable of the talents from Matthew 25:14-30. Matthew writes, "For it will be like a man going on a journey, who called his servants and entrusted to them his property. To one he gave five talents, to another two, to another one, to each according to his ability" (Matt. 25:14-15). During the time of the New Testament, one talent was worth a lot of money. Some scholars estimate that one talent was worth about 20 years of wages. The master entrusted his servants with a lot of money! The one who had five talents turned it into ten talents. And the one who had two turned it into four. But the one who had only one talent was scared and went and hid it in the ground, producing no more talents. Once the master returned, he praised the two who had been faithful and reproduced what they were given. However, the servant who did nothing with what his master gave him was punished for his unfaithfulness. Although each of the servants had different levels of ability, the master trusted each of them to take care of his property and be faithful with what he gave them.

A couple of points from this story apply to the work of discipleship today. First, Christians should be found faithful with what God has given them. If Jesus Christ returns tomorrow, we want Him to find us being faithful doing the work He called us to do. As a disciple of Christ, don't hide or put to waste what God has entrusted you with. Be a disciple who makes disciples. Second, everyone has different levels of ability when it comes to making disciples. Paul tells the Corinthians, "Be imitators of me, as I am of Christ" (1 Cor. 11:1). I'm sure the Christians in Corinth felt like imitating Paul was an impossible task! Paul tells Timothy, "what you have heard from me in the presence of many witnesses, entrust to faithful men, who will be able to teach others also" (2 Tim. 2:2). Notice the only qualification Paul gives for what type of people Timothy should teach and train: those who are faithful. Paul doesn't tell Timothy to pick the smartest or best looking, the richest or most respected. He tells Timothy to find those who are faithful, those who are working for the King while waiting on the King.

The servants in the parable of the talents had different abilities, and the master left them his property according to their ability. All followers of Jesus Christ have different gifts and abilities. Some people have the ability to make lots of disciples. They may have an incredibly high capacity for diverse relationships, or they may simply have lots of free time to meet with and equip people to be followers of Jesus. Others may only have the capacity and time to disciple one or two people. Someone may have years of training and experience with disciples making, while others may have never discipled anyone in his or her life. It's okay! God knows the abilities you have; He created you! He's gifted and equipped you with the ability to make disciples. God doesn't desire a resume of your abilities; He desires your faithfulness. While we wait on the King, let's also work for the king.

WORSHIPPING THE KING—REVELATION 21-22

Revelation is one of, if not the most, complicated and confusing book in the Bible. Revelation falls under the genre of apocalyptic literature. While apocalyptic literature is a genre most readers today are not familiar with, Jews and early Christians reading John's letter were quite familiar with the style. Books like Ezekiel and Daniel have sections within them that are apocalyptic. Apocalyptic literature, particularly Revelation, is comprised of symbolic visions that display God's heavenly perspective of historical and present events in light of the final outcome of history. Revelation is also a prophecy (Rev. 1:3), meaning John sees himself within the long line of prophets who God uses to both warn of coming events and to provide future hope of God's ultimate restoration of heaven and earth. Revelation, then, acts as a capstone to not only all of the previous prophetic messages but also the entire biblical story.

Revelation is also a letter, meaning it had a distinct purpose for those who first read it. Revelation is a circular letter that John wrote to seven different churches in Asia Minor. Some of the churches struggled with apathy, immorality, and affluence, while others were being persecuted for their faith. Through John, Jesus Christ warns these churches that the persecution and tribulation they are facing will continue and increase, and all Christians will be faced with a choice: either compromise to the will and standards of Rome or remain faithful to Jesus Christ and suffer persecution, or even death. For those who endure, there is a beautiful promise of reward in the new heaven and new earth (Rev. 21-22).

Between the messages to the seven churches (Rev. 1-3) and the promise of new creation (Rev. 21-22), there is a lot that goes on in the book. This lesson will not provide information about or an interpretation of everything that happens in those 17 chapters. For this lesson, you simply need to realize that the letter was written to Christians who were likely going to be forced to make a choice: worship Rome or worship Jesus. For those who remained faithful and worshipped Jesus, they would receive the promise of being with Jesus Christ in new creation. For the church today, the message remains the same. Though Christians today are not under Roman rule, many Christians are suffering and being persecuted. Those who are not being persecuted face the struggle not to be like the churches in Revelation who were apathetic, addicted to affluence, or wrought with immorality. Either way, the church today is forced to make the same choice: worship Rome (or whatever ruler is in place) or worship Jesus. Only those who remain faithful to and worship Christ will be with Him in new creation. In new creation, followers of Jesus will worship Him forever, unencumbered by sin, the flesh, and death.

SUMMATION OF ALL THEMES

Throughout this study, we've learned about many of the themes in the Bible that run from Genesis to Revelation. Though we didn't learn about or cover every possible theme, we looked at a lot of the major and important ones. Revelation 21-22 is the summation of all the themes, the place where all the themes in the story have been pointing to and moving toward—new heavens and new earth. John provides his readers with a glimpse into eternity. Remember, he's having a symbolic vision; therefore, a lot of what he sees represents a greater reality. For example, at one point, he sees new Jerusalem coming out of the sky, but he describes it in very odd terms. Essentially, he describes a beautiful city that is as wide as it is long as it is deep, which is a cube. Now, I don't think John means the new heaven and new earth will be a cube; instead, John is forcing us to think about the presence of God throughout Scripture. The holy of holies was a cube, and it was the place where heaven and earth met. In the future, John says, the presence of God will no longer be veiled or restricted because of sin. Rather, God's presence will always be with His people. Heaven and earth will meet fully and wonderfully in eternity.

New creation is the eternal promised land. It's where the presence of God dwells with His people. God's intention for the garden to spread is fulfilled when His glory covers the whole face of the earth. In new creation, humanity will be able to worship and obey God in the garden temple with no chance to mess it up, because sin and death will be no more. What once was a marriage between man and woman in the garden will then be a marriage between Christ and the church, lasting and eternal. The first gospel promised in Genesis 3:15 finds its fulfillment in Christ, who provides life for all those who trust in Him. In new creation, sacrifice and atonement aren't necessary because Jesus Christ accomplished both perfectly at the cross. The salvation God provides in Christ is consummated in new creation. Whereas wilderness used to represent separation from God's presence, in the new heaven and new earth, wilderness won't exist because God's presence will be ubiquitous. In new creation, the covenant promised to Abraham is fulfilled; the covenant promised to Moses is fulfilled; the covenant promised to David is fulfilled; and the new covenant, made possible because of Jesus Christ, is ultimately fulfilled because of His perfect birth, life, death, and resurrection.

In new creation, there will be no evil powers, like Pharaoh, who will attempt to stand in opposition to God. The people of God will not be slaves to the flesh or any other ruler; rather, they will rule and reign with Christ as slaves to righteousness. The true and better Passover lamb, Jesus Christ, will forever cover and save His people. Just as Israel crossed through the waters of death into life, the family of God will, in an eternal manner, pass through death into eternal life with their Savior. In new creation, God's children will be able to freely follow God's law and commands and will do so joyfully and faithfully. New creation will be the once-and-for-all meeting place of heaven and earth. God's presence will dwell among his people, with no boundaries or stipulations. His children will be able to bask in the abundant beauty of His presence forever. God's kingdom will be fully realized in the new heavens and new earth. He will reign over His people in the place He has prepared for them, and they will be able to worship and obey Him eternally. Every bit of the hope of future restoration the Prophets promised will be proven gloriously true in new creation. God's people will no longer be in any form of exile but eternally restored to their Savior. And it's in new creation that all the nations of the earth will be blessed. Every tribe, tongue, and nation will be represented around God's throne, worshipping Him for who He is and what He has done, forever.

All of these things will be true in new creation, and it's all because of Jesus Christ. Without Christ, His work, and the good news of the gospel, new creation isn't possible. It's through Jesus Christ that new creation will come to fruition. It's Jesus Christ, our Savior, our hope, our King, who we will worship for eternity. Revelation 21-22 is a promise, and God is faithful to keep His promises, which means the church should worship Jesus Christ now as it will for eternity. As we wait for the King, let's be faithful to work for the king, and as we work for the king, let's be sure to worship Him for who He is, what he Has done, and the glorious future He's promised to His people.

CONCLUSION

That's it! You made it from Genesis to Revelation! You've learned about some of the themes that connect the two books and every one in-between. This study is not meant to be comprehensive or all-encompassing. Hopefully, this study in biblical theology helped spark your interest in the whole story of Scripture, and will motivate you to continue learning more about how the various parts of the Bible fit together. Once you have a good grasp of biblical theology, you can begin moving into other areas of study like systematic theology and historical theology. Studying biblical theology is more than an academic exercise; it's also an act of worship. As Christians, we want to think rightly about God and His word in order to live rightly before Him. We want this study to deepen your love for God, His word, and the wonder of the gospel. Continue reading and learning about how the various parts of the Bible fit together to tell the most amazing story ever told. And don't keep it to yourself! Help others learn, as well. Part of working for the King is helping others see His beauty and worship Him as well. Next week we'll learn how to be faithful disciples who make disciples.

In your group, reflect on the following questions:

1. What stands out to you most about Revelation 21-22?

2. What is something new you learned from these verses?

3. What themes or ideas above help you think well about Revelation and the summation of all the themes we've studied to this point?

Model the Word

1. Take time for each member to explain an important aspect of Revelation 21-22.

2. How would you teach the importance of these two chapters to someone else? What aspects or ideas would you emphasize?

Share the Word

1. Think about reading these chapters from the perspective of an unbeliever. How could you use it to share the gospel or begin a gospel conversation?

2. Why is it helpful to understand Revelation 21-22, and how the story of the Bible ends? How can you use these ideas as you share the gospel?

Pray the Word

1. As a group, spend time praying for each other to have a better understanding of God's Word.

2. Pray for opportunities to share the gospel with others. Pray that God will give you boldness to share with those in your family and at your job.

Daily Bible Reading

Day 1: Psalm 24 and Proverbs 24
Day 2: Psalm 25 and Proverbs 25
Day 3: Psalm 26 and Proverbs 26
Day 4: Psalm 27 and Proverbs 27
Day 5: Psalm 28 and Proverbs 28

33. Life on Mission

Know the Word

Read Matthew 28:16-20

1. What do you see? (Observation)

2. What does it mean? (Interpretation)

3. What do you do? (Application)

4. How should you pray?

You made it to the final week! Over the past 32 lessons, you've learned what a disciple is, does, looks like, and lives like. You've learned about the church and its purpose. And you've learned about biblical theology, how the Bible is connected from Genesis to Revelation, and why every section of Scripture is important for you to know and understand. Each lesson in this study has been preparing you for this moment. This is where the rubber meets the road. It's time for you to go and make disciples. Hopefully all the things you've studied and learned to this point have been instrumentally helpful for you, your walk with Christ, and your understanding of God's Word and discipleship. However, if you walk away from this study and don't actually do the work of discipleship, it's all been for nothing. Maybe you're asking, "why?" Why do I need to go and make disciples? The simple answer is this: making disciples is the responsibility of every follower of Jesus Christ. Discipleship isn't optional. Today we'll learn why. Making disciples is part of living your life on God's mission. What, then, is God's mission? What is your role in it? And why is discipleship so crucial to seeing it through? Let's jump in.

MISSION AND VISION

Before learning about the mission of God, we need to understand what mission is. Mission is a specific task with which a group or person is charged. Good companies all have mission statements, which define the aims and values of the company. Mission statements define how a person or group is going to achieve the desired outcome or vision of the company. What is vision? Vision is the goal, dream, or desired future of a person or group of people. Good companies also have vision statements, which provide a picture of what that company desires its future to look like. Vision statements answer the question: "where do we want to go?" or "what is our dream?" Good vision statements provide inspiration and hope. Take Amazon, for example. Amazon's vision statement is, "To be Earth's most customer-centric company, where customers can find and discover anything they might want to buy online." This is what Amazon desires to be; it's their inspiration. How are they going to make their vision a reality? Through their mission. Their mission statement is, "We strive to offer our customers the lowest possible prices, the best available selection, and the utmost convenience." Therefore, Amazon is going to become the world's most customer-centric company by offering customers the lowest possible prices, the best selection, and the most convenience possible. Amazon is everywhere! From Alexa to next day shipping of anything you could want, Amazon is working hard on their mission to see their vision come true, right? Mission and vision go hand in hand.

Understanding the relationship between mission and vision is crucial; the two go hand-in-hand. Think about this: mission without vision is pointless. Without vision, there is no reason to accomplish the mission. Why would Amazon work so hard at offering low prices, the best selection, and convenience if they had no goal in mind? They would have no reason for providing the best service if there wasn't a goal in mind or something to aspire toward. On the other hand, vision without mission is impossible. Amazon may desire to be the world's most customer-centric company, but if they only sold books and baking supplies every other month to states that start with the letter "M," their vision would never become a reality; their vision would be impossible. Mission without vision is pointless; vision without mission is impossible. Therefore, to rightly understand the mission of God, we must also understand the vision of God and how the two relate.

THE MISSION AND VISION OF GOD

Matthew 28:16-20 is often called the Great Commission. Commission simply means an instruction or command given to a person or group of people, which means these verses define the mission God has for His people. Jesus tells His disciples, "All authority in heaven and on earth has been given to me. Go therefore and make disciples of all nations, baptizing them in the name of the Father and of the Son and of the Holy Spirit, teaching them to observe all that I have commanded you. And behold, I am with you always, to the end of the age" (Matt. 28:18-20). The main command here is "make disciples." Discipleship is at the very heart of God's mission. Jesus also defines the target audience for discipleship: all nations. People from all nations need to be discipled. Finally, Jesus defines the work of discipleship: baptizing people from the nations, teaching them all He commanded, and teaching them how to obey what He commanded. "Disciple the nations" is God's mission statement for His people, but why? Remember, mission without vision is pointless. There must be a reason God desires His people to participate in His mission. We must, then, identify the vision of God.

There are a few different places in the Bible we could look to see God's vision for humanity and creation. The book of Revelation provides the clearest picture of God's vision. John writes in Revelation, "After this I looked, and behold, a great multitude that no one could number, from every nation, from all tribes and peoples and languages, standing before the throne and before the Lamb, clothed in white robes, with palm branches in their hands, and crying out with a loud voice, "Salvation belongs to our God who sits on the throne, and to the Lamb!'" (Rev. 7:9-10). As John sees the throne room of God, people from all nations are represented. The vision John has holds a promise: every tribe, tongue, and nation will be represented around God's throne. "Every tribe, tongue, and nation around the throne" is God's vision statement, and He promised it will be a future reality. This vision should compel and motivate God's people to participate in His mission. Remember, vision without mission is impossible. How will God's vision come true? Through God's mission. The only way people from all nations will be around God's throne is if God's people go and make disciples of all nations.

THE TASK AHEAD

Well, how is the church doing on God's mission? Are people from every tribe, tongue, and nation reached with the gospel? Sadly, the answer is a resounding no. That doesn't mean the church hasn't been faithful to reach the lost with the gospel and make disciples; they have. There are just a lot of people around the world who are lost. About 7.7 billion people are living on Earth today. There are 195 self-governing countries in the world, and there are several other individual states or places that are dependent on one of the 195 countries. If Jesus meant for the church to reach the 195 countries in our modern-day, the mission of God would already be accomplished. However, the word "nations" in Matthew 28:19 comes from the Greek word ethnē or ethnos, which gives us our English word ethnicity. Think about how many different ethnicities make up the population of the United States. Modern countries aren't the "nations" Jesus was referring to. Moreover, think about how small Jesus starts: reach the tribes! Tribes are small groups of people with a closely connected culture and language, among other things. How, then, will we know when every tribe, tongue, and nation is reached?

Technically it's impossible to know the exact way to define every tribe, tongue, and nation. However, researchers dedicated to seeing the mission of God fulfilled have worked hard to locate and define different "people groups" around the world. A people group is the largest group within which the gospel can spread as a church planting movement without encountering barriers of understanding or acceptance. Some people groups are quite large. For example, the Japanese people group is one of the largest in the world at 125 million. The overall population of Japan is 126 million, which means only around 1 million people in Japan aren't ethnically Japanese. Therefore, if a church planting movement took place in Japan, it would be relatively easy for the gospel to spread to every part of the country. The Japanese people share the same language and culture, meaning there are few barriers to the spreading of the gospel among Japanese. People groups can also be really small. The Dakpa people group is Buddhist and lives in the mountainous northwest corner of India. There are around 100 people in the Dakpa people. Although Hindi is one of the main languages in India, the Dakpa people primarily speak Brokpake. Because of their location, culture, and language, it would be difficult for a church planting movement to transfer to the Dakpa people from Hindi speaking Indians from a Hindu background. Some countries, like India and China, have thousands of different people groups.

According to the Joshua Project, there are 17,094 people groups that make up the 7.7 billion people living on Earth. That's a lot of people groups! Many of these people groups are reached with the gospel or have easy access to the gospel. For example, the population of the United States is 331 million people, and there are about 490 people groups. Around 70% of Americans identify as "Christian," which may mean Evangelical, Protestant, or Catholic, among others. Therefore, America is considered reached with the gospel. However, there are groups and places in America that are unreached. What do these terms reached and unreached mean? When a people group is comprised of 2% or more evangelical Christians, that group is considered reached. Reached doesn't mean that every person in the group is a Christian, but there is enough of a gospel presence for there to be multiplication of disciples and churches to reach the rest of the population. Unreached is when a people group is comprised of less than 2% evangelical Christians. 2% may seem like an arbitrary or low number, but when the Christian population gets to at least 2%, it becomes sustainable and reproducible. Unengaged is another term used to describe people groups. Unengaged people groups are those that are less than 1% evangelical Christian and have no Christian missionary currently working to reach them. The final classification of people groups in this discussion is uncontacted. Uncontacted people groups are those that have no contact or interaction with the outside world. These people groups are few and small (it's impossible to know how many there are because of the lack of contact, but it's likely less than 100). Most of these people groups are tribes in the Amazon Rainforest or on islands like the Andamans tribe off the coast of India. Therefore, there are unreached people groups (UPG's), unreached and unengaged people groups (UUPG's), and unreached, unengaged, and uncontacted people groups (UUUPG's).

Of the 17,094 people groups on the planet, 7,165 are unreached with the gospel of Jesus Christ. Those 7,156 groups are comprised of 3.2 billion people. That means 41.6% of the world population is unreached. 7,165 groups that are less than 2% evangelical Christian, and the reality is that most of those groups are far less than 2%, closer to 0%. There are a little over 3,000 people groups that are unreached and unengaged. There are around 300 million people who make up those 3,000 groups (remember, a lot of these groups are very small). Think about those numbers for a minute. 3.2 billion people are lost, dying, and going to hell. 3.2 billion people who likely haven't and never will hear the gospel of Jesus Christ. 3.2 billion.

All of those numbers are overwhelming. The task seems impossible. You may be asking yourself, "What can I possibly do about 3.2 billion people?" The reality is that more than 3.2 billion people are lost. Just because some places have access to the gospel doesn't mean every person is a follower of Jesus. There are people in your life—family, friends, neighbors, and coworkers—who have plenty of access to the gospel but are not believers. "Oh no! What can I do about more than 3.2 billion?!?" Don't worry. God hasn't called you to reach billions of people. He's called the church to reach them, brothers and sisters around the world working together for the advancement of the gospel. You don't need to start with many, just start with a few.

START WITH A FEW

Isn't it interesting how Jesus spent his time? While He often had compassion on large crowds and would spend some time with them, the majority of His time during his ministry was spent with twelve people. Even within the twelve close to Him, Peter, James, and John were the closest, and it was those three who became the pillars of the church along with Paul. Jesus certainly understood the task at hand. He knew the vast lostness around Him. Jesus could have spent His time with large crowds and lots of people, but He chose to invest in a few in order to reach many. Jesus chose to make disciples. The three years Jesus spent with His disciples had more impact on the world than any of the time He spent with the crowds. Once the disciples received the Holy Spirit, they began to turn the world upside down. Thousands were saved on the first day, and thousands more after that. What started small grew exponentially large. Today, the church is all over the world and is comprised of hundreds of millions of people.

What were those who followed Jesus doing to have such an impact on the world? They made disciples. Think back to Lesson 3 on Sharing the Gospel. What is the first step in making disciples? Sharing the gospel! Jesus' disciples shared the gospel wherever they were. When people repented and believed, they would baptize them, and teach them to obey all Jesus commanded. Many of the 12 stayed in one spot most of the time. While they did travel and share the gospel with people in places far away, most of them usually stayed in one spot and made disciples where they were. They would share the gospel with family, friends, neighbors, and coworkers. When someone came to faith, they would baptize them and teach them to obey everything Christ commanded. They made disciples. Some, like Paul and Barnabas, traveled from city to city, proclaiming the gospel and making disciples. Once their disciples were trained and ready to make disciples on their own, they would leave and go to some other city that didn't have the gospel or followers of Jesus. They acted like modern-day missionaries. It didn't matter if they were full-time missionaries or worked and lived in one spot their whole lives; the followers of Jesus made disciples where they were or where they went.

You don't have to reach 3.2 billion people. You just need to reach a few. If you make three disciples, and each of those goes and makes three disciples, that's twelve total disciples made. Continue to do the math, and the number of disciples will grow exponentially. That's how Jesus started. He taught and trained twelve people who ended up affecting hundreds of millions. Your task in the mission of God is to be faithful to make disciples. Maybe one day you will be the person who goes to the unreached and unengaged people groups to share the gospel with them and make disciples. Maybe not. I hope and pray you will be involved in international missions by going when you can, giving what you can, and praying for the salvation of the nations. Perhaps you will move somewhere else in America that is unreached with the gospel. Perhaps you will live right where you do now for the rest of your life. Guess what? It's your task and responsibility to make disciples of those around you who are lost, wherever you are! God has called you onto His mission of making disciples of all nations. He has equipped you through the power of the Holy Spirit to do the work. And He is using people, tools, and resources to prepare you to do the work. Allow the vision of God to inspire, compel, and motivate you to participate in the mission of God. Start with a few and trust that God will use your faithfulness to reach many.

CONCLUSION

Who are your few? Who are a few people in your life right now that you know need to hear the gospel of Jesus Christ, possibly for the first time? I challenge and encourage you to have a gospel conversation with them. Who are some people you know who are followers of Jesus Christ but have never been discipled? Talk with them and see if they would like to meet with you and go through this material. Many people in the church have never experienced genuine discipleship. They have never had someone invest in their life and teach them how to be a disciple of Christ. I guarantee there are Christians you know who are desperate for discipleship. Your life is meant to be a life on mission. God didn't only save you from your sin; He also saved you for His mission. No one can force you to make disciples. I hope as you've spent time being discipled you understand the importance of it in the believer's life. Be faithful to God's mission. Go and make disciples!

In your group, reflect on the following questions:

1. What stands out to you most about Matthew 28:16-20?

2. What is something new you learned from these verses?

Model the Word

1. Take time for each member to explain an important aspect of Matthew 28:16-20.

2. How would you teach the importance of these verses to someone else? What aspects or ideas would you emphasize?

Share the Word

1. Think about reading these verses from the perspective of an unbeliever. How could you use it to share the gospel or begin a gospel conversation?

2. What is the relationship between evangelism and discipleship?

3. Who are three people in your life you know need to be discipled? Write those names down and begin praying God would provide an opportunity for you disciple them.

Pray the Word

1. As a group, spend time praying for the names you wrote down.

2. Pray for opportunities to share the gospel with others. Pray that God will give you boldness to share with those in your family and at your job.

3. Pray for the salvation of the nations. Consider what your part in God's mission should be.

Daily Bible Reading

Day 1: Psalm 29 and Proverbs 29
Day 2: Psalm 30 and Proverbs 30
Day 3: Psalm 31 and Proverbs 31
Day 4: Psalm 32-33
Day 5: Psalm 34-35

Made in United States
Orlando, FL
08 February 2024